POSTMODERN CRISES
From *Lolita* to Pussy Riot

ARS ROSSICA

Series Editor
DAVID BETHEA (University of Wisconsin—Madison)

POSTMODERN CRISES

From *Lolita* to Pussy Riot

Mark LIPOVETSKY

BOSTON / 2017

Library of Congress Cataloging-in-Publication Data:
A bibliographic record for this title is available
from the Library of Congress.

Names: Lipovetskii, M. N. (Mark Naumovich), author.
Title: Postmodern crises : from *Lolita* to Pussy Riot / Mark Lipovetsky.
Other titles: Ars Rossika.
Description: Brighton, MA : Published by Academic Studies Press, 2017. |
  Series: Ars Rossica
Identifiers: LCCN 2016042029 (print) | LCCN 2016045161 (ebook) | ISBN
  9781618115584 (hardcover) | ISBN 9781618115591 (e-book)
Subjects: LCSH: Postmodernism (Literature)—Russia (Federation) | Russian
  literature—20th century—History and criticism. | Russian
  literature—21st century—History and criticism. | Postmodernism—Russia
  (Federation) | Motion pictures—Russia (Federation)—History and
  criticism.
Classification: LCC PG3027.5.P67 L56 2017 (print) | LCC PG3027.5.P67 (ebook)
  | DDC 891.709/0044—dc23
LC record available at https://lccn.loc.gov/2016042029

Copyright © 2017 Academic Studies Press
All rights reserved.

ISBN 9781644696651
ISBN 9781618115591 (electronic)

Cover design by Tatiana Vernikov.
On the cover: film-still from *Short Stories*, dir. Mikhail Segal, 2012.

Published by Academic Studies Press in 2017
28 Montfern Avenue
Brighton, MA 02135, USA
press@academicstudiespress.com
www.academicstudiespress.co

To Tanya,
my favorite coauthor and critic,
who has read it all already anyway

Contents

Preface	8
LITERATURE	
The War of Discourses: *Lolita* and the Failure of a Transcendental Project	13
The Poetics of the ITR Discourse: In the 1960s and Today	33
The *Progressor* between the Imperial and the Colonial	53
Cycles and Continuities in Contemporary Russian Literature	87
Fleshing/Flashing the Discourse: Sorokin's Master Trope	109
Pussy Riot as the Trickstar	130
The Formal Is Political	145
FILM	
Post-Soc: Transformations of Socialist Realism in the Popular Culture of the Late 1990s–Early 2000s	169
War as the Family Value: *My Stepbrother Frankenstein* by Valery Todorovsky	195
A Road of Violence: *My Joy* by Sergei Loznitsa	219
In Denial: *The Geographer Drank His Globe Away* by Aleksandr Veledinsky	230
Lost in Translation: *Short Stories* by Mikhail Segal	240
Works Cited	248
Index	262

Preface

Among the articles collected under this cover, the earliest was written in 1996 and the latest, a couple of months ago, in 2016. Consistency is not what one would expect from such a long stretch. I did not select articles according to a certain plan—just ones available in English and ones I was not exceedingly ashamed of, from today's perspective. Many of these texts were triggered by the desire to react to the most recent cultural irritants, and although English tends to quench most flammable emotions, these articles can hardly pretend to offer an objective history of the given (and worse, contemporary) period in Russian culture.

Nevertheless, I was surprised to detect at least two themes that seem to thread through this motley assemblage. One of them is the cultural crisis that we, for lack of a better word, call postmodernism. This is why I included in this collection an article about *Lolita*—a seminal novel that, in my opinion, marked the crisis of the transcendental cultural paradigm. Next to it I placed two articles discussing the culture of the Soviet scientific intelligentsia of the 1960s, which, as I try to argue, signified the crisis of the posttotalitarian Enlightenment project. Articles about Vladimir Sorokin and Pussy Riot, as well as about the "misuses" of postmodernism in post-Soviet popular culture, naturally belong to the same analytic thread. Nowadays, Fredric Jameson, the foremost theorist of postmodernism, says that "it would have been much clearer had I distinguished *postmodernity* as a historical period from *postmodernism* as a style" (Jameson 2016, 144; emphasis in the original). I also accept this distinction. Postmodern crises do not necessarily require postmodernist poetics for their manifestation—for example, all the films that I address here can hardly qualify as postmodernist by their aesthetics; yet they are undoubtedly postmodern, as they all display discursive discordances resulting from multiple breakdowns of cultural communication and the collapse of stable binaries. These are the characteristics of postmodernity, but they are also central to postmodernist aesthetics (which also necessarily includes deconstruction of binaries).

Any attempt to reflect on recent cultural phenomena cannot help relating—directly or not—to the political context surrounding the works under analysis. The articles in this collection are not about politics (obviously not my field), and yet inevitably they are. I didn't plan it this way, but the twenty years between 1996 and 2016 include at least three distinct periods in contemporary Russia's history—the anarchic 1990s, the "stabilized" 2000s, and the repressive 2010s. Recently, I can't help writing about the cultural reasons behind the failure of the perestroika aspirations for a new, liberal Russia and the recent turn toward a new yet old (or vice versa) nationalist, imperialist, conservative, and isolationist Russia. There is also the question of the liberal intelligentsia's responsibility for today's state of affairs. Another painful question concerns the relationship between postmodern crises and today's crisis of Russian society, with its notorious 86 percent of the public supporting Putin's political course and the marginalization and repression of everything subversive, critical, and countercultural. Strangely enough, I believe that this "signified" can be detected not only in texts written after the failure of the anti-Putin protests but also prior to these events. This is certainly an aberration in perception, but I prefer to stick with it.

Such a collection also offers the wonderful chance to thank from the bottom of my heart all the friends and colleagues who tirelessly improved my ungainly English by editing, proofreading, and sometimes (re)translating my texts. My gratitude goes to Helena Goscilo, Birgit Beumers, Eliot Borenstein, Vladimir Makarov, Dirk Uffelmann, Tine Roesen, Klavdia Smola, Irene Masing-Delic, Helen Halva, Yana Hashamova, Lacey Smith, Julia Gerhard, and, of course, my oldest, strictest, and most sarcastic editor—Daniil Leiderman. Ben Peterson has done a lot of work to smooth the stylistic differences between disparate texts in this collection, for which I am very grateful to him.

I am also profoundly grateful to Birgit Beumers, Natascha Drubek, Ingunn Lunde, Helen Halva, Irene Masing-Delic, Williams Stephen Matthew, Marina Mogilner and Ilya Gerasimov, and Benjamin Kloss for their permission to reprint articles that first appeared in the following publications:

"The War of Discourses: *Lolita* and the Failure of the Transcendental Project." In *Набоков/Nabokov: Un'eredita letteraria*, edited by Alide Cagidemetrio and Daniela Rizzi, 49–66. Venice: Universitá Ca'Foscari Venezia, 2006.

"The Poetics of ITR Discourse: In the 1960s and Today." *Ab Imperio* 1 (2013): 109–31.

"The *Progressor* between the Imperial and the Colonial." In *Postcolonial Slavic Literatures after Communism*, edited by Klavdia Smola and Dirk Uffelmann, 29–58. Postcolonial Perspectives on Eastern Europe, vol. 4. Frankfurt am Main: Peter Lang, 2016.

"Cycles, Continuity and Change in Contemporary Russian Culture." In *Russia's New Fin de Siècle*, edited by Birgit Beumers, 29–45. Bristol: Intellect, 2013.

"Fleshing/Flashing Discourse: Sorokin's Master-Trope." In *Vladimir Sorokin's Languages*, edited by Tine Roesen and Dirk Uffelmann, 25–47. *Slavica Bergensia*, vol. 11. Bergen: Bergen University Press, 2013.

"Pussy Riot as the Trickstar." *Apparatus* 1 (2015): http://www.apparatusjournal.net/index.php/apparatus/article/view/5.

"The Formal Is Political." *Slavic and East European Journal*, vol. 60, 2 (2016): 185-204.

"Post-Soc: Transformations of Socialist Realism in the Popular Culture of the Recent Period." In "Innovation through Iteration: Russian Popular Culture Today," special forum issue, *Slavic and East European Journal* 48, no. 3 (Fall 2004): 356–77.

"War as the Family Value: Failing Fathers and Monstrous Sons in *My Stepbrother Frankenstein*." In *Cinepaternity: Fathers and Sons in Soviet and Post-Soviet Film*, edited by Helena Goscilo and

Yana Hashamova, 114–36. Bloomington: Indiana University Press, 2010.

With Tatiana Mikhailova. "In Denial," review of Alexander Veledinsky's *The Geographer Drank Away the Globe*. *Kinokultura* 43 (2014): http://www.kinokultura.com/2014/43r-geograf-MLTM.shtml.

"Lost in Translation." Review of Mikhail Segal's *Short Stories*." *Kinokultura* 50 (2015): http://www.kinokultura.com/2015/50/fifty_rasskazy.shtml.

Many thanks to Mikhail Segal for the kindest permission to use takes from his film *Rasskazy* and for sharing with me high-quality photographs of the selected scenes. Last but not least, my warmest gratitude goes to Igor Nemirovsky, Kira Nemirovsky, and Faith Wilson Stein, without whom this book would have never happened.

Boulder, July 2016

Literature

The War Of Discourses:
Lolita and the Failure of a Transcendental Project

In *Lolita* (1955), perhaps for the first time in all his works, Nabokov transfers unto his hero *all* the traits of the author-narrator. Similar forms of discursive organization have appeared before in the novel *Despair* (1934) and the novella *The Eye* (1930). In these and all other previous works, however, we are presented with the narrating character's inner monologue, whereas in *Lolita* the reader faces a *text*, written by Humbert before his death in prison. Thus, the protagonist is here situated in the space-time of writing ("creative chronotope," to use Bakhtin's term), which Nabokov, by all indications, believes to be the sole realm where freedom of the self may be realized. In this respect, *Lolita* lends its voice directly to the metafictional tradition: it is a narrative of the creative process, though one that extends beyond the flatness of the page and into life—a narrative in which the hero becomes the author. At the same time, and as related in his own words, this introspective narrative details Humbert's attempt to realize his artistic vision in life itself, reminding us that the author-creator is not eclipsed by the hero-narrator or even by the hero-author. In the greater scheme of the evolution of modernism, however, this sentiment appears waning in importance: H.H. is truly the creator sui generis, and in his life he leads to the absolute extreme all that was distinctive in Nabokov's favorite characters.

One of the defining traits of Humbert's novel-spanning confession is its inner paralogy, structured on the polemical intertwining of two separate codes of aesthetic world-modeling. One of these codes extends from Nabokov's perennial topic of banality and totalitarianism (*poshlust*), though here it adopts a new form through association with mass (that is, pop) culture. The other is entirely monopolized by Humbert himself and lies at the basis of his personality, his philosophical and aesthetic self-definition; this code is identifiable by the *literary* intertexts of Humbert's confession.

A literary scholar, H.H. blueprints his artistic project through dialogue with numerous traditions of world literature, from Ovid and Catullus to Russian symbolists and Joyce.[1] If one judges by the frequency of allusions, the paramount positions in Humbert's model are held by Edgar Allan Poe ("Annabel Lee") and Prosper Mérimée (*Carmen*), followed by Shakespeare and Dante, then Blok,[2] Dostoevsky, Flaubert, Verlaine, Rimbaud, Baudelaire, and Joyce. What do these writers have in common, aside from being part of the canon of "high literature"? Of most likely significance to *Lolita*, it is that they all are somehow linked to romanticism—whether as its forebears, its classics, or its modernist progeny. On the whole, we can state that the romantic tradition, as the predecessor and foundation of the modernist sensibility, formulates Humbert's consciousness and project. Moreover, we can say that its influence is something of a double-edged sword.

First, romanticism endows Humbert (as well as Nabokov's other "creative" characters) with a well-developed discourse of transcendence. The narrator's transcendental fixation is initially visible in the intensive allusions to Edgar Allan Poe, and particularly to his poem "Annabel Lee," wherein the full scope of Humbert's love is established. His passion for Lolita becomes one link in an endless chain of surrogates and analogies: Lolita finally, after repeated failures, "replaces" Humbert's lost childhood love "Annabel," who in turn is reminiscent of Poe's Annabel, who in

---

[1] For more detail, see Proffer (1968) and Appel (1991).

[2] Blok's intertexts in *Lolita* are analyzed by Senderovich and Shvarts (1999).

turn reminds Poe of his youthful dead wife, Virginia. All these recursive substitutions serve as metaphors for transcendental escape beyond the boundaries of reality, beyond time and death. Poe's love for Annabel transcends her passing; for Humbert, the mythical nymphets are so unlike merely pretty girls that they exist on an "intangible island of entranced time" (Nabokov 1977, 21).[3] It is not lust that moves the hero but in essence a desire to surpass the passage of time and to return to the heavenly garden of eternal childhood.[4] "Ah, leave me alone in my pubescent park, in my mossy garden. Let them [the nymphets] play around me forever. Never grow up" (ibid.), he proclaims at the beginning of the novel, inciting a theme that blossoms steadily throughout the text.

Before their first "rendezvous," Lolita appears in the famous "davenport scene" with Humbert, holding in her hands a "banal, Eden-red apple" (58), and while she sits in his lap, H.H. writes, "Lolita was safely solipsized.... What I had madly possessed was not she, but my own creation, another fanciful Lolita; overlapping, encasing her; floating between me and her, and having no will, no consciousness—indeed, *no life of her own*" (60, 62; emphasis mine). The imagery harks back to the motif of daydreaming, a device as characteristic to romanticism as it is to modernism, symbolizing escape into a transcendental dimension. (Nabokov himself used it before in *The Luzhin Defense*; *King, Queen, Knave*; *The Gift*; and *Invitation to a Beheading*.) Humbert achieves a transcendental reverie in the davenport scene—if not daydreaming, then a sort of in-between dream and reality—which is accompanied by the *erasure* of Lolita, the deprivation of her own will, consciousness, and even life.

At many points in *Lolita*, particularly throughout the novel's second part, such romantic dreaming seamlessly morphs into a waking nightmare. The termination of transcendental endeavors in reality produces for Humbert grim and surreal effects. It is telling

---

[3] All further quotations from the novel refer to this edition.

[4] There is an obvious parallel between this project and Nabokov's habitual idealization of his own childhood. Notably, *Lolita* was written immediately after Nabokov's Russian autobiography, *Speak, Memory*, in which this idealization reaches its highest point.

that the indications marking this transition from transcendental exercise to psychological plague arise immediately after Humbert attains his desired goal: the sexual possession of Lolita, without resorting to violence or subterfuge but rather at the girl's own initiative. Humbert's state of mind is far from satiation, despite his success: "Why then this horror that I cannot shake off?" (135), "an ashen sense of awfulness" (137), "a paradise whose skies were the color of hell-flames" (166). This arc culminates in Quilty's murder, which Humbert carefully adorns in the trappings of the romantic tradition: the hero, all in black, comes to kill his twin and reads the verdict in white verse—the scene is practically a quotation from Poe's "William Wilson" or Lermontov's *The Masquerade*. Yet Humbert's authorial fancy is insufficient: throughout the murder scene, the tone of a nightmare ("a daymare") overshadows any feeling of romantic grandeur.

The second feature of romanticism to be actualized in Humbert's narrative is one linked with the romantic discourse of chaos—with the romantic abyss. This aspect emerges in the forbidden and transgressive nature of Humbert's desire. An intertextual parallel is formed by the appearance of Mérimée's "Carmen" as a trivialized but still distinctively romantic theme of criminal desire—or, rather, desire that provokes crime. (Another important parallel in this context is Flaubert's *Madame Bovary*, though the role of that intertext is much more complex.) Humbert's confession continues to incite argument over the morality or immorality of the novel to this day, resurrecting the romantic-chaotic thread of moral ambivalence. From the perspective of morality and law, the protagonist's infatuation with an underage girl is repulsive and criminal, but Nabokov, having given Humbert the power of his own oratory and having fixed his composition in the context of the romantic tradition, not only makes this passion aesthetically appealing but compels the reader to sympathize with the criminal hero, and ever to wish him luck in his efforts to seduce a twelve-year-old child. (This dynamic persists at least until the first chapters of the book's second half.)

More broadly, though still molding to the notion of the romantic abyss, *Lolita* presents us with a story of destructive and self-destructive love, in which love *inevitably* predicates death. Given that we are told in the very first pages that he has already died in prison, Humbert's fate comes as no surprise. The device of the confession at death's door, although it is not known what crime brought him there, is deeply rooted in romanticism. With this criminal motif intertwines that of madness—not only in terms of Humbert's frequent visits to the mental hospital before his introduction to Lolita but also in his characterization as a romantic lunatic, or a "demented diarist," in the words of John Ray. Madness is perhaps the most typical manifestation of the abyss in romantic and modernist culture; tellingly, the motif persists throughout the text of *Lolita*.

In the davenport scene, Humbert sees himself "suspended on the brink of that voluptuous abyss" (60), associating this abyss with escape into the transcendental dimension. A comparable sensation, that of "the teasing delirious feeling of teetering on the very brink of unearthly order and splendor" (230), accompanies Lolita playing tennis, a scene that Nabokov categorized with several other episodes as the book's nervous system ("the nerves of the novel," 316). In direct relation to this description of the "brink," the novel invokes an ironic paraphrase of two classical quotations (Poe plus Dostoevsky): "Winged gentlemen! No hereafter is acceptable if it does not produce her as she was then, in that Colorado resort, between Snow and Elphinstone" (230). The abyss and its promised transcendence, then, are linked in this case with admiration of Lolita's beauty. However, the abyss opens again before Humbert when Lolita flees from him with Quilty: amid the ringing of church bells in Elphinstone, he comprehends how he has wronged her and finds himself on the edge of the "friendly abyss" (307; another of the book's "nerves"). His chase after Lolita formerly transported him to the verge of this abyss, causing at once unearthly pleasure; now, the bliss has vanished, and all that remains is to fall madly into the yawning chasm.

One can find virtually innumerable manifestations of the romantic abyss in Humbert's autobiography. His curse (an appetite for nymphets), his self-destruction, and the ruin Humbert brings to his beloved—Annabel, Charlotte, Lolita (only Valechka manages to evade him; is that why he has such vehemence for her?) — all of these signify the void opening before H.H. and finally consuming him. Given the context of romantic discourse through which Humbert's literary sensibilities lead him to intersect his own story, this abyss is in essence the binary opposite of transcendence, and the toll for it.

If the presence of romantic motifs is so prominent here, why is it that in the famous afterword "On a Book Entitled *Lolita*" (1958) Nabokov responds with no little umbrage to a comment from critic John Hollander declaring *Lolita* a "record of a love affair with the romantic novel"? Perhaps Nabokov's reply is meant to remind us that the romantic code is but one aspect of the discursive spectrum of *Lolita*, and to reduce the whole novel to these terms alone is, in principle, a faulty approach.

In accordance with the logic of Nabokov's style, Humbert's "literary" code is not contrary to that of "life" but rather to the "cultural" code—to an entire bouquet of like codes. These codes are crude and pseudoromantic and belong to a sphere of popular or mass culture—or, in Nabokov's terms, the sphere (or rather the discourse) of *poshlust*. Humbert presents in the most excruciating detail a whole host of pop-culture gibberish, from the *Youth* and *Young Homemaker* magazines to the fictional *Campfire Girl* (whose author bears the familiar name "Shirley Holmes"). He invents a pop song about "little Carmen," recreates scenes from a Western, and burrows into the tourist subculture, complete with its fake fetishes and seductive brochures. In describing family life with Charlotte, he does not fail to admit that "the two sets were congeneric since both were affected by the same stuff (soap operas, psychoanalysis and cheap novelettes) upon which I drew for my characters and she for the mode of expression" (80). Pop literature's sentimental clichés clearly resound in Charlotte's letter to Humbert, and even when H.H. himself, especially in the first half of his narrative, proclaims on occasion, "All New England for a lady-writer's pen" (49). In the course of banal codes, an honored place is afforded to Freudianism (which Nabokov mocked with succinctness and consistency). Humbert's resentment of Freudianism is quite understandable, as psychoanalysis mocks and overturns the romantic worldview: if Humbert negates the "lower" with high poetry, then psychoanalysis contrarily divines a sexual complex behind all poetry, thus denying any transcendental values.

Lolita, too, is a product of this culture. The many pedagogical institutions to which she is subjected all manufacture the banal, from Charlotte's by-the-book child-rearing efforts, to "Camp Q" with its cabins named after Disney creatures and sex games under the guise of water sports, to the "good old Beardsley School," whose director presents an entire curriculum of mass-cultural education, following the thesis that "we live not only in a world of thoughts, but also in a world of things. Words without experience are meaningless. What on earth can Dorothy Hummerson care for Greece and the Orient with their harems and slaves?" (178). Later, Humbert explicitly defines his beloved as an exemplary demographic and consumer of pop culture: "She it was to whom ads were dedicated: the ideal consumer, the subject and object of every foul poster" (148).

A particularly important position in the book's pop culture discourse is held by all things associated with Hollywood, as Alfred Appel discusses in *Nabokov's Dark Cinema* (1974). Films, real and imagined, watched by the heroes of the novel (not excluding Humbert) occupy many of the novel's pages. Charlotte, like her daughter, carefully imitates film stars, even on the surface resembling a "weak solution of Marlene Dietrich" (37), and she fashions her relationship and even dialogue with Humbert after the patterns of movie love. Humbert dispenses astronomical degrees of sarcasm in his exposure of the inconsistencies, or even the blatant idiocy, of Hollywood characters and plots, in which "real singers and dancers had unreal stage careers in an essentially grief-proof sphere of existence wherefrom death and truth were banned" (170). It is little wonder that Clare Quilty, the popular playwright, "the American Maeterlinck," who has authored fifty-two Hollywood scripts, whose cigarette-commercial portrait seems to hang on every surface (including the wall in Lolita's bedroom), who stands at the epicenter of the world of banality, is the one to steal Lolita from Humbert.

The unlikelihood of the events on the silver screen (as well as those described in tourist booklets, magazines for girls and women, etc.) is clearly juxtaposed to analogous situations within the lives of the novel's characters (the collision of the rebellious daughter seeking her freedom in show business and the doting father, crime and punishment, a battle with an adversary away from civilization). In most cases, the lives of the heroes carefully emulate expectations cultivated by Hollywood. However, nothing turns out quite as sleek and pretty for them as it does in the movies, and the novel's characters suffer far more than their models do. To some degree, the interplay between the ideals promoted by mass culture and the events of the novel reveal the paradox later explored by Jean Baudrillard in his Disneyland example: "Disneyland is presented as imaginary in order to make us believe that the rest is real. [. . .] It is no longer a question of false representation of reality (ideology) but of concealing the fact that the real is no longer real, and thus of saving the reality principle" (Baudrillard 1994, 13–14).

The delusive indistinguishability of life and film is exemplified not only by Charlotte and Lolita but also by many passing characters and even by Humbert himself. (Quilty is excepted, as he understands the price of these illusions.) The Hollywood "dream factory" is the first significant enterprise of the "hyperreality of the simulacrum," which is why the earliest of its "products" is not the imaginary but rather the real. Of course, even the romantic discourse to which Humbert belongs and from which he derives his facetious attitude toward Hollywood, is also a "dream factory" in a sense. It is apparently not the dreams themselves that aggravate Humbert, but their careful insulation of the consumer from grief and pain, abysses and tragedies. In absence of this threshold, the two-dimensional flatness of inevitable happiness precludes the need for transcendence. For instance, in "Annabel Lee," an obvious precursor to Humbert's transcendentalism, love acquires its full transcendental meaning only after the beloved's death. Likewise, only the death of his "Annabel" permits Humbert to glimpse the abyssal dimension of his passion. Later, the death of Lolita, obfuscated in John Ray's prologue, imparts the highest romantic intensity in Humbert's self-judgment and final profession of love for Lolita. All such feeling is impossible in the void of the flat simulacra of life and love shaped by Hollywood. In this sense, Humbert shares Nabokov's point of view: he, like his creator, rejects *poshlust*, here represented by the discourse of pop culture as traitorous in its appeal, a beguiling, disorienting *simulacrum of transcendence*.

In this lies the greatest problem of *Lolita*: by handing the reins of authorship to Humbert, Nabokov does not allow us to accept one aspect of Humbert and reject another. We cannot agree with him on, for example, his disdain for mass culture and his faith in the transcendental qualities of love, and simultaneously reject, say, the practical realization of his philosophical-aesthetic program.

Despite the contrasting nature of the romantic-modernist discourse and the discourse of pop culture, the intertwining of *Lolita*'s motives and images demolishes the implied dichotomy of poetry and *poshlust*. To be more precise, while Humbert strives to enforce just such a dichotomy, the subtleties of the text repeatedly demonstrate the futility of such an undertaking. The artistic optic of *Lolita* is multidimensional, and nearly every image and every plot device illuminates the symbol system of high culture and the context of mass culture as its doppelgänger.

These codes interweave most noticeably in relation to Lolita herself. It is essentially this duality, according to Humbert, that yields the greatest mystery of the nymphets: "What drives me insane is the twofold nature of this nymphet—of every nymphet, perhaps; this mixture in my Lolita of tender dreamy childishness and a kind of eerie vulgarity, stemming from the snub-nosed cuteness of ads and magazine pictures [. . .] and then again all this mixed up with the exquisite stainless tenderness seeping through the musk and the mud, through the dirt and the death" (44). As we can see, vulgarity and *poshlust*, directly traced to their source, pop culture ("the snub-nosed cuteness of ads and magazine pictures"), intersect here with transcendental motifs of unearthly innocence, eternal childhood ("tender dreamy childishness," "exquisite stainless tenderness"), and the abyss ("the musk and the mud, through the dirt and the death").

This is exactly why Lolita becomes the subject of dispute in an invisible battle between two antipodes: Humbert and Quilty, the poet and *poshlust* incarnate. H.H. and Lolita's first kiss, imagined as an elevated moment in Humbert's code, turns out to be a "bit of backfisch foolery in imitation of some simulacrum of fake romance"

(113). Even the longed-for copulation transpires on Lolita's—that is, teenagers', which means pop-cultural—not Humbert's, terms. When Lolita, "at a kind of slow-motion walk" (120) or as if in a dream (passage into the transcendental dimension), attends to the gifts brought to her by Humbert, the romantic discourse subtly morphs into stereotypical falsity: "She crept into my waiting arms, radiant, relaxed, caressing me with her tender, mysterious, impure, indifferent, twilight eyes—for all the world, *like the cheapest of cheap cuties*. For that is what nymphets imitate—while we moan and die" (120; emphasis mine). A romantic dream becomes a selection of pop culture stereotypes, a Hollywood simulacrum. This is precisely why Humbert is unable to take advantage of Lolita's dream: his traditional romantic chronotope does not possess, as is discovered in the course of the plot, the expected autonomy over banal, pop-culture-saturated reality.

For the very same reason, Humbert fails miserably in the various operations of his transcendental project, be they to resurrect Annabel in Lolita by copulating on the shore of the sea, or peacefully to observe nymphets playing in the school yard opposite the house at Beardsley ("On the very first day of school, workmen arrived and put up a fence some way down the gap. . . . As soon as they had erected a sufficient amount of material to spoil everything, those absurd builders suspended their work and never appeared again"; 179). It is then no surprise that the poetically charged roster of Lolita's class transforms in her own retelling into a rogue's gallery of "low" pleasures; thus the "Shakespearean" Miranda twins "had shared the same bed for years," and Kenneth Knight (chivalry indeed!) "used to exhibit himself wherever and whenever he had a chance" (137).

In a similar fashion, the Enchanted Hunters Hotel—its name romantic as well as evocative of Humbert's pursuit of the nymphet—appears initially in Charlotte's memory as a symbol of bourgeois comfort, then becomes actualized as a destination, where H.H. spends his first night with Lolita. It is significant that in this hotel Humbert unknowingly crosses paths for the first time with Quilty, who has come there to compose his play "The Enchanted Hunters." Lolita will later be cast in a school production of this very drama as a "little nymph" (the nymphet), will grow intimate with Quilty, and finally will elope with him, abandoning Humbert. Even more poignantly, the story of the play, per Humbert's retelling, reads much like an unconscious parody of his own confession.

Humbert himself falls under the spell of what may be called the "enchanted hunters" effect—a turn that reveals just how rare it is that an element of *Lolita*'s poetics belongs solely to either the romantic-transcendental discourse or the mass-culture discourse, a combination or shuffling of both being most commonly the case.[5] Humbert's appearance is, at first glance, cloaked in a romantic aura, though many of these same descriptions inspire quite banal associations: for instance, "dark-and-handsome" (188) or "first time I've seen a man wearing a smoking jacket, sir—except in movies, of course" (189). Humbert's behavior, too, can be matched to the conventions of the criminal love story, evincing such tropes as the corrupter and the seduced, the fortunate competitor, the elopement, vengeance brought on the thief, and so on. On the other hand, Humbert unwittingly prophesizes the outcome of his story by ironically improvising to the tune of a pop song: "Drew his .32 automatic, I guess, and put a bullet through his moll's eye" (62). H.H. will put a bullet in a rival rather than some "moll"—but it's the gesture that counts. Humbert's brawl with Quilty nearly qualifies as a spoof of a Hollywood shootout: the hero's recitation of the verdict of death, in verse, to his nemesis—is this not drawn from melodrama? Humbert's capability "of shedding torrents of tears

---

[5] The applicability of Freudian interpretation to Humbert's psychological development is another example of such double encoding. Jenefer Shute argues, "Almost every possible interpretation of Humbert's predicament has been anticipated, planted in the text, and wired to explode at the first Viennese advance. Thus the first problem to confront a psychoanalytical reading is not the absence of recognizable analytical configuration but the fact that such configurations are in no sense 'latent': they constitute a system of signifiers in their own right rather than any ultimate signified of the text" (1995, 417). Later she adds, "Psychoanalytic economies of desire are invoked only to be denied, named only to be negated, but on the other hand they remain essential to the disposition of the text. The psychoanalytic structure is inscribed and then effaced by parody, yet it remains intact, in place, and wholly legible" (419).

throughout the other [sexual] tempest" (207) could potentially be read as an extension of the romantic code of the nineteenth century, but in the twentieth such imagery has been universally annexed by sentimental pop culture.

Considering his abyssal lust and romantic transgressivity, it is no surprise that H.H. fits with such precision the characteristics of the demonic hero and the specifics of demonic eroticism. Alongside these features in Humbert's depiction, there are hints of a prominent archetype of romantic mythology: the vampire Dracula—who, coincidently, had already been thoroughly exploited in popular culture by the 1950s. It is not only the more blatant references to this archetype that are worth noting; for instance, just after their first night at the Enchanted Hunters Hotel, H.H. writes of Lolita, "Nothing could have been more childish than her snubbed nose, freckled face or the *purplish spot on her naked neck where a fairytale vampire had feasted*" (139; emphasis mine). Like Dracula, Humbert commands a colossal erotic force. Like the vampire's victim, Lolita "freezes" in the same state as she was first "bitten" by Humbert. She does not turn into an adult woman and, in essence, dies a nymphet-adolescent.

If one is inclined to accept the principle of the Beardsley School, then the discourse of pop culture operates through *things*, whereas romantic transcendentalism is limited to a circle of *ideas*. The discourse of the commercial corresponds best to things, while transcendental ideas manifest most potently through the medium of art. As Dana Brand (1987) notes, the transformation of art into the commercial, or rather that of the transcendental discourse into the discourse of pop culture, is finely interwoven into the changes in Humbert and Lolita's relationship after H.H. "possesses" her, in every sense of the word—including that connoting a commodity. This diagnosis seems fair, and would explain the ever more determined melding of pop and romantic discourses that occupies the second half of the novel.

The intensifying collision between the romantic and *poshlust* codes appears also in how Humbert, in his capacity as Lolita's "owner," comes to resemble Charlotte more and more: "Charlotte, I began to understand you" (149). Even his complaints reverberate a note of hypocrisy characteristic to "a woman with principles": "I am now faced with the distasteful task of recording a definite drop in Lolita's morals" (183); "Lolita, when she chose could be a most exasperating brat" (148); "I have just retracted some silly promise..." (169). Charlotte educates her daughter by the instruction of *A Guide to Your Child's Development*, while Humbert's manual bears the "unintentionally biblical title *Know Your Own Daughter*" (174). Although he fails to notice, Humbert sends Lolita to the very Beardsley School of which Charlotte dreamed. Even Lolita's and Humbert's new home "bore a dejected resemblance to the Haze home" (176).

Humbert's fatal attraction to nymphets, although transgressive, is certainly not alien to American cinema of the 1940s and '50s, with its oddly sexualized child stars—Shirley Temple foremost among them. As Appel, who first drew attention to this parallel, notes, "The willful asexuality of screen adolescents is an interesting contrast to sexual charades indulged by the same stars when they resemble children... Except for the crude low-budget films, the charades of the child stars seem to complement, rather than burlesque adult behavior, as though the performers were adults alchemically reduced in size..." (1974, 94–95). Appel also cites the characteristic judgment of Graham Greene, who, as is well known, first championed *Lolita*: "Shirley Temple acts and dances with immense vigor and assurance... but some of her popularity seems to rest on a coquetry quite as mature as Miss Colbert's and on an oddly precocious body as voluptuous in gray flannel trousers as Miss Dietrich's" (100).

A similar duality marks other fairy-tale images, which play a vital role in conjuring a poetic aura around Humbert's nympholepsy. It was in the 1950s that Walt Disney's cartoons achieved the status of the hyperreality of simulacra, pushing aside or dominating other fairy tales. The original Disneyland was constructed in 1954, two years after the novel's heroes die; otherwise, Lolita would have certainly insisted that they visit this fairy-tale province.

Finally, even the differences between Humbert and Quilty do not annul their deep inner likeness. It is no coincidence that the first mention of Quilty comprises a coded paraphrase of Humbert's fate, as read in the names of Quilty's plays: "author of *The Little Nymph, The Lady Who Liked Lighting . . . Dark Age, The Strange Mushroom, Fatherly Love* and others" (31). Nabokov's Russian translation of the text stresses the resemblance of the two men in their initials, G.G. and K.K. (in their English variants, these equate to H.H. and C.Q.). On the wall in Lolita's bedroom, Quilty's posing in a cigarette advertisement corresponds to another commercial idol, that which "Lo had drawn in a jocose arrow to the haggard lover's face and had put in block letter: H.H. And indeed, despite a difference of a few years, the resemblance was striking" (69). Following Quilty's tracks and parsing his "clues," Humbert admits that "his genre, his type of humor—at its best at least—the tone of his brain, had affinities with my own. [. . .] His allusions were definitely highbrow. He was well-read. He knew French. [. . .] He was an amateur of sex lore" (249–50). Quilty speaks candidly of his kinship to Humbert: "We are men of the world, in everything—sex, free verse, marksmanship" (301). Quilty, like Humbert, is no stranger to transcendental aims. At the very least, he professionally imitates them; it is not in vain that he claims the epithet "the American Maeterlinck," squaring him with perhaps the most mystical playwright in European theater.

There are many possible interpretations of the similarities between Humbert and Quilty. Most often, Quilty is read as the doppelgänger or Jungian "shadow" of Humbert, manifesting his low, animal side. (There is a strange irony in how Humbert, the romantic, is the one who repeatedly rapes Lolita, while Quilty the lecher proves to be impotent, and instead exploits her for "visual" pleasure, planning to use her in pornographic home videos.) However, we cannot deny that, in killing Quilty, Humbert not only reaps vengeance on a competitor and not only extinguishes his "shadow," but passes judgment on himself. Through the act of murder, he performs a sort of suicide, bringing retribution on himself for what he has done to Lolita. It is telling *how* he surrenders to the police yet is unaware of the crime—knowingly breaking the laws of traffic, Humbert leaves the murder scene by driving on the wrong side of the road.

Quite logically, the intermingling of romantic and pop-culture imagery most frequently and most effectively corresponds to the atmosphere of surreal horror that accompanies the realized transcendental project. A strong example is the mystical and, in essence, transcendental vision of an enormous film screen that Humbert passes on the eve of the premeditated murder: "While searching for night lodging, I passed a drive-in. *In a selenian glow, truly mystical in its contrast with the moonless and massive night*, on a gigantic screen slanting away among *dark drowsy fields, a thin phantom* raised a gun, both he and his arm reduced to tremulous dishwater by the oblique angle of that receding world—and the next moment a row of trees shut off the gesticulation" (293; emphasis mine).

The mutual transformations of the discourse of transcendentalism and the simulacra of mass culture in Humbert's narrative form a principally new artistic philosophy in *Lolita*, distinct from both the earlier and later works of Nabokov. In essence, the high romantic/modernist code proves undivided from the cheap codes of pop-culture, or the "cultural industry" (in Adorno and Horkheimer's understanding of this term). Nabokov thus comes in *Lolita* to a postmodernist perception of culture, showcased by a disruption of the autonomy of the high (elitist) and low (popular) cultures. The novel does not, however, posit a favorable synthesis of the two; rather, it depicts the tragic indistinguishability of transcendence and simulation.

Both of these forces work alike to devalue and destroy Lolita herself. Humbert, discerning and guilty, writes of her victimization, "She groped for words. I supplied them mentally ('*He* [Quilty] broke my heart. *You* merely broke my life')" (279). Humbert's project of romantic transcendence replaces her single, brief life with an idea of eternity, reducing Lolita to a stand-in for Annabel, delineating the utopia of childhood as an individual paradise and offering an attempt to return to this utopian "island"—this is how H.H. breaks her life. Meanwhile, the flowing tide of mass culture substitutes all that is truly individual and alive in her with a celluloid simulacrum; this is why Quilty, whom Lolita loves, breaks only her heart. In both cases the principal victim is Lolita, crushed and burned away.

Interestingly, both projects fail in spite of their sacrificial toll on Lolita. Humbert, as we have seen, flunks his pursuit of the "transcendental Other." Lolita does not permit him into her secret world, guarded by a barricade of stereotypes, and Humbert realizes too late "that quite possibly, behind the awful juvenile clichés, there was in her a garden and twilight, and a palace gate—dim and adorable regions which happened to be lucidly and absolutely forbidden to me" (284). In the debris of his collapsed mission and its unrealized poetic significance—the return to childhood, to the "intangible island of entranced time"—only Quilty's project of the enslavement and possession of Lolita's body, by comparison uncomplicated and straightforward, remains. Yet he likewise cannot submit her to his will (though she loves only him), as she refuses to participate in his "films"; she evidently does possess some individuality, which reaches beyond the steadfast stereotypes of pop culture.

Nonetheless, she is ultimately effaced in the scramble for her soul waged by coveted transcendence and assimilating mass culture. Humbert's worship of the poetry of childhood effectively dissolves Lolita's childhood, ravaging her life without mercy. After all, the real Lolita concerns him little. It is only once he has lost Lolita that Humbert recalls the words she spoke that revealed her pain and commences his autotribunal. Ellen Pifer is right when she asserts, "It is Humbert's riotous imagination that, paradoxically, leads to his betrayal of the highest values of imagination: the spontaneity, vitality, and originality emblemized by the child. In striving to obtain his ideal world or paradise, he selfishly deprives Lolita of her rightful childhood—and betrays the principles of romantic faith and freedom" (1995, 317). In other words, attainment of the individual freedom enjoyed by the modernist or romantic creator is accomplished at the cost of the total eradication of even the potential freedom of the Other—in this instance, of Lolita.

It is no coincidence that Humbert and Lolita's story is framed by the image of a burned house. H.H. first arrives at the Haze abode because the home of Mr. McCoo, where he had previously arranged to live, "had just burned down" (35). At the very end of the novel, this imagery reemerges in the tale Lolita tells about her escape from Quilty's ranch: "It had burned to the ground, *nothing* remained, just a charred heap of rubbish. It was so strange, so strange" (277). In the

Russian variant, to emphasize the repetition of this motif, Humbert adds, "Well, McCoo had a similar name and his house also burned down" (Nabokov 2001, 315).[6]

Other motifs advancing death as a hopeless and inevitable outcome (and not the transcendental signified) populate the entire novel. Humbert arrives to Charlotte's house in "a limousine, in a marvelously old-fashioned, square-topped affair" (35–36), and the first thing he observes on entering Quilty's home in the finale is "a black convertible for the nonce" (294) — in Russian translation, "a black car resembling an undertaker's limousine" (2001, 37).[7] Gazing at his beloved after their first night together, he feels "as if I were sitting with the small ghost of somebody I just killed" (140). At the home where the lovers reside in Beardsley, Humbert remarks, "One of the latticed squares in a small cobwebby casement window at the turn of the staircase was glazed with ruby, and that raw wound among the unstained rectangles [. . .] always strangely disturbed me" (192). Lolita comments, on receiving Humbert's bouquet in the hospital at Elphinstone, "What gruesome funeral flowers" (243). Later, hunting for traces of Lolita, Humbert leafs through jumbled newspapers in the library, "turning the enormous and fragile pages of a coffin-black volume almost as big as Lolita" (262). And finally, we note how Lolita presses herself to the door to let Humbert into her modest domicile at their last encounter, a tragic expression lurking within a seemingly mundane gesture: "Against the splintery deadwood of the door, Dolly Schiller flattened herself as best she could (even rising on tiptoe a little) to let me pass, and was crucified for a moment, looking down, smiling down at the threshold, hollow-cheeked with round pommettes, her water-milk-white arm outspread on the wood" (270).

Through these subtle yet insistent signals, entropy and death acquire an allegorical signification in *Lolita*. Thanks to the (fictional) foreword by Dr. John Ray, we know from the very start that all

---

[6] «. . . сгорело дотла, *ничего* не оставалось, только черная куча мусора. Это ей показалось так странно, так странно. . .»

[7] «в погребальном лимузине».

the major characters of the novel—Humbert, Lolita, Charlotte, and Quilty—have died. As strange as it may sound, even the hero-author himself is conscious of this fact: the novel ends by noting his stipulation that "A Confession of a White Widowed Man" is to be published not only after his own death but after Lolita's as well. Placing this restriction, he is unaware that Lolita will follow him in death by a mere few months. Thus, the text of *Lolita* illustrates with remarkable accuracy Derrida's vision of the ruin, which "appears not after the work, but remains [. . .] as its origin. In the beginning there was a ruin [. . .] with no hope for the reconstruction" (Derrida 1990, 68–69). For Derrida, the ruin is the very experience of an individual, his or her ontological self-portrait. Conversely, Walter Benjamin considers ruin the most expressive allegory for history: "History finds its embodiment in this form [of a ruin] not as the form of the process of an eternal life so much as that of irresistible decay. [. . .] In the process of decay, and in it alone, the events of history shrivel up and become absorbed in setting" (Benjamin 1978, 179).

Nabokov himself seems to construct the ruin from within his hero-author's text. By colliding the discourses of romantic transcendence and pop culture, he leads them to annihilate one other, leaving behind "ruins," fragments of this or that discourse behind which there is only an abyss. Nominating nine episodes as "the nerves of the novel," Nabokov selects either those in which the code of romantic culture imperceptibly transmorphs into its *poshlust* double ("that class list of Ramsdale school," "Lolita in slow motion advancing towards Humbert's gifts," "Lolita playing tennis," "Charlotte saying 'waterproof,'" "the pictures decorating the stylized garret of Gaston Godin," "the hospital at Elphinstone," 316) or those in which, behind the net of cultural codes, suddenly appears naked death—not as a transcendental dimension but as *nothing*: "The Kasbeam barber (who cost me a month of work)" (ibid.) and "pale, pregnant, beloved, irretrievable Dolly Schiller dying in Gray Star (the capital town of the book), or the tinkling sounds of the valley town coming up the mountain trail . . ." (ibid.).

It is most telling that Lolita's status, subjected to the cultural aggression of Humbert, does not fit the boundaries of cultural codes. This is demonstrated, for instance, in her expression "of helplessness so perfect that it seemed to grade into one of rather comfortable inanity just because this was the very limit of injustice and frustration" (283) and in "her sobs in the night—every, every night" (176), as soon as Humbert feigns sleep. In these expressions, unsullied by words, "reality" ("one of the few words which mean nothing without quotes," as Nabokov remarks in the afterword; 312) does not erupt from behind the screen of devalued discourses, nor is a shining "otherness" revealed. "The nerves of the novel" signify nothingness as the last horizon of being.

From this point of view, we can clearly see that culture, cultural models, and stereotypes, deconstructed in *Lolita*, are in principle necessary to guard against such a hopeless essence of existence. The exception of Humbert, trying to manufacture life as a work of literature, is different only in that he follows the models provided by Edgar Allan Poe and Mérimée, and not those by Marlene Dietrich and Humphrey Bogart. He denounces Quilty as the epitome of *poshlust*; but how guilty is Quilty? He is simply one architect, or one mold, of those flat cultural models (simulacra of transcendence) by which millions live. It seems there is no exit: life in the existential wilderness is unbearably horrifying, while life in the shell of cultural stereotype, high or low, is self-destructive and innately catastrophic.

Life, and especially Lolita's childhood, is desiccated and withheld by two competing discourses: the romantic and the pop cultural. Humbert and Quilty find common ground in how they confiscate the individuality and freedom of Lolita, leaving naught but an empty husk, which each of the heroes (and the discourses they represent) struggles to fill with his own meaning. This battle ends with the death of Lolita "in childbed giving birth to a stillborn girl, on Christmas Day 1952" (4). The irrecoverability of childhood, even anew in the life of Lolita's daughter, is poignantly underscored by the date of this twofold tragedy: an aborted Christmas places the final punctuation on Humbert's and Quilty's "projects." (The conclusion is foretold, though goes unnoticed, on the second page of the novel.) This grim affirmation opens onto the historical (per Benjamin) aspect of Lolita, positioning the entire composition as a requiem for modernity, with all its logos manifested in the various discourses that aim to order life into a correspondence with the ideal. As Lolita teaches, these endeavors yield only the extinction of innocent life—of Lolita's precious, vanquished childhood. The whole history of modernity, in the end, becomes a history of cataclysm, self-destruction that propagates from toe tip to scalp, and concludes only in the undoing of its own origin—the liquidation of the Nativity and of the Birth.[8] Probably, this is the point where the history of postmodernism begins.

---

[8] This idea was introduced by the late Marina Kanevskaya, who planned to develop it in her book *The Madonna of Gray Star: Fallacies of Modernity in "Lolita."* Marina's tragic death interrupted her work on this project.

The Poetics of the ITR Discourse: In the 1960s and Today*

Back in 2010, I wrote a column for the popular Russian web portal OpenSpace titled after a line from Mandelstam: "O, that abyss of technical intelligentsia."[1] I summed up in that piece my various grievances about the modern cultural mainstream as well as outlined its limitations, which derive from the discourse of the *nauchno-tekhnicheskaia intelligentsia* (scientific and technological intelligentsia). Originally formulated in the 1960s, this discourse has undergone some dramatic transformations in the subsequent decades. The column caused a certain stir on its publication, and it seemed that I had touched a nerve, so to speak, in the 2010 state of things. This impression was followed within a year by the "snow revolution": former technical intelligentsia, along with newly emerged white-collar workers (known in Russia as the "office plankton," whom I view as the direct heirs of the technical intelligentsia's culture) and those composing a complex community of the humanities, stood up in union with the Left, and even with the nationalists, to form a new social and political entity. It is no wonder that the term "creative class," borrowed from Richard

---

* Translated from Russian by Vladimir Makarov. "ITR"—*inzhenerno-tekhnicheskii rabotnik*, engineer/technical employee.

1 "О, эта бездна ИТР . . ." from Mandelstam's draft of the poem "О, эта Лена, эта нора . . ." in the Voronezh notebooks.

Florida's book of the same title, so rapidly gained use. (I will reserve my appraisal of whether the phrase was relevant until later.) Like everyone else, I was fascinated by the social scope and the cultural energy of this movement: at first glance, it had disproved my pessimism regarding the prevailing cultural conditions.

I was not the only commenter to draw a quick parallel to the days of perestroika (see, for example, Belkovskii 2012a and 2012b). Excepting the availability of the Internet, the two movements had much in common: a clear consensus that the odious presiding regime is the common enemy, a very vague apprehension of what is to come in the wake of that regime, a stagnant hope that new and honest conditions will simply figure themselves into place following the regime's collapse, a winged euphoria and a sense of involvement and concurrence with fellow thinkers who proved to be so very numerous . . . This probably all-too-subjective pattern of thought was immensely gratifying at first, but later gave way to a certain unease: Could it be true that the whole experience of Russia's post-perestroika cultural history has been in vain? Is the intelligentsia actually returning to its state of the late—or even early—1980s, having learned nothing in more than twenty years, save access to the Internet? This discomfort—which, again, could be quite subjective—imparted a new meaning to my experience of grappling with the discourse of the technical intelligentsia of the 1960s, which I see as the foundation and core of the specifically late-Soviet and post-Soviet strands of liberalism.

"ITR" (*inzhenerno-tekhnicheskii rabotnik*, engineer/technical employee) was surely a misnomer as the cultural milieu unified by the scientific intelligentsia's discourse incorporated a far broader company than these laborers alone. This ITR class, distinguished from the "bourgeois specialists" who were their predecessors, emerged in the 1930s. Sheila Fitzpatrick has suggested that it was designed to become the Soviet middle class, which was to form the basis of Stalinist socialism, and subsequently it was conceived of as the late-Soviet version of this middle class by the likes of Boris Dubin, Lev Gudkov, and Alexei Levinson. Western analysts as far back as the '60s described the technical intelligentsia as the most educated echelon of the Soviet elite, coining the name "priviligentsia." It was this subsection of the intelligentsia who offered the most vigorous and massive support to the "Thaw" and became the core of the liberal Soviet intelligentsia in the '60s. It was the ITRs who crowded in the lecture halls of the Polytechnic Museum, who were the chief audience of Galich and Vysotskii, whose jokes spread to the masses on the waves of *KVN* (a televised competition of wits) and whose compositions formed the sounds of the KSP (*klub samodeiatel'noi pesni*, amateur song club) movement.

The members of this class secured their freedom of thought as a precondition for scientific efficiency even before Stalin's death. In the years of the Thaw, marked by an exponential growth in the numbers of the technical intelligentsia,[2] the nurturing efforts of restricted-access research institutes finally kindled this free thinking to the point where it exceeded the bounds of the privileged stratum. Albert Parry, author of *The New Class Divided: Science and Technology versus Communism* (1966), was at the same time quite sure that "if in our permissive society American scientists, engineers, and other technical experts do not constitute one class or even a group, then under the much more restrictive conditions of the Soviet sociopolitical order the comparable Soviet intelligentsia has even less of a chance to get together as a unified force to challenge the Communist Party" (23). As we can clearly see now, Parry missed the mark; it was precisely the presence of the Communist Party and the Soviet power, their role as common enemy, that both rallied the technical intelligentsia and promoted its ideology to an undisputed new rank: the flagship of liberal modernization. In the words of Vladislav Zubok, "Scientists became the first group of highly educated people in the late 1950s and early 1960s whose influence on society and cultural life far surpassed their professional competence" (2009, 131).

As the same author argues, writers during the Thaw failed to wrest control of literary matters, while the technical intelligentsia ever more vigorously purged itself of ideological control and cultivated

---

[2] According to Vladislav Zubok, in the period from 1950 to 1965, the number of jobs in science and research grew in the Soviet Union from 162,000 to 665,000, increasing at the highest rate in world history (2009, 132).

the intellectual freedom so conspicuously absent in the humanities (see Zubok 2009, 137). It is no coincidence that many of the famous dissidents of the 1970s began as hard scientists: Valentin Turchin and Boris Al'tshuler as physicists; Sergei Kovalev, Vladimir Bukovskii, and Zhores Medvedev as biophysicists; Vladimir Al'brekht, Vladimir Kormer, and Aleksandr Esenin-Vol'pin as mathematicians. Vadim Delone, although a graduate of the philology department, came from a family of leading mathematicians and studied at a specialized mathematical secondary school. Liudmila Alekseeva was a history major at Moscow University, but her mother was another prominent mathematician, who authored several university textbooks, worked at the Institute for Mathematics, and taught at the prestigious Bauman Moscow State Technical University.

As Petr Vail' and Aleksandr Genis wrote in *The Sixties: The World of the Soviet Man*:

> Scientists became more than just heroes. The public opinion turned them into the aristocrats of the spirit. [. . .] Scientists were to succeed politicians. Hard science would replace imprecise ideology. Technocracy, instead of partocracy, would lead the country towards utopia. [. . .] This is how the scientists' view was expressed by [Petr] Kapitsa, member of the Soviet Academy of Sciences: "To be ruled democratically and lawfully, every state must have independent institutions, serving as arbiters for every issue. [. . .] It looks like this moral function in the Soviet Union falls on the lot of the Academy of Sciences." (Vail' and Genis 2003, 616–19)

Andrei Sakharov took a similar stance, opening his "Progress, Coexistence and Intellectual Freedom" with the following passage:

> The views of the author were formed in the milieu of the scientific and scientific-technical intelligentsia, which manifests much anxiety over the principles and specific aspects of foreign and domestic policy and over the future of mankind. *This anxiety is nourished, in particular, by a realization that the scientific method of directing policy, the economy, arts, education, and military affairs still has not become a reality.* We regard as "scientific" a method based on deep analysis of facts, theories, and views, presupposing unprejudiced, unfearing open discussion and conclusions. The complexity and diversity of all the phenomena of modern life,

the great possibilities and dangers linked with the scientific-technical revolution and with a number of social tendencies demand precisely such an approach, as has been acknowledged in a number of official statements. [. . .] *International affairs must be completely permeated with scientific methodology.* (Sakharov 1968; emphasis mine)

Despite a very cautious assertion of the compatibility of the suggested models with "a number of official statements," the notions of freedom and progress born among the scientific community very soon ran contrary to official dogmas. Lev Landau, according to his KGB dossier, declared as far back as 1956, "Our system remains fascist and simply cannot change. It is ludicrous to hope that this system can lead us to something good" (quoted in Zubok 2009, 138). Landau added that "if our system cannot collapse peacefully, then a third world war with all its horrors is inevitable. Therefore, the issue of a peaceful dissolution of our system is the vital issue for the future of all humankind" (ibid.). He was much more pessimistic than, say, Sakharov, foreseeing an inevitable war as the extension of the Soviet political regime: "The current state of things cannot last for long. My opinion is, if our system is liquidated without a war, no matter whether by evolution or revolution, the war will be no more. No fascism, no war" (Bessarab 2003). Certainly, fascism here stands for the Soviet system rather than its political opponents.

I would like to argue that an understanding of modernization, which in the 1960s morphed into the ITR discourse, very soon became a rallying platform for the *whole* liberal intelligentsia—or, rather, for the intelligentsia that considered itself liberal. This is a crucial distinction since the concepts of freedom and personality within the scientific intelligentsia's discourse, having originated in Soviet ideological constructs, bore little in common with what was known as liberalism outside the USSR. As a result, the boiling point for European and American liberalism—the 1968 student revolution—went virtually unnoticed by Soviet liberals (it was overshadowed by the Prague Spring's destruction). Additionally, and for the same reason, the political agendas of today's liberals in Russia are frequently closer to those of U.S. Republicans than to those of any liberal party proper.

However, it would be an exercise in imprecision to limit our study to politics alone. Throughout the whole Soviet period, politics remained indivisible from cultural phenomena. Moreover, it was in the field of culture that central political processes actually transpired.

The first authoritative confirmation of the ITR discourse as a *cultural phenomenon* was the now nearly forgotten incident known as the debate of "physicists and lyricists."[3] Konstantin Bogdanov (2011), in his detailed analysis of this once very lively forum, aptly points out the "heated grandiloquence and empty rhetoric" that characterized these arguments. Such a description was warranted, most likely, by the rhetorical tendency to substitute actual problems with false ones. Feuds over what was more useful for mankind, "the culture of feelings" or scientific progress, were utterly meaningless; these subjects—mere placeholders for an ulterior contest. Behind the façade of the debate, the intelligentsia of the Thaw was deeply disappointed with the squandered potential of art and literature, seeing contemporary authors' works as trussed up and permeated by ideological mythologies and Socialist Realism's lies.[4] In such a context, science and scientific pursuits were perceived not only as liberated from Soviet ideology but as openly opposing it.[5] As Vail'

---

[3] A letter to *Komsomol'skaia Pravda* by Igor' Andreevich Poletaev, a specialist in cybernetics, in the words of Vladislav Zubok, "was a revolutionary claim for the supremacy of science as a cultural form replacing the previously dominant poetry and highbrow novels" (2009, 133). This interpretation is unlikely to be correct, as the debate had its hidden "signifier" in the dominance of socialist realism rather than in actual "highbrow literature." Poletaev made it clear that his reaction to an article by Ilya Ehrenburg condemning a certain Iurii the ITR for his lack of interest in literature and art was quite calm: "The trouble starts when an idiot, an uneducated bohemian, a poetaster calling himself a poet for the lack of better examples, approaches a hard-working engineer and starts annoying him and calling him 'uncultured', since the engineer has nothing to do with poetry" (ibid., 19).

[4] The debate began before the publication of Solzhenitsyn's *One Day in the Life of Ivan Denisovich*; like Pasternak's *Doctor Zhivago*, the works of Nikolai Arzhak and Abram Terts, along with other samizdat texts, remained unknown to the mass reader and could not be discussed in Soviet media.

[5] "Studies of music, fine arts, theater and literature Dau considered

and Genis remarked later, "After it was discovered that words tell lies, equations were more trustworthy" (2003, 612). The impossibility of addressing the real underlying issue ultimately conducted all the demagogic effusions of "physicists vs. lyricists."

This debate was often analytically paired with the famous article by C. P. Snow about two cultures—the sciences and the humanities—that have lost any point of contact whatsoever (see Snow [1956] 1998). The actual Soviet situation, however, was vastly different from this model. As Zubok explains it, "Even the literary vanguard during the Thaw seemed to recognize the supremacy of scientists. For all their personal candor and linguistic experimentation, the young poets of the Thaw could not and did not offer a universal and global alternative to the discredited official ideology" (2009, 140). Agents of science could and did offer such an alternative. Lacking any authoritative opposition from the visible public culture of the humanities, with its excessive dependence on ideology, the technical intelligentsia began to build its own cultural milieu. Physicists did not limit themselves to joke writing (anthologized in the popular book *Fiziki shutiat* [*Physicists' Jokes*, 1966]), but also produced undeniably fine poetry such as that of atomic scientist Gertsen Kopylov[6] or neurobiologist Dmitrii Sukharev. Scientists could spread their wings in professional prose as well: among the most triumphant examples are Vladimir Makanin, a graduate of the Faculty of Mechanics and Mathematics (*mekhmat*) at Moscow State University, whose novel *Priamaia liniia* (*A Straight Line*) made him famous in 1965, and Elena Venttsel', a professor of mathematics known since 1962 by her pen name, I. Grekova (from *igrek*, a Russian pronunciation of the algebraic symbol y).

    'pseudoscience' and usually referred to them as 'the deception of the working people.' It was impossible to make him change his mind" (Bessarab 2003).

[6] Under the pen name of Semen Telegin, Kopylov published the article "Kak byt'" ("How to Be," 1969?), which was known to have evoked Solzhenitsyn's indignation, in samizdat. Among other things, the article described how "physics' powerful methodology" gives rise to "a new philosophy of life," and "dozens of discipline-specific and local subcultures are putting forth in the drawing rooms of design bureaus, in research institutes' lobbies, in the halls of the Academy of Sciences."

The social science fiction by the Strugatsky brothers (Boris, an astronomer, and Arkady, an interpreter); *Deviat' dnei odnogo goda* (*Nine Days of One Year*, 1952) by Mikhail Romm; *Kollegi* (*Colleagues*, 1959) and *Zolotaia nasha Zhelezka* (*Our Golden Iron*, 1973) by Vasilii Aksenov, a medical doctor by education; *Idu na grozu* (*Into the Storm*, 1962) and *Eta strannaia zhizn'* (*This Strange Life*, 1974) by Daniil Granin, a graduate of the Leningrad Polytechnic; *Bratskaia GES* (*The Bratsk Power Station*, 1965) by Evgenii Evtushenko, of the Institute for Literature; *Oza* (1964) by Andrei Voznesenskii, an architect by degree; *Vertikal'* (*The Vertical*, 1967) by Stanislav Govorukhin, who graduated from the school of geology and subsequently the VGIK (State Institute of Cinematography)—these are but a few of the conspicuous cultural out-churnings in which the ITR discourse honed and polished its rhetoric and attitudes toward life. But the particular diploma that this or that person had was largely unimportant in the 1960s and '70s since the cultural values born unto the technical intelligentsia were spread further (even furthest) by people outside the ITR class. It is highly indicative that Shurik, the hero of Leonid Gaidai's tremendously popular movie trilogy, joins a polytechnic university in *Operatsiia "Y"* (*Operation "Y,"* 1965) and in *Ivan Vasil'evich meniaet professiiu* (*Ivan Vasilievich: Back to the Future*, 1973) invents a time machine. Although in *Kavkazskaia plennitsa* (*Kidnapping, Caucasian Style*, 1966), he suddenly appears as a philologist studying folklore in the Caucasus, Shurik is indeed an archetypal ITR. It is also worth remembering that Iurii Lotman's appeal to literary studies to become a real *nauka*—a word used in Russian for both science and scholarship—meant not only untethering itself from ideological pressure but also embracing scientific methods. It was on this very foundation that mathematical linguistics and Russian versions of structuralism and semiotics originated.

In its development, the scientific intelligentsia's discourse has absorbed a number of related entities (among them the "youth prose" and the "bard" tradition of songwriting) and distanced itself from others, which at first seemed cognate but later proved incompatible with the liberal concepts framed by this discourse. The ITR discourse's boundaries thus began to seem eroded and blurred.

At the same time, however, the discourse itself has preserved an internal structure, albeit one drastically reformed in the post-Soviet period. Ultimately, as my hypothesis goes, it is the ITR discourse that has in fact shaped the cultural mainstream of late-Soviet and post-Soviet liberalism.

The ITR discourse was, of course, far from the only intellectual and cultural formation of the 1960s and '70s. On one side of this spectrum of developing thought, almost concurrent to the discourse of the ITR, arose the nationalist discourse, in all of its "white" and "red," "Orthodox" and "pagan" varieties. On the other, stirring to life deep in the underground, the proto- and postmodernist discourse was conceived at the same moment—with many brands of its own, from Moscow conceptualism to Leningrad religious modernism.

In this context, the Sakharov-Solzhenitsyn rift remains quite urgent, as well as both indicative of and very important in shaping the two wings of Soviet anti-Sovietism (liberal vs. nationalist, or rather, Enlightenment vs. romanticism). Solzhenitsyn remains irrefutably a product of the scientific and technical milieu, first tied to the Department of Physics and Mathematics at Rostov University, then to the Marfino *sharashka* (a secret research institute staffed by political prisoners). However, his sociocultural agenda is radically divergent from the ITR discourse, though they belong to a common intellectual paradigm. I would venture to explain this affinity as follows: both Sakharov's and Solzhenitsyn's concepts of modernizing Russia are built on *essentialist concepts*. In the case of Sakharov, this means the notion of *progress*; for Solzhenitsyn, that of *nation*. This essentialism—the idea that intellectual constructs have an objective and invariable nature—stems not solely from a scientific and technical mind-set. To a certain degree, it is a mirrored version of Soviet ideological essentialism and imports from this parent discourse two of its pillars: "the progress of mankind" and "the Soviet people."

Solzhenitsyn scrutinizes the influence of "nation" as subsuming personality and opposing both "the Soviet people" and the cosmopolitan intelligentsia's notion of individuality: "Nations are very much living entities, to whom all moral senses are available, including, however painful it might be, remorse" (1973). Sakharov centers conversely on "progress," also understood to be an absolute value, and one construed primarily as an extension of personal freedom: "I am likewise convinced that freedom of conscience, together with the other civic rights, provides the basis for scientific progress and constitutes a guarantee that scientific advances will not be used to despoil mankind, providing the basis for economic and social progress, which in turn is a political guarantee for the possibility of an effective defense of social rights. At the same time I should like to defend the thesis of the original and decisive significance of civic and political rights in molding the destiny of mankind. This view differs essentially from the widely accepted Marxist view, as well as the technocratic opinions, according to which it is precisely material factors and social and economic conditions that are of decisive importance" (1968). In this instance, Sakharov is speaking of a person liberated from national, religious, ideological, and many other suprapersonal dependences.

It is this abstract vagueness of "person" as a category within the ITR discourse that gave rise to so many subsequent transformations and reorientations, seeking "roots" in religion, blood and soil, or imperial supremacy (i.e., inclining toward Solzhenitsyn's position). However, this uncertainty also begot *irony*—to the present culture, the ITR subject's most attractive feature. Irony comprises a distancing of oneself from most (though not all) metanarratives—primarily from the Soviet quasi religion—and articulated increasing disappointment in the supposed Communist utopia. Such areas as science, progress, and personal freedom generally remained immune to irony. Hence, texts and movies discovered a fresh, popular device: the *shestidesiatnik* ("one of the generation of the '60s"), an ironist who seemingly doesn't give a penny for anything yet heroically sacrifices himself—frequently for the sake of science. (As an aside, it should be noted that the ironic hero of the ITR culture is always or almost always a man. The major bodies of the scientific intelligentsia's discourse, such as the KSP and tourist or alpinist subcultures, have formulated a cult around educated versions of machismo, with a "real man" stifling a woman into the second-rate role of an obedient lover or "war bride." In this sense, the distance between Romm's *Deviat' dnei odnogo goda* and Govorukhin's *Vertikal'* is remarkably slight.)

Thus, essentialism and the binarism that derives from it have become the most important facets of the ITR discourse. Emanating into the cultural domain, these traits "ontologize" culture, consequently representing it as a set of "eternal" values rather than a dynamic and paradoxical process. This perspective consigns culture to rubber-stamping premade ideas instead of problematizing values, seeks unwavering loyalty to lessons long learned rather than producing creative discomfort, and promotes reverent protection of established hierarchies rather than subversion. It denies, in a word, the "un-coziness" of culture (as described by Leonid Batkin and in a different way by Giorgio Vattimo): "Knowledge itself among the intelligentsia was and still is imagined as a sum of ready-made truths, objectively existing somewhere, to be found and utilized. [...] Any issue of importance that could cast doubt on and relativize the existing views and ideas, was ousted. [...] In other words, the mechanisms of the intelligentsia's culture give their sanction to the value of subjectivity only as a collective good, an ideological symbol, a collective resource, inherited from the completed tradition, the 'classics'" (Gudkov and Dubin 2009, 133, 136).

It was on this foundation that the *neotraditionalist turn* (as diagnosed by Gudkov [2004]) transpired in the first decade of the twenty-first century. It cannot, of course, be entirely written down to the role of the ITR discourse, but being a core of the cultural liberal mainstream, it proved to have little or no resistance against new political trends essentializing nation and empire. The essentialization of culture above all is accountable for the ITR discourse's tendency to binarize, simplify, and resist complexity. It is why the community of Gaidai's Shuriks, avid readers of Hemingway and the Strugatskys, admirers of Evtushenko and Voznesenskii, of bard songs and *KVN*, has ebbed quietly past and yielded its shores to the fans of Veller and Minaev, Luk'ianenko and Prilepin, Grishkovets and Emelin, *Nasha Russia* and *Comedy Club*, and so on. It is why each and every cultural player in today's liberal mainstream functions as no more than a substitutive tremor to a late-Soviet counterpart.

The resistance to complexity erected by the scientific intelligentsia's discourse, an attempt at revitalizing the Enlightenment by its nature, either completely overlooks or willfully ignores the critique of the Enlightenment that has been simmering in Europe and America since 1968. This critique—spawned in the wake of the Second World War by Theodor Adorno and Max Horkheimer and fostered by Foucault, Derrida, Lyotard, and later Agamben and Jean-Luc Nancy—led in time to the creation of a new cultural paradigm, which can be called, with a good deal of reserve, post-structuralist. Rather, it should be termed post-ideological or post-utopian, as it methodically and consistently undermines belief in progress as a category and in the unambiguity of scientific knowledge, as well as traces the link between violence and metaphysics, between power and the seemingly natural "order of things." Most important, it demonstrates how the zeal of enlightenment forms a basis for terror. The late-Soviet cultural milieu cannot claim total ignorance of these ideas (consider Iurii Levada's sociological circle or Merab Mamardashvili's philosophical influences), yet on the whole, the late-Soviet and post-Soviet scientific intelligentsia's discourse has lain on the other side of the divide.

The Enlightenment fever—based in a belief in progress and supported by the strength of reason, science, and technologies (including those with political ends)—struck the promoters of the ITR discourse with a twofold opposition: to the state and the "people," and to the absurdity of the regime, on the one hand, and to the insurmountable idiocy of the "uneducated masses," on the other. Sakharov (1968), in his manifesto, exposed the peril resultant to free thinking: "Freedom of thought is under a triple threat in modern society—from the deliberate opium of mass culture, from cowardly, egotistic, and philistine ideologies, and from the ossified dogmatism of a bureaucratic oligarchy and its favorite weapon, ideological censorship." "Mass culture" and "philistine ideology" appear as interchangeable here, as both terms are really de facto synonyms for the Soviet ideologeme of "the people" (*narod*).[7]

---

[7] Solzhenitsyn and his nationalist followers employ an analogous strategy:

The ITR discourse's preservation of the Soviet notion of "philistinism" (*meshchanstvo, obyvatel'shchina*) is curious. Whereas the Soviet discourse repurposed *meshchanstvo* from a generic term for the third estate into a political label inciting hatred of conventional norms of living and everyday comfort, the ITR discourse makes the *meshchanin*, or philistine, an antonym to the free Man (capitalization mandatory), or rather, a euphemism for the sacral Soviet category of "the people." This contrast is most notably exhibited by the Strugatsky brothers (more on them below), with the most exemplary case being *Ulitka na sklone* (*Snail on the Slope*, 1966), in which Peretz skirmishes with the bureaucratic machine while Candide is devoured by the Woods as an allegorical feast of *narod*.

The theme of this collision finds a reduced (or rather, a travestied) treatment by Sergei Luk'ianenko in his *Vselennaia "Dozorov"* (World of Watches) series of novels (popularized by Timur Bekmambetov's *Night Watch / Day Watch* film diptych). Through the undying clash between the Dark and the Light, the author portrays a supernaturally tinged melee that pits constructive, impersonal powers of the state against destructive forces of individualist freedom. One description of the Light is most indicative:

> A burning heart, clean hands and a cool head. [. . .] Small wonder that in the days of the revolution and the civil war the Light almost in full strength joined the Cheka. And those who hadn't, mostly perished. From the hands of the Dark, yes, but more often from the hands of those whom they were trying to protect. From human hands. From human stupidity. From human stupidity, meanness, cowardice, hypocrisy or envy. (Luk'ianenko 2006, 273)

A similar friction in Dmitry Bykov's *ZhD* (2006; published in English as *Living Souls*, 2010) takes the shape of a civil war between the Varangians (proponents of a strong state) and the ZhD people

---

he, too, renames the categories that do not fit into his ideologemes. Thus, he terms a not-quite-national and irreligious intelligentsia *obrazovanshchina* ("people with superfluous education"), and people who lost their national or ethnic roots become the "masses" (as opposed to *narod* and *natsiia*, "nation").

(liberals), with the two sides depicted as equally injurious. Acting both as perpetual victim and as stumbling block to the warring parties are the Vas'ki, the true "people" of the region, who struggle to protect their secret culture and identity.

It was just such a twofold conflict as these authors imagine that induced the particular liberalism of the ITRs, at once antidemocratic and antitotalitarian. Such oxymoronic pairings as idealism and pragmatism, total irony and hierarchic consciousness, anti-Marxism and reliance on implicit Marxist dichotomies, populism and a particular brand of sectarianism (intellectual clubs, KSP, *KVN*, tourist clubs)—all of these are attributable to what may be defined as the double negativity of the ITR discourse.

Double negativity deposits the intelligentsia protagonist in a position of exceptionalism. The intelligentsia may be compared to magicians and wizards, as in the Strugatsky brothers' *Ponedel'nik nachinaetsia v subbotu* (*Monday Begins on Saturday*, 1965), or encircled with a halo of heroic self-sacrifice, as in Romm's *Deviat' dnei odnogo goda*. When this conceptualization extends to the dissident movement, seen as a struggle for social progress, the exceptionalism is augmented by the illumination of a profoundly tragic alienation. As the scientific intelligentsia's discursive tributaries roll ever more robustly into the mainstream, this exceptionalism drenches the whole liberal intelligentsia, essentializing itself along the way. Vladimir Kormer, among others, has examined the ensuing complex:

> No one has ever been alienated from their country and their state to such an extent as the Russian intelligentsia. No one has ever felt so alienated—not from others, or society, or God—but from their land, their people, their statehood. It was this peculiar feeling that the heart and mind of an educated Russian felt in the late nineteenth–early twentieth century. It was realizing this collective alienation that made him part of the intelligentsia. [. . .] In spite of all the transformations that happened to Russia and its educated layer over this amazing 60 years, this layer has remained unchanged in its main feature, still being the intelligentsia in the only true sense of the word. (1970)

Kormer also explains how the exceptionalist or alienated consciousness nurtures what he defines as the intelligentsia's "double consciousness":

> The intelligentsia does not accept the Soviet power, they repel it, sometimes hate it. On the other hand, they both are in a symbiotic relationship: the intelligentsia feeds and nurtures it, at the same time waiting for the collapse of the Soviet power and hoping that it collapses sooner or later. On the other hand, the intelligentsia collaborates with it. The intelligentsia suffers because they have to live under Soviet control and, at the same time, aspires for its own well-being. The intelligentsia would prefer to think of Soviet power as of something external, as of a tribulation that came on them from somewhere, but fails to think this way consistently, hard as they try to stick to such a viewpoint. (1970)

Kormer's statements from an article published in 1970 under the pen name O. Altaev can be further expounded by two quotations, one detailing the early phases of the complex in question and the other considering its post-Soviet repercussions. The first comes from the book by Petr Vail' and Aleksandr Genis *The Sixties*, written in the 1980s: "It is worth recalling that the Soviet physicists did not have Hiroshima-type moral sufferings. The image of a Frankenstein was not present in the Russian imagination" (2003, 614).[8] And the second comes from Dina Khapaeva's *Goticheskoe obshchestvo* (*The Gothic Society*, 2007):

> Mass idealization of the West that permeated Russian society in the late 1980s and early 1990s was a way of living through the changes that led the Russian mind to deny any connection with the Soviet past. [. . .] The more detailed, thanks to westernizers' efforts, the picture of the ugly [Soviet] past became, the stronger the impulse to identify this past with the hostile regime rather

---

[8] Nevertheless, the omniscient recording devices preserved the following statement by Lev Landau, which runs counter to Vail' and Genis's sureness: "One must use every available power to steer clear of the nuclear affair. At the same time, any attempt to refuse or exempt oneself from such affairs should be done most carefully. The aim of a clever man, who wants to live a happy life, as far as this is possible, is to exempt oneself from the tasks put forth by the state that is built on repression" (Bessarab 2003).

> than themselves. The "condemnation of Stalinism" made the Soviet past turn alien, an alien history which had nothing to do with those who had made up their mind to "rebuild Russia" anew. [. . .] To clear up the path toward the West for Russia, the Soviet past had to disappear in the abyss of oblivion. Otherwise, its continued presence would destroy the belief in progress. (89–91)

The absence of any feeling of responsibility for the devastating military might of the Soviet regime is typical among many (though certainly not all) representatives of the technical intelligentsia of the 1960s. This is a notable instance of the class's double consciousness, possibly in its purest form. Khapaeva has shown how the double consciousness propped up by the liberal scientific intelligentsia's discourse begets the hefty issue of the Soviet past failing to be "worked out." This issue looms over every acre of post-Soviet culture. (It is remarkable how close, almost verbatim, Khapaeva comes to Kormer's words.) The Soviet catastrophe's not being "worked out," as has been many times corroborated by research and analysis, leads both to nostalgia for the Soviet past and to the replication of many cultural and social practices of late socialism (more on this in upcoming chapters).

Curiously, the absolutization of progress has been abandoned by the ITR discourse in the post-Soviet period. The proof of this lies not only in the retrospective fantasies of mathematician-turned-historian Anatolii Fomenko but also in the well-elaborated, four-stage cyclical schematic of Russian history (reforms—crackdown—thaw—stagnation or dementia) that Dmitry Bykov has advanced for more than ten years (see Bykov 2003a). Although these conceptions of history leave no place for progress, they do preserve the exceptionalism complex that appoints the intellectual as an agent of liberal modernization.

The post-Soviet transmutations of the scientific intelligentsia's discourse can be demonstrated perhaps most clearly by the Strugatsky brothers and by Viktor Pelevin, whose works have served as the preeminent mouthpieces for critical periods of the ITR discourse—in the 1960s and '70s, and in the '90s and 2000s, respectively. The subsequent article in this collection analyzes the Strugatskys' trope of the progressor as the central element of the ITR discourse. As for Pelevin, the younger author's personal pedigree is, likewise, that of the ITR. Pelevin graduated from the Moscow Power Engineering Institute, after which he was employed by the magazine *Khimiia i zhizn'* (*Chemistry and Life*), while his first independent compositions were exercises in social sci-fi. However, Pelevin's characters feature one important distinction from their ITR parentage: positivist faith in reason and science is replaced with a belief in the irrational, also understood as a certain *technology*, at times demanding chemical catalysts—that is, drugs. This technology transforms the mind, and with it the world. The substitution is quite in line with the overall evolution of the ITR discourse proper; in the 1980s and 1990s, the technical intelligentsia was fascinated with religion, mysticism, and the occult, fields that came to succeed the fully dispersed "grand narratives" of ideologies.

Pelevin's texts, from the very start, might seem to invest no illusions in their characters toward improving the world. At best, these characters are found deep in self-improvement; at worst, trying to acclimate to a world that reinvents itself blazingly fast, jostling them in unwelcome, unknown directions. But this impression is mistaken: these individuals really do influence the world around them. Their strategy (Pelevin's favorite, it seems, visible most overtly in the conclusion of *Chapaev i Pustota / Buddha's Little Finger* [1996]) is to erase "reality" and ascend into the beautiful and boundless world created by their own imagination. One can construe this self-deliverance as an essentially solipsistic response to the defeat of a particular ITR variation of utopia: basically, we have tried to change society's consciousness, but nobody cares about our ideas, so let us not expend our effort on the ungrateful; we shall instead create a perfect world for ourselves and our loved ones with the same mind-altering technique.

Generation "P" (1999) employs a different, yet more significant, scenario, also derived from the disillusionment of former progressors: technologies, albeit with an irrational background, are aimed at manipulating mass conscience in order to secure the nearly absolute power of a new-generation ITR (here with an Institute for Literature degree). This rule is founded on deception and self-deception, on dreams and illusions and, most importantly, on the blinding, pervasive, and hypnotic desire for *the dough*. Nevertheless, as the novel's finale reveals, the authority situated on such a foundation is just as illusory and demands that Tatarsky, now verging on divinity, be both literally and metaphorically *depersonalized*. His face, endlessly copied and plastered across every advertisement, becomes a symbol of power and forsakes its significance as a personal identifier.

Pelevin carries the Strugatskys' motifs further, albeit with a tangible irony: whereas one Strugatsky character becomes a *liuden* and vanishes transcendentally into the vast expanses of open space, almost every protagonist of Pelevin's, from *Omon Ra* to his latest works, must become a god, with each new metamorphosis more monstrous than the last. I read this disparity between the authors as signaling a transformation in the technical intelligentsia's exceptionalism/alienation complex.

Tatarsky is the first in Pelevin's line of *polittekhnologi* (spin doctors), who, like their prototypes from Georgii Shchedrovitskii (see Kukulin 2007) to Gleb Pavlovskii, so vibrantly embody cynical modernization: as described by Peter Sloterdijk, "that modernized unhappy consciousness, on which enlightenment has labored both successfully and in vain" (1987, 33). Indeed, Sloterdijk expresses exactly the outcome of the ITR modernizers' enterprise:

> Today the cynic appears as a mass figure: an average social character in the upper echelons of the elevated superstructure. [...] The key social positions in boards, parliaments, commissions, executive committees, publishing companies, practices, faculties, and lawyers' and editors' offices have long since become a part of this diffuse cynicism. A certain chic bitterness provides an undertone to its activity. [...] They know what they are doing, but they do it because, in the short run, the force of circumstances and the instinct for self-preservation are speaking the same language, and they are telling them that it has to be so. Others would do it anyway, perhaps worse. Thus, the new, integrated cynicism even has the understandable feeling about itself of being a victim and of making sacrifices. (32–33)

Sloterdijk's statement fits Pelevin's cast of characters perfectly, with one minor caveat: their cynicism is far from diffuse. On the contrary, it is a very proud and defiant cynicism. However, its sources lie in the same double consciousness that permeated the intelligentsia of the 1960s and '70s (including the exceptionalism complex and the self-sacrificial volunteerism), as described by Kormer.

As is well known, the participants of the protest movement of the winter of 2011–12 chose to identify themselves with the phrase "creative class." Out of this descriptor stems the question I have been saving: Can the modern liberal intelligentsia, molded, inter alia, by the ITR discourse, broadly be deemed the "creative class"? For the famed sociologist Richard Florida, from whose books the term is borrowed, the creative class entails a strange unity of software engineers, architects, designers, university professors, people of art—in a word, all those marketing the products of their creative activity and capable of developing "meaningful new forms." Having studied the areas where their concentration is the highest, Florida discovered that although this social group is highly mobile, professionals of this sort prefer to live in a few particular U.S. cities and towns over, say, any old stead where jobs are available. Comparing his own map of the creative class's residential hot spots with a colleague's study examining the concentration of gay communities, Florida found the maps to be nearly identical. He arrived at the conclusion that those individuals assembled under the "creative class" designation are linked together not only by their seat in the economic system and the type of commodity they produce but also by the aspects of lifestyle.

In the process of becoming a social force, creativity, as Florida's work demonstrates, demands a specific code of values, in opposition to those of both orthodox and pragmatic standpoints. Protestant ethics is replaced here by a cult of individuality reaching into the eccentric, a fascination with everything "foreign and exotic," a rejection of traditional religions, and an imperative of racial, gender, and sexual diversity. The issue of whether a company is ready to provide insurance to homosexual partners is substantial to the creative class regardless of one's own sexual orientation. At the same time, Florida insists, "Members of the Creative Class resist characterization as alternative or bohemian. These labels suggest being outside or even against the prevailing culture, and they insist they are part of the culture, working and living inside it. In this regard, the Creative Class has made certain symbols of nonconformity acceptable—even conformist. It is in this sense that they represent not an alternative group but a new [. . .] mainstream of society" (2000, 82).

To mechanically cross apply all of these traits to Russia's protest-minded intelligentsia would surely be an empty gesture. However, it is quite remarkable that the debates in the Russian Internet community (i.e., the new intelligentsia, a candidate to the position of Russia's creative class) have in recent years been raging around exactly the same values that Florida cites among those definitive of the creative class in the United States.

Reactions to Pussy Riot's performance in the Cathedral of Christ the Savior in February 2012 for the first time have linked together at least three crucial and yet-unresolved issues in the modern intelligentsia's mind-set: the attitude toward the church and traditional religiosity in general, the attitude toward contemporary art and its eccentric and postmodernist "obscenity," and the attitude toward feminism. A newly adopted law of 2013 prohibiting "homosexual propaganda" also triggered an intense debate and uncovered another chord of dissonance within the protest-thirsty intelligentsia—the attitude toward gay culture and homosexuality. The new round of discord began after the annexation of Crimea in 2014 and the war in eastern Ukraine, marking the neo-imperialist and isolationist turn of neotraditionalism. The chasm around values of the empire and nationalism indicates a new step away from the ITR discourse. Will this process continue, or will it prove to be reversible? Is essentialism supported in the ITR discourse fading away under the new historical and cultural conditions, or is it getting stronger in confrontation with new political repressions? These questions deserve close monitoring since they surely define whether the future of Russian culture will be different from its past.

The *Progressor* between the Imperial and the Colonial

> I was a Progressor for three years only, I was bringing good, only good and nothing but good, but, God, how they hated me, those people! And they had a right to do so. Because gods have come without asking permission.
> —*Arkady Strugatsky and Boris Strugatsky*[1]

> We are progressors, enlighteners, a landing party. We do not need to be liked by the electorate. We do not care if they like us or not.
> —*Valeriia Novodvorskaia*[2]

Within "Imperial Situation"

Alexander Etkind's monograph *Internal Colonization: Russia's Imperial Experience* (2011) has accomplished a good measure more than to contribute a novel perspective to the ongoing conversation

---

[1] «Я был Прогрессором всего три года, я нес добро, только добро, ничего, кроме добра, и, господи, как же они ненавидели меня, эти люди! И они были в своем праве. Потому что боги пришли, не спрашивая разрешения» (2000–2003, 8:631). All translations from Russian in this chapter are mine.

[2] «Мы прогрессоры, просветители, десант. У нас нет обязанности нравиться избирателям. Нам абсолютно безразлично, нравимся ли мы или нет» (Sobchak 2012).

about the Russian Empire as a cultural entity. It has also presented a new paradigm for the discussion of Soviet, late-Soviet, and post-Soviet cultural experiences. Etkind's concept, wherein the methods of colonial domination were exercised upon both colonial and noncolonial subjects, dissolves the dichotomy of "external" and "internal" colonization by the revelation of a constructed, rather than an essentialized, notion of the "colonial Other." Following the author's logic, one may find that the effects of the "colonial boomerang" (an idea introduced by Hannah Arendt in her book *On Violence*) spread two-directionally. In its "classical" interpretation, the colonial boomerang concept suggests the adoption of colonial methods of repression within metropoles. By the same token, the Soviet colonization of Eastern Europe evinces the "externalization" of Communist methods of internal colonization developed in the USSR in the 1920s–30s, through the "cultural revolution," collectivization, industrialization, and the Great Terror.

However, this historical approach is complicated by openly anticolonial Soviet rhetoric and practices in former Russian colonies that result in the paradoxical "affirmative action empire" (see Martin 2001). Ilya Gerasimov, Sergei Glebov, and Marina Mogilner explicate the complex nature of Soviet empireness as one that has already integrated its anticolonial and postcolonial aspects:

> The Soviet regime established on much of the territory of the former Russian Empire [...] after 1917 made anticolonialism one of its priorities in both domestic and foreign policies. [...] The Soviet version of anticolonial rhetoric and politics contained a genuinely postcolonial quality. It unmasked the hidden hegemonic agenda of even the most benevolent bourgeois *mission civilisatrice*, and underlined the clash between the authentic and spontaneously revolutionary class consciousness of the oppressed, and the false consciousness of the colonial ideology of capitalist modernization imposed by the oppressors. Most importantly, the Soviet regime dared to counter the very hegemonic discourse of the "West" with an alternative version of modernity as its cornerstone category. [. . .] The claim to be a "Second World" was the claim for an alternative version of history, the claim for historical subjectivity and independence in articulating the discourse of modernity. (2013, 109, 117)

While answering Mogilner's query about the applicability of his concept to Soviet society, Etkind tellingly avoids generalizing statements, emphasizing the continuity between certain aspects of the Soviet project with the imperial period's internal colonization:

> Internal colonization is not an ideal sort (having corresponding "versions"), but a vector that connects geographic, political, and cultural impulses. A vector always has a direction, it starts from one point and aims at the other. Certainly among a huge diversity of Soviet practices there were many that were directed towards the center. I think, soon one will not be able to write a history of the Gulag, or, for example, the history of Soviet urbanization without involving the concept of internal colonization. (Mogilner and Etkind 2011, 124–25)

Other scholars (myself included) have attempted to apply Etkind's scheme to Soviet and post-Soviet periods on a much broader scale. Contributors to the volume *Tam, vnutri* (*There within*; Etkind, Uffelmann, and Kukulin 2012) have extended Etkind's logic to Soviet and post-Soviet forms of modernity. In the introduction to the volume, its editors, while observing the fusion of repressive methods of internal colonization in the USSR of the 1920s–50s, exemplified by the Gulag ("an extreme form of internal colonization" [29]), describe the post-Soviet period as postcolonial, yet complicated by neo-imperialist tendencies. Kukulin, through the analysis of a massive body of literary texts (with a special attention paid to Fazil' Iskander, Aleksandr Solzhenitsyn, and Semen Lipkin), has demonstrated how Russian literature between the 1970s and 2010s explored the hybridity of a Soviet subject (see Kukulin 2012). According to this scholar's conclusions, the late Soviet subject exemplifies an amalgam of features characteristic of the "colonizer" and the "colonized," while the post-Soviet subject exhibits the crumbling of this hybridity, triggered by the emancipation from dependence on and continuous dialogue with the state power. Kukulin argues that both phases resonate with the postcolonial paradigm; indeed, the melding in the Soviet subject of the qualities of imperial master and colonial subaltern recall Homi Bhabha's idea of postcolonial mimicry: "the desire for a reformed unrecognizable Other, *as a subject of a difference that is almost the same but not quite*" (Bhabha 1994, 86; author's emphasis).

Since 2014 neo-imperialist rhetoric has surged in Russia's state media and political (as well as cultural) discourse alongside the annexation of Crimea and the dispatch of support to separatist enclaves in the eastern part of Ukraine, reinforced by the enthusiasm of an overwhelming majority of the Russian population. Such widespread zeal indicates a more dimensional presence of neo-imperialist tendencies in post-Soviet culture than a mere lingering shadow of the postcolonial late-Soviet mainstream. In this environment, the concept of the *cognitive turn* acquires new relevance. This concept has been developed by a circle of scholars affiliated with the historical magazine *Ab Imperio*. In a series of publications, these scholars have argued that revisionist studies of modern empires induced the crises in traditional dichotomies between premodern and modern, and between overseas and continental empires, and planted doubts about "the assumed fixity of boundaries between metropoles and colonial periphery" (Gerasimov et al. 2009, 8). Yet such labels as "racialized discourse, Orientalism, modern politics, ideologies, and techniques of the 'gardening empire'" have demonstrated much greater stability in the characterization of modern empires than those supposedly "objective" dichotomies (8–9). In accordance with some Western researchers of modern empires (see Beissinger 1995; Brubaker 1998; Suny 2001; Burbank, von Hagen, and Remnev 2007), the *Ab Imperio* historians urge us to focus "on empire as a mental construct or a system of thinking that accommodates the different types of human and spatial diversity" (Gerasimov et al. 2009, 15), an approach that entails understanding empire as a "context-setting framework of languages of self-description of imperial experience." According to these scholars, the concept of the "imperial situation," defined by "the complex of [imperial] languages of self-description and self-rationalization" (17, 20), appears to be more flexible than the concrete terms of *empire*. Furthermore, the ideal sort of empire presupposes "the situation of uncertainty, incommensurability, and indistinction [. . .] as the quintessential characteristic of 'imperial formation'" (21; authors' emphasis).

From this perspective, I would like to revisit the functions and implications of the *progressor*. This figure is an agent of a highly developed civilization covertly planted into the repressive bog of a backward society, who tries not to interfere with the natural course of the "alien" history, but instead to help or alleviate the suffering of select denizens of the host world—mainly its intellectuals and those to whom the progressor grows attached. Surprisingly, this character type has maintained its currency beyond its formative appearances in the works of Arkady (1925–1991) and Boris (1933–2012) Strugatsky, and into the era of post-Soviet literature, as will be exemplified by analysis of widely popular contemporary authors such as Dmitry Bykov, Viktor Pelevin, Boris Akunin, and Sergei Luk'ianenko. I argue here that the trope of the progressor signifies the cultural dramaturgy of internal colonization, and in this capacity it has become a form of imaginary self-identification for late-Soviet and post-Soviet liberals who opposed the Communist regime in the 1980s and have confronted authoritative, as well as nationalist and neo-imperialist, tendencies in post-Soviet politics.

The progressor's role can hardly be defined as postcolonial, since the character primarily offers an identification not with a "colonized" but with a "colonizer," a bearer of enforced progress to the passive and backward community of "natives"; such a stance typically predicates Orientalization of aborigines as a part of the "package." At the same time, as I will attempt to show, progressors tend to expose internal contradictions in the implied sociopolitical identification, frequently despite the respective authors' intentions. Most significantly, the progressor signifies the interconnectedness and mutual influence of seemingly incompatible positions, one based on the imagined or real cultural (and sometimes political) superiority and another on the imagined or real external or internal subalternity. Thus, this cultural trope in many ways epitomizes the nature of late Soviet postcolonial mimicry, representing "the sign of a double articulation; a complex strategy of reform, regulation and discipline, which 'appropriates' the Other as it visualizes power" (Bhabha 1994, 86).

As will be demonstrated, the progressor's selfhood and strategy undergo significant problematization both in the late-Soviet works of the Strugatsky brothers and in post-Soviet literature. These reevaluations, however, do not contradict the "strategic relativism" of the "imperial situation"; rather, they signify its mature, self-reflexive stage: "An *imperial situation* cannot be described within one noncontroversial narrative or typified on the basis of rational and equally noncontroversial classificatory principle" (Gerasimov et al. 2009, 24; emphasis in the original). Nevertheless, the self-reflexive state of the imperial discourse may be also described as *postimperial*, as it tangibly connects the Soviet empire's final decades with its post-1991 remnants, including the contemporary revival of imperialist rhetoric. Arguably, the Soviet "imperial situation" fully takes shape only when it becomes post-Soviet (i.e., "postimperial") and its subjects enter "the situation of uncertainty, incommensurability, and indistinction." This very atmosphere descended on the liberal Soviet culture around 1968 and continues to hold its humid fog into the present moment.

The Internal Colonizer

The progressor, and his incognito operations on a remote planet in a repressive, medieval, or totalitarian society, serves as the centerpiece for many of the Strugatsky brothers' science fiction novels of the 1960s–80s: most notably, *Popytka k begstvu* (*Escape Attempt*, 1962), *Trudno byt' bogom* (*Hard to Be a God*, 1964), *Obitaemyi ostrov* (*Inhabited Island*, 1967), *Ulitka na sklone* (*Snail on the Slope*, 1966–8), *Zhuk v muraveinike* (*Beetle in the Anthill*, 1980), and *Volny gasiat veter* (*The Time Wanderers*, 1985), as well as the 1964 short story "Bednye zlye liudi" ("Poor, Angry People," initially titled "Trudno byt' bogom"). The theme is also addressed, albeit not front and center, in other of the coauthors' works including *Ponedel'nik nachinaetsia v subbotu* (*Monday Begins on Saturday*, 1965), *Khishchnye veshchi veka* (*Predatory Things of the Century*, 1965), *Vtoroe nashestvie marsian* (*The Second Invasion of Martians*, 1968), *Otel' "U pogibshego al'pinista"* (*The Dead Alpinist Hotel*, 1970), *Malysh* (*The Space Mowgli*, 1971), *Piknik na obochine* (*Roadside Picnic*, 1972), *Gadkie lebedi* (*The Ugly Swans*; written in 1967, published abroad in 1972, in the USSR in 1987), and *Paren' iz preispodnei* (*The Kid from Hell*, 1974).

It would not be an exaggeration to claim that the Strugatsky brothers enjoyed a veritable cult following during the decline of the Thaw (1964–68) and the period of stagnation (1968–85), especially among the ITR class.³ Besides one of the brothers, Boris, personally belonging to the ranks of the technical intelligentsia as a professional astronomer, the duo's vision of the communist future was but minimally informed by the official ideology from the very start of their joint career. Rather, their premonitions reflected the cultivation of creative freedom, in association with the world of the scientific intelligentsia. In brother Arkady's words:

> We were writing about the country of "junior researchers." About people who, as we thought back then, have already been embodying features of their descendants in the communist future. About people for whom the main value of life has been associated with the "adventures of the spirit." (Strugatsky and Strugatsky, 2000–2003, 11:335)⁴

Furthermore, the brothers' novels have in many ways shaped the symbolic core of liberal ideology in late-Soviet and post-Soviet Russia. Their science fiction offered an indirect narrativization of contemporary Soviet social contradictions and conflicts, through seemingly distant and fantastic collisions between different civilizations of the future, predicated on an ideological process. According to Clifford Geertz, "Thinking, conceptualization, formulation, comprehension, understanding, or what-have-you, consists not of ghostly happenings in the head but of a matching of the states and processes of symbolic models against the states and processes of the wider world" (1973, 214).

---

3   For a discussion of the specific understanding of modernization and of the cultural ethos of the Soviet scientific intelligentsia in the 1960s–80s, see a debate (with articles by Vladislav Zubok, Maxim Waldstein, Zinaida Vasil'eva, Benjamin Nathans, Artemii Magun, Pal Tamas, Jan Kubik, Alaina Lemon, and Mark Lipovetsky) in *Ab Imperio* (2013, 1:133–219).

4   «Мы писали о стране 'младших научных сотрудников'. О людях, которые, как мы тогда считали, уже сегодня несут в себе черты потомков из коммунистического завтра. О людях, для которых главные ценности бытия — именно в 'приключениях духа'».

The very genre of the Strugatsky brothers' oeuvre—allegorical sci-fi with political subtexts—best of all corresponded to the function of symbolic models described by Galanter and Gerstenhaber and cited by Geertz as definitive for the production of ideology: "Imaginal thinking is neither more or less than constructing an image of the environment, running the model faster than the environment and predicting that the environment will behave as the model does" (Geertz 1973, 214). Among these models, the progressor trope holds a central seat, offering the Soviet/post-Soviet liberal *intelligent* an appealing platform for identity construction on the basis of interiorized internal colonization—in Dirk Uffelmann's terminology, "self-colonization" (2012, 62–67)—which is molded into the oppositional intelligentsia's ideologeme in the 2010s.

As Alexander Etkind has argued in *Internal Colonization* (2011), the logic of internal colonization elucidates the nature of Russian modernity. The figure of the progressor, a modern intellectual wading through a totalitarian backwater, has provided a powerful focal point of self-identification for the Soviet scientific intelligentsia, which was spawned by the Soviet imperial project and naturally assumed an imperial position in the national context as well. The Foucauldian transformation of knowledge into power—symbolic and cultural in this case—serves as the most logical explanation for this phenomenon. According to Etkind, it is not racial, ethnic, or political differences but a cultural disparity that predicates internal colonization: "Where there is no cultural distance—there is no colonial situation" (2003, 111).[5]

---

[5] Cf. in Said's *Orientalism*: "We are left at the end with a sense of the pathetic distance still separating 'us' from an Orient destined to bear its foreignness as a mark of its permanent estrangement from the West" (1979, 244). "For every idea about 'our' art . . . another link in the chain binding 'us' together was formed while another outsider was banished. Even if this is always the result of such rhetoric, wherever and whenever it occurs, we must remember that for nineteenth-century Europe an imposing edifice of learning and culture was built, so to speak, in the face of actual outsiders (the colonies, the poor, the delinquent), whose role in the culture was to give definition to what *they* were constitutionally unsuited for" (228, author's emphasis).

In the Strugatskys' oeuvre, the culture gap between the progressors and the subjects of their mission constitutes the nexus of the authors' genre and its artistic conventions. This cultural distance is even externalized, both in the interstellar spatial distance between the communist Earth and the progressed planets, and as the historical distance between the futuristic World of the Noon, to which the progressors belong, and the medieval (*Trudno byt' bogom*) or totalitarian (*Obitaemyi ostrov, Paren' iz preispodnei*) worlds they visit.

The Strugatskys' early output (from 1959 to 1963) featured a wholly unproblematized glorification of intervention on distant planets by progressive communist intellectuals. Quite tellingly, in *Dalekaia raduga* (*The Distant Rainbow*, 1963) the term "colonization" is used without any negative connotations: "This is a planet colonized by science and needed for physical experiments. All of humanity awaits the result of these experiments" (Strugatsky and Strugatsky 2000–2003, 3:219).[6] In their later novels, the colonization theme is predominantly associated with educational practices, through which children may be culturally distanced from their parents, as one can see in *Gadkie lebedi*. This scholastic emphasis also emerges in the plots of *Malysh* and *Paren' iz preispodnei*.

However, the Strugatskys also stress "cultural relativity" in the later works by bringing into play nonhumanoid civilizations that developmentally eclipse the society of the progressors. The earthlings' contact with these superior alien races is varyingly explored from observation (*Malysh*) to misunderstanding (*Otel' "U pogibshego al'pinista"*), from sacralization (*Piknik na obochine*) to persecution (*Zhuk v muraveinike*) and immigration (*Volny gasiat veter*). This "double bind" of the progressors' engagement with both more backward and more advanced civilizations narrativizes one of the key facets of the late-Soviet and post-Soviet "imperial situation." The duality of the progressors' self-awareness as both agents and victims of colonization grounds the Strugatskys' discourse.

[6] «Это планета, колонизированная наукой и предназначенная для проведения физических экспериментов. Результата экспериментов ждет все человечество».

In Ilya Kukulin's words, "the depiction of the Soviet person as a hybrid phenomenon, who combines in a conflicted way features of a 'subaltern' and 'master'" (2012, 850) has become foundational for the late-Soviet postcolonial discourse, which, for this reason, can equally be interpreted as postcolonial—depending on which side of this hybrid dominates. Furthermore, the Strugatskys were probably the first to detect the mutual transformability of postimperial and postcolonial complexes of the late Soviet subject. As I will attempt to illustrate further, this quality lays the foundation for post-Soviet subjectivity, in which identification with the position of power (postimperial) does not preclude self-representation as a colonial subaltern (postcolonial): the dominance of each of these models depends on circumstances, immediate needs, context, and so on.

Symptomatically, the novella *Popytka k begstvu*, which the authors considered the dawn of the "real Strugatskys," also marked the progressors' inauguration: "This is our first work in which we have discovered for ourselves the theme of the Progressors, although this term was not yet conceived. There was only a question: should a highly advanced civilization interfere with a backward one—even with the most noble intentions?" (2000–2003, 3:679).[7] In the novella's plot, adventuring earthlings from a distant future start acting as, in essence, freelance progressors after coming across an extraterrestrial Gulag. Ultimately it is revealed that Saul Repnin, who initiated their expedition and eventually decides to stay on this nightmarish planet, is a time-displaced survivor of a Nazi concentration camp seeking to settle historical scores. (The reader of the 1960s was accustomed to Aesopian substitution of the Gulag with the Nazi camp.) Thus, a profound connection between potential (and unsuccessful) progressors and the subjects of their progressive efforts is established in this novel through allusion to

---

[7] «Это первое наше произведение, где мы открыли для себя тему Прогрессоров, хотя самого этого термина еще не было и в помине, а был только вопрос, следует ли высокоразвитой цивилизации вмешиваться в дела цивилизации отсталой—даже с самыми благородными намерениями».

real historical trauma inflicted by state-imposed colonial violence. In this context, we might rethink the meaning of the Zone in *Piknik na obochine*: while in the novel it signifies the effects of contact with a superior civilization, the more literal meaning of the word *zona* yields a clear association with the Gulag, suggesting another potent symbolic evocation of the trauma of internal colonization by the totalitarian state.

Alongside imagining far-off realms subjected to progressors' intercessions, the Strugatsky brothers have methodically saturated these chronotopes with motifs and realia promoting an interpretation of these planets as sociopolitical metaphors for the Soviet world. Don Reba in *Trudno byt' bogom* is readable as a slightly distorted anagram of Beria. The same novel's depiction of persecuted intellectuals, torture chambers, and the fascist coup; the division of intelligentsia into hounded "degenerates" (dissidents) and well-paid (yet suffering) conformists; the mysterious transmitted waves that cause patriotic exaltation in some and unbearable headaches in others (a transparent metaphor for the propaganda machine); the concentration camps that figure in *Popytka k begstvu* and *Obitaemyi ostrov*—all these and alike motifs in the brothers' works compact the light-years between planets into an ironic allegorical device, emphasizing the *internal* vector of the quasi-sci-fi representation.

Under these conditions, the progressor's alienation from his immediate historical environment precipitates a powerful symbolic mirror for enlightened Soviet intellectuals who find themselves confronted by a *culturally distant* social milieu. Meanwhile, the accompanying sci-fi conventions *essentialize* cultural differences by presenting the unenlightened masses as—literally—aliens. The second, and much more significant for the Strugatskys' readers, layer of metaphorical interpretation enveloping these "distant worlds" is an ironic problematization of the Orientalizing essentialism, thus displaying the "self-referential and performative character of internal colonization" (see Etkind, Uffelmann, and Kukulin 2012, 16–17; cf. Uffelmann 2012, 72). Nonetheless, we should note that this problematization, however ironic, also effectively accents the progressor's authority, expressly unearthing its roots in his intellectual and cultural superiority, and thus amplifies the postimperial overtones of this trope.

Due to the duality of their position (power/powerlessness, master/subject), and contrary to the model described by Etkind, the Strugatskian progressor conducts a double Orientalization, targeting both the masses and the state power. Through the eyes of the progressor, the "local authorities" are no more than better-dressed "savages," while the repressed subalterns inspire no empathy (either in the progressor or the reader) in light of their enthusiastic complicity with their repressive overlords. The authorities and the masses are typically represented by the writers as symbiotically conjoined and culturally codependent, if not entirely indistinguishable from one another. Aleksei German, in his cinematic take on *Trudno byt' bogom* (2013), underscores this inseparability through the uniformly putrescent visual texture of the film, which makes the royal palace indiscernible from a pigsty. In Ignatiy Vishnevetsky's words, "If *Hard to Be a God* isn't the filthiest, most fetid-looking movie ever made, it's certainly in the top three. Everyone seems to be continually kicking each other, spitting on each other, or beating each other—and if they're not, it's because they're busy picking things out of the mud, poking bare and dirty asses with spears, or smelling what they just wiped off their boots. It is grotesque and deranged and Hieronymus Bosch-like, and damn if it isn't a bona fide *vision*" (2015; emphasis in original). Other critics, Russian and Western alike, unanimously share this impression.

The visual logic of German's film blossoms directly from the source text's narrative, in which "the cold-blooded brutality of those who slaughter" matches only "the cold-blooded meekness of those who are slaughtered" (Strugatsky and Strugatsky 2014, 173–74).[8] The hero, a progressor, alias Don Rumata Estorian, summarizes the situation in the Arkanar kingdom as a quasi-medieval fascist coup d'état: "Wherever grayness triumphs, black robes come to

---

[8] «Хладнокровное зверство тех, кто режет» — «хладнокровная покорность тех, кого режут» (Strugatsky and Strugatsky 2000–2003, 3:380).

power" (171).⁹ Rumata's diagnosis, expressed by this chromatic formula, eludes a consummate translation: "grayness" stands here for mediocrity and the ignorant masses, while "blackness" could signify the black gowns of the religious order employed by Don Reba, the Soviet "black hundreds" (i.e., the Russian party), or the uniforms of the SS.

The oneness of the oppressive state and the masses is uncovered in even harsher light in *Ulitka na sklone*, where the action takes place on the planet Pandora and the Stugatskys' typical hero, the paradigmatic Soviet *intelligent*, is divided into two protagonists.¹⁰ The first, Peretz, desperately appeals to the Kafkaesque Directorate of the Woods for permission to access the mysterious and tantalizing world of the Woods. The second, Candide, is stranded in these very woods by a helicopter crash and hopelessly seeks escape. The novel's depiction of the natives of the Woods bears all the markers of Saidian Orientalization: they are thoroughly passive, and their existence comprises the same daily rituals in cyclical repetition: the same lies ever spun, the same conversations ever reiterated, and the same desires forever unfulfilled. In short, they are portrayed as beings in chronic lack of agency. Like Arabs in the Orientalist discourse, they "have an aura of apartness, definiteness, and collective self-consistency such as to wipe out any traces of individual Arabs with narratable life stories" (Said 1979, 229). The representation of the aboriginal mind-set in *Ulitka* perfectly resonates with the words, as cited by Said, of T. E. Lawrence: "They think for the moment, and endeavor to slip through life without turning corners or climbing hills. In part it is a mental and moral fatigue, a race trained out, and to avoid difficulties they have to jettison so much that we think

---

⁹ «Там, где торжествует серость, к власти всегда приходят черные» (ibid., 378).

¹⁰ The inseparability of this novel from the progressors' discourse can be supported by its first edition, published in the late 1980s and titled *Bespokoistvo* (*Anxiety*), in which the protagonist Gorbovskii, who in the Strugatskys' other texts is depicted as a superprogressor, contemplates the destiny of the Woods.

honorable and grave: and yet without in any way sharing their point of view" (228–29).

At the same time, in the Peretz portions of the novel, the bureaucratic gears of the Directorate, despite its centralized and hierarchical nature, produce the same effect of senseless repetitions and meaningless routines, imprisoning the protagonist and driving him to stagnant despair at the futility of his efforts to reach the beckoning Woods. The only detectable difference between the indigenous society's customs and the bureaucratic regime of the Directorate is that the natives passively obey the incomprehensible logic of the Woods, while the colonizers, with a cruel persistency, demolish the unknowable realm with their machinery, exercising a purely imperial power.

The melding of the colonizing and liberating perspectives is not new for postcolonial discourses, especially in their Soviet reduction. Accordingly, confrontations of the intellectual with both the Orientalized masses and the oppressive power, as well as the mutual mirroring of these two "others," have been typical for the Soviet legacy of internal colonization since the 1920s (see the previous chapter). However, the Strugatsky brothers' treatment of this symbolic configuration appears to differ from, say, Olesha's *Zavist'* (*Envy*, 1927). The intellectual was stigmatized in the '20s and beyond as impotent (see Rutten 2012), while his opponents proved strikingly energetic and proactive. To the contrary, the Strugatskys imagined a world in which both the "people" and the "power" are marked by the *lack of agency*, while the progressors' agency fuels each narrative arc. This willpower stems from the progressors' commitment to the two basic principles of the Enlightenment: rationality (manifested by science) and humanism (manifested in their aversion to violence). Rumata's recourse to violence in *Trudno byt' bogom* is represented as morally ambivalent, although it is obvious that his decision to kill — notably, not with the unparalleled technology he possesses, but instead with a common sword — results from his humanism:

> My brothers, thought Rumata. I'm yours, I'm the flesh of your flesh! He suddenly felt with tremendous force that he was no

god, shielding the fireflies of reason with his hand, but instead a brother, helping a brother, a son saving a father. I'll kill Don Reba, he thought. What for? He's killing my brothers. (Strugatsky and Strugatsky 2014, 148)[11]

Budach said quietly, "Then, Lord, wipe us off the face of the planet and create us anew in a more perfect form. . . Or even better, leave us be and let us go our own way."

"My heart is full of pity," Rumata said slowly, "I cannot do that." (ibid., 209–10)[12]

In *Trudno byt' bogom* the Strugatskys use subtle colors to mark the mutability of the progressor's position, with motifs of violence that indicate the transformation of the progressor's symbolic power from that of the Enlightenment agent into a political force pregnant with (imperial) domination. In *Zhuk v muraveinike* this change becomes central: the head of the progressors' agency, Rudolf Sikorski, organizes a witch hunt against the progressor Lev Abalkin, whom he suspects to be an incognizant vessel for a destructive program implanted in his body (or his mind, maybe) by the superior civilization of the Wanderers. Sikorski's climactic murder of Abalkin remains unjustifiable in the eyes of the novel's narrator, Maxim Kammerer (also a progressor, and the protagonist of *Obitaemyi ostrov*). Even if Abalkin is indeed the "robot" Sikorsi believes him to be, preprogrammed by the Wanderers to commit some horrible atrocity despite his will, his assassination at Sikorski's hands clearly illumines a political paranoia that incriminates (perhaps rashly) any and all "Others" capable of questioning or subverting the imperial rule on the basis of progressism. *Zhuk v muraveinike*, thus, can be

---

[11] «Братья мои, — подумал Румата. — Я ваш, мы плоть от плоти вашей!» С огромной силой он вдруг почувствовал, что никакой он не бог, ограждающий в ладонях светлячков разума, а брат, помогающий брату, сын, спасающий отца. «Я убью дона Рэбу. — За что? — Он убивает моих братьев» (Strugatsky and Strugatsky 2000–2003, 3:360).

[12] «Будах тихо проговорил:
—Тогда, господи, сотри нас с лица земли и создай заново более совершенными. . . или еще лучше, оставь нас и дай нам идти своей дорогой» (ibid., 407).

read as the Strugatskys' version of Arendt's colonial boomerang, "the process in which imperial powers bring back their practices of coercion from their colonies back home" (Etkind 2011, 7)—in other words, of the postimperial discourse.

Sikorski himself, however, validates his decision to kill by citing the imperative to defend Earth from colonization by the Wanderers—that is, to protect Earth from an imagined or real state of powerless colonial subalternity. Despite disapproving of his actions, Kammerer shares his boss's conviction: "Yes, there are intelligent beings in the world who are much, much worse than you, whatever you may be. And it's only then that you develop the ability to divide the world into friend and foe, make instantaneous decisions in acute situations, and learn the courage of acting first and thinking later. In my opinion, that is the essence of a Progressor: the ability to decisively divide the world into friend and foe" (Strugatsky and Strugatsky 1980, 7).[13]

Progress vs. Power

Ulitka na sklone similarly uncovers the progressor's fear of potential subjugation. Among the many "races" inhabiting the Woods, authority and agency seem to belong solely to a community of women who possess magic powers over the Woods and its creatures. They are true goddesses of the Woods. Without the touch of a finger, by their intangible will alone, they are able to inspire life in the dead and dispel it from the living. Monstrous *mertviaki*, feared by all humans, including Candide, appear to be their servants, controllable automatons not unlike zombies.

These mystical witches seem to gain sympathy from neither the hero nor the authors. They steal Candide's wife, Nava, and treat

---

[13] «Существуют на свете носители разума, которые гораздо, значительно хуже тебя, каким бы ты ни был. И вот только тогда ты обретаешь способность делить на чужих и своих, принимать мгновенные решения в острых ситуациях и научаешься смелости сначала действовать, а потом разбираться. По-моему, в этом сама суть прогрессора: умение решительно разделить на своих и чужих» (Strugatsky and Strugatsky 2000–2003, 8:12).

him with unveiled contempt, disregarding his knowledge and his good intentions. In the close-knit matriarchy of witches, males are either sterilized or discarded as useless and detrimental beings. Although the women are prepared to make an exception for our hero and enfold him into their world, Candide opts to run away; he apprehends that this "adoption" entails his diminution into a subordinate deprived of autonomy. In lieu of this fate, he returns to the Woods' passive subalterns, over whom he can preserve his status as progressor.

The Strugatskys themselves interpreted this episode as the intellectual culmination of *Ulitka na sklone*. As Boris wrote,

> Historical truth here is on the side of the highly unpleasant, alien and unsympathetic to him [Candide], complacent and arrogant Amazons. The protagonist's compassion fully belongs to the dumbish, ignorant, and helpless men and wives, who, nonetheless, have saved him, given him a wife and house, admitted him as one of their own. [. . .] What is a civilized person to do when he realizes where the progress that appalls him goes? How should he relate to this progress if he despises it?! (Strugatsky and Strugatsky 2000–2003, 4:613–14; author's emphasis)[14]

The emotional incandescence of this commentary hides a few significant contradictions. Through their depiction of the paranormal women of the Woods, the Strugatskys, on the one hand, revitalize and invoke ancient myths of the Great Goddess or Great Mother (one of the women is pregnant; another turns out to be Nava's long-lost mother), spirits who occupy the liminal border between life and death. Their linkage with the *mertviaki* and drowned women

---

[14] «Историческая правда здесь на стороне крайне неприятных, чужих и чуждых ему [Кандиду], самодовольных и самоуверенных амазонок. А сочувствие героя целиком и полностью на стороне этих туповатых, невежественных, беспомощных и нелепых мужичков и баб, которые его, все-таки, как-никак, а спасли, выходили, жену ему дали, хату ему дали, признали его своим. [. . .] Что должен делать, как должен вести себя цивилизованный человек, понимающий, куда направлен *отвратительный* ему прогресс? Как он должен относиться к прогрессу, если этот прогресс ему поперек горла?!»

hints at pagan mythological figures like the *rusalki* and Baba Yaga. On the other hand, the writers openly mock Western feminism, or at least the typically distorted image by which it was known to the late Soviet intelligentsia (see Goscilo 1996, 5–31). The association of these powerful women with Western feminism validates their characterization as the embodiment of progress that is appalling to Candide (and the authors).

But why exactly is this progress so appalling? The Strugatskys methodically underscore the negative traits of the Woodland hostesses—they are condescending, they humiliate Candide on the basis of his gender, they are unwilling to recognize the man's personal merits. All these behaviors are meant to emphasize their role (and defuse Candide's) as the colonial lords of the Woods. However, on closer inspection, it becomes clear that the goddesses' power—the occult and the colonial—is not extrinsic to the territory. Unlike humankind's Directorate of the Woods, their influence is inseparable from the Woods' internal life, wherein it manifests its highest form, which remains unattainable to the progressor, who has fallen, literally, from the sky. The Strugatskys cannot imagine a power that is not divorced from the masses by a cultural gulf. (Perhaps this is a reflex of internal colonization?) Nonetheless, the witches' might is not imperial, and in fact is much more effectual and rational than the strength of Earth's science and civilization, imported by the Directorate. Women's power resists Orientalization, yet it is still depicted in a critical, quasi-imperialist, color.

Only partially can this paradox be explained by the fact that Candide's supremacy dissolves before the women of the Woods, meaning that he ceases, at this point, to be *the* progressor. He could concede their truth and surrender his authority in exchange for admission to their community as the most "progressive" and enlightened, but this fails to pass for reasons only of *gender*. Gender relations, as is well known, ordinarily replicate colonial configurations of mastership and subalternity; Candide cannot accept the dominion of women because it contradicts his—not only patriarchal but also (post)imperial—conception of power. According to Said, whose observation fully harmonizes with the Strugatskys' progressor material, "Latent Orientalism also encouraged a peculiarly (not to say invidiously) male conception of the world. [. . .] This is especially evident in the writing of travelers and novelists; women are usually the creature of a male power-fantasy. They express unlimited sensuality, they are more or less stupid, and above all they are willing" (Said 1979, 207). The magic-wielding woodswomen of *Ulitka na sklone* patently defy this model: they are definitively more progressive than women, as scrutinized through the Orientalist lens, they "should be." Yet this progress is loathsome to the male protagonist, as it strips him of his own power. His self-identification, to which this power is vital, appears to supersede the notion of progress.

This sentiment resonates with certain other subplots in the Strugatskys' library of progressor stories. One might recall the turbulent relationship of the progressor Lev Abalkin with his mistress Maia Glumova, whom he subjects to physical (in childhood) and psychological (in adulthood) abuse as an expression of his love for her. We also might notice how the Strugatskys' progressors, in cross textual opposition to *Ulitka na sklone*'s witches of the Woods, constitute a veritable boys' club. The same can be said of the utopian commune of scientist-wizards in *Ponedel'nik nachinaetsia v subbotu*; in neither instance is the gender bias of the progressors or the reasons behind this exclusivity ever plainly articulated.

Orientalism—that toward Soviet authorities and the masses but also, as we can see, the "gender Orientalism" toward women—appears to be inscribed into the progressor trope. The imperial situation in late-Soviet society materializes, alongside other discourses, through internal Orientalism, justified by a cultural distance, and emerges as a pillar of the intelligentsia's (symbolic) power. The phantasy of the progressor, while manifesting Orientalist complexes, simultaneously serves up a thoroughly romantic image for the intelligentsia's identification. Yet this model necessarily involves a logic of binary oppositions as the predicate for the progressor's power. Despite his professed humanism, the progressor strives for the Other, and the process of othering (as *Zhuk v muraveinike* demonstrates) is inextricable from his mission.

The distinct division of the world into "us" and "them" begins to crumble, however, in the Strugatskys' later works. If, in the novels of the 1960s, the roster of "they" was unambiguous—medieval Berias and the brutal masses in *Trudno byt' bogom,* or the "Fathers" with their bustling propaganda machines in *Obitaemyi ostrov*—the clarity of this category harshly waned in the novels of the 1980s. In *Zhuk,* the wanted "Other" Abalkin is encircled by an aura of compassion, while Sikorski, the appointed defender of "us" and "our" independence, repulses the narrator. Thus, binaries foundational for the progressor discourse appear to destabilize—and this erosion resonates with the shift in the progressor's focus, from the strategic acceleration of a subordinate society's intellectual stock to the preservation of the progressor's own identity. In other words, the progressor becomes increasingly concerned not with becoming *like them* but with the project of *advancing* them and improving their lives. This new interest first reaches center stage in *Ulitka*: illuminatingly, Boris Dubin interpreted both protagonists of this novel—Candide confronting the Woods and Peretz confronting the Directorate—as Soviet versions of existentialist "strangers" (see Dubin 2010, 162–63).

The hazard of becoming like the masses is rooted chiefly in the progressor's resistance to the former's collective fatalism and passivity, but the progressor's alliance with the rulers likewise prefigures conformity to the imperial body. (Furthermore, either of these avenues implies the acceptance of violence.) The two scenarios, in fact, correlate precisely to the dual roles scripted by the imperial discourse: by resisting the gravitation of both the "masses" and the "authorities," the progressor charts the path between the positions of imperial power and colonial subjectivity. He wishes to avoid the clutches of both and yet to remain the colonizer, colonizer-liberator, colonizer-enlightener.

As demonstrated in the Strugatskys' late novels—*Grad obrechennyi* (*The Doomed City*; written in 1975, published in 1988–89), *Volny gasiat veter,* and *Otiagoshchennye zlom* (*Overburdened with Evil,* 1988)—the identity of the enlightened colonizer, paradoxically, cannot find any other means for its realization than self-isolation, which, in turn, evicts all concern for the progressor's mission. Heroic service to intergalactic Enlightenment is usurped by the instinct of self-preservation and its resistance to the allure of conformism.

Promises of the most refined exemplification of this change of attitude lurk in the prospect for a novel that remained unwritten due to Arkady's death in 1991. The book, tentatively titled *Belyi ferz'* (*The White Bishop*) or *Operatsiia "Virus"* (*Operation "Virus"*), was to have followed Maxim Kammerer's exploits in the Island Empire on the planet Saraksh. Revising its depiction in *Obitaemyi ostrov* as a cannibalistic and militaristic Nazi-like state, in the new novel the world of the Empire would have consisted of three circles. The first, "hell," is the region reserved for the masses: "Dregs of society [. . .] drunkards, outcasts, trash [. . .] they didn't fear punishment and lived by laws of brute force, baseness and hatred. [. . .] By this circle the Empire bristled up against the rest of the universe, defended itself and attacked the others" (Strugatsky and Strugatsky 2000–2003, 8:725).[15] The second circle, "purgatory," houses the "ordinary people"—presumably, the philistines and conformists—while the center, "paradise," comprises a replica of the ideal world of the Noon Universe, whose values progressors have tried to export to remote worlds: "And in the center reigned the World of Justice. 'Noon. 22nd Century.' Warm, friendly, a safe world of spirit, creativity and freedom, inhabited exclusively by talented, nice, and friendly people keeping holy faith in the commandments of the highest morality" (725).[16] Naturally, this society—this *Empire*, to be more emphatic—requires segregation and discrimination as a precondition for its prosperity: "Everyone born in the Empire inevitably would find 'his own' circle, the society would gently (and if necessary, crudely) push him to where he belongs according to his talents, temper and moral potential. This distribution happened either automatically or with the help of a corresponding social

---

15 «Подонки общества [. . .] вся пьянь, рвань, дрянь [. . .] тут не знали наказаний, тут жили по законам силы, подлости и ненависти. [. . .] Этим кругом Империя ощетинивалась против всей прочей ойкумены, держала оборону и наносила удары».

16 «А в центре царил Мир Справедливости. "Полдень. XII век." Теплый, приветливый, безопасный мир духа, творчества и свободы, населенный исключительно людьми талантливыми, славными, дружелюбными, свято следующим всем заповедям самой высокой нравственности».

mechanism (something like a vice department of the police). This was a world in which the principle 'To each his own' triumphed in its broadest interpretation" (725).[17]

The Strugatskys surely remembered that the inscription "Jedem das Seine"—a translation of the Latin expression *Suum cuique* ("To each his own" or "Everyone gets what he deserves")—adorned the entrance to Buchenwald, the infamous Nazi concentration camp (as well as, after the war, the NKVD Special Camp no. 2), a reference that leaves no doubt as to the true nature of this utopia. It is no wonder that Boris Strugatsky described the unwritten novel as "some summary of the whole worldview. Its epitaph. Or—a sentence?" (726).[18]

There is also no doubt that the worldview in question corresponds to the standpoint of the Soviet modernizing intellectual, epitomized by the progressor figure and his accompanying discourse. Most likely, the novel-to-be would have lowered an indictment on the progressor's utopia. The similarity of the book's proposed design to blueprints of colonial settlements exposes the core of the progressor project. As it turns out, even through self-isolation, the progressor cannot maintain the seat of an enlightened internal colonizer without mutating into an imperial power of aggression and domination.

Post-Soviet Reevaluations of the Progressor

The perseverance of the progressor device in the post-Soviet period testifies not only to the continuity between the "imperial situation" of the 1960s–80s and the "post-imperial situation" of the 1990s–2010s; it also sheds a certain light on the various meanings of the *post-*

---

[17] «Каждый, рожденный в Империи, неизбежно оказывался в "своем" круге, общество деликатно (а если надо—и грубо) вытесняло его туда, где ему было место—в соответствии с талантами его, темпераментом и нравственной потенцией. Это вытеснение происходило автоматически, и с помощью соответствующего социального механизма (чего-то, вроде полиции нравов). Это был мир, где торжествовал принцип "Каждому—свое" в самом широком его толковании».

[18] «Некий итог целого мировоззрения. Эпитафия ему. Или приговор?..»

prefix, revealing a diverse plethora of vectors, each differently connoting the rhetoric of modernization based on cultural distance and entailing internal Orientalization. Despite certain variations between representations of progressors in the works of such disparate artists as Aleksei German, Boris Akunin, Dmitry Bykov, Viktor Pelevin, and Sergei Luk'ianenko, one structural feature unites all of these recent progressor and progressor-like creations: as I will attempt to demonstrate further, post-Soviet progressors invariably operate as "switches" between imperial and colonial rhetorical modes, between the external and internal, between the enlightening shepherd and the repressed lamb. The progressor as a character type exemplifies the coexistence and mutual influence of postimperial and postcolonial models and forms of self-identification within post-Soviet culture.

One may isolate three prevailing treatments that the progressor receives in post-Soviet culture: (a) the progressor is *heroized* as a tragic figure embodying a nostalgia for lost historical opportunities and, more specifically, for the lost connection with the spirit of Enlightenment and humanism; (b) the progressor is *relativized* and emerges as a metaphor for the intelligentsia's psychological mechanism of coping with historical catastrophe; or (c) the progressor is *satirized* as a byproduct or agent of the Western cultural or political colonization of Russia.

The finale of Aleksei German's screen adaptation of *Trudno byt' bogom* opts to venerate the progressor, presenting this reverence in perhaps the most direct and impressive manner yet achieved. The film's ending differs radically from that of the Strugatskys' novel: while, in the text, Rumata leaves the affairs of Arkanar behind and returns to Earth, where a few red drops of strawberry remind of the blood he has spilled, German concludes his three-hour-long fresco with a stark, snow-coated landscape (visually reverting the mud and grime of the preceding scenes) and Rumata traveling in a sledge through the blinding white, breathing a soulful tune on some clarinet-like reed. The camera zooms in on his face, on which a smile of strange amazement, bordering insanity, has been fixed. Such a conclusion hardly signifies the hero's liberation—or, if so, it grants his liberation only through death, through departure from life, with all its dirt and dismay. Alternatively, this finale may be read as the procession of Rumata's exile, or escape, from Arkanar, where he can no longer stay. Yet even in this case, the scene effects a visual requiem to the progressor and his attempts to uphold humanist values despite their inexorable defeat. According to German's visual logic, however, the progressor's cause had been lost before it began. Rumata's dedication to behaving as an enlightened human being in an inhumane age is a mark of the truly tragic hero, who acts as the one of greater power, while aware of his incapacity to either dominate or improve this world, drowning in its own shit.

In Boris Akunin's historical novella *Ognennyi perst* (*The Fiery Finger*, 2014), written as one of the fictional "illustrations" to the first volume of his megaproject *Istoriia rossiiskogo gosudarstva* (*The History of the Russian State*, 2013–), a progressor appears in a less tragic light, yet with a more pronounced connection to imperial power than in the works of German and the Strugatskys. The author here directly establishes the connection between the protagonist of his novella and the Strugatskys' Rumata. Two central characters, both *amintes*—secret agents of Byzantium, sent to the land of the Slavs—have the following dialogue:

> "Did you notice how the prince's guards you killed were looking at us? What was the look on their faces?"
>
> "Fear. For Slavs—we are aliens, who possess unfathomable knowledge, and therefore are frightening."
>
> "To them we are not human, but superhuman beings. Here we are gods, who have descended as humans."
>
> "With just one difference: that we're also mortals," noted Damianos. (Akunin 2014, 246)[19]

---

[19] — Ты обратил внимание, как на нас с тобой смотрели дружинники, которых ты убил? Какие у них были лица?
— Боязливые. Мы для славян — люди чужие, обладающие непонятным знанием, а потому страшные.
— Мы для них не люди, а сверхъестественные существа. Здесь мы — боги, спустившиеся к смертным.
— С той лишь разницей, что мы тоже смертные, — заметил Дамианос.

Damianos is indeed believed to be of divine genesis: a Slavic girl called Radoslava, who falls in love with him, is certain that he is a forest deity. Consummating the parallel with Rumata, Akunin brands his Damianos with a birthmark on the forehead, reminiscent of Rumata's "third eye" (although for the latter man, this is a hidden camera that documents his mission).

Damianos is assuredly a progressor: he undertakes to exterminate the marauding Viking bands and dreams of the blossoming of a yet-small and innocuous Kievan princedom into a formidable Byzantine outpost, a colonial megalopolis beside the regional Slavic tribes. He is dispatched to urge local princes and warlords toward decisions that are beneficial to Byzantium. On his execution of this charge, Akunin argues, hinges the fate of ancient Russia: a European path or an Asian one. (The first installments of Akunin's *Istoriia* are illuminatingly titled *Chast' Evropy* [*A Part of Europe*] and *Chast' Azii* [*A Part of Asia*].) Thus, the writer presents his "historical progressor" (albeit with a slight touch of irony) as one who could directly and monumentally affect the historical trajectory of the entire country. His power to change the course of history is, no doubt, derivative of the imperial might that he represents. Akunin depicts Constantinople as an exemplar of national success, and its intellectual leader and father (literally) of all *amintes* as an advocate of benevolent imperial hegemony, delivering the light of civilization unto "wild" and "backward" clans. But, unlike his father, Damianos cannot detach himself sentimentally from the "natives": when both he and his beloved Radoslava drink poisoned wine, Damianos gives his antidote to the Slavic girl and admits death. His self-sacrifice, however valorous in the present, undoes all beautiful, far-reaching prospects for Russia.

In German's film and Akunin's novella alike, the progressor's putative godlike status epitomizes the essentialization of cultural distance in the imperial ruler-subaltern relationship. However, both Rumata and Damianos fail to be true gods. To be a god means to adopt a wholly external position toward base "savages"; instead, both heroes choose to remain human. Their stance signals the minimization of Orientalist attitudes and affirms that the life of the colonial subaltern is no less (or more) valuable than the progressor's.

Inevitably, the humanistic choice spells doom to the progressor and to his mission.

Considering the reliably liberal leanings of both German and Akunin, one may argue that the elevation of the progressor as a martyr of Enlightenment ideals and values (in German's film), or as the embodiment of lost historical alternatives (in Akunin's novella), serves as a foundational layer of the contemporary liberal Russian imagination. Quite tellingly, Valeriia Novodvorskaia (1950–2014), a famous dissident and the founder of the Democratic Union Party, when asked in one of her final interviews how she sees her role in Russian society, referred to herself and her followers as "progressors" (see epigraph).[20] Novodvorskaia backed up this self-definition with a perfectly Orientalizing description of the Russian "electorate" as *nedeesposobnyi*—passive and lacking rational direction:

> A people that is not capable of electing a normal president, normal organs like parliament or Senate. A people that begs for alms from the authorities, that agrees with everything. And the majority, about 60%—this is "Putin's mattress." On such a mattress he can spend not just two but three terms. [. . .] This people has no agency. (Sobchak 2012)[21]

Novodvorskaia's characterization probably most blatantly reveals the interconnectedness of seemingly opposite concepts within the progressor trope: the sense of his tragic doom and Orientalizing attitudes toward the masses. It is the essentialization of cultural distance that, while precipitating Orientalization of the "natives," at the same time predicates the inevitable failure of the progressor's utopia.

---

[20] Notably, Novodvorskaia wrote a critical article on the Strugatsky brothers. See Novodvorskaia 2012.

[21] «Народ, который не в состоянии избрать нормального президента, нормальные органы типа парламента или Сената. Народ, который выпрашивает у власти подачки. Народ, который на все согласен. А большинство, около 60%—это 'Путинский матрас.' На этом матрасе можно пролежать не только два, но и три срока. [. . .] А этот народ не дееспособен».

Dmitry Bykov—who, along with Akunin, has become an intellectual leader of the anti-Putin movement and its protests in 2011–14—aims with his adaptation of the progressor to deconstruct the essentialist notion of cultural distance and thus to abolish tragic fatalism. His novel *Evakuator* (*The Evacuator*, 2005) at first glance replicates a conventional progressor plot: computer engineer Igor', initially in jest but then with gradually greater sincerity, convinces his lover Katia that he is an emissary of an idyllic civilization located in a remote star system, and that he has been sent to Earth as an observer and evacuator of select humans. Subsequently, he persuades Katia and five random strangers to fly away in his spaceship from Moscow, which in the meantime slips into chaos under a torrent of terrorist attacks.

Throughout this story, Bykov methodically overturns all the key components and plot points of the progressor narrative. First, the progressor and his beloved are followed in their departure by a second spaceship, ferrying a herd of Katia's relatives and their friends, from all of whom she dreamed to escape. Second, the progressor's home planet turns out to be as devastated as Russia. Third, the unfamiliar inheritors of this formerly perfect planet eventually outcast Igor' and Katia as inessential to their mundane needs and incompatible with their xenophobic worldview, forcing the lovers to fly away once again. And, finally, the entire tale of interplanetary exodus is revealed to be but a fruit of Igor' and Katia's joint fantasizing, while they spend the night together in apprehension of a massive, preannounced terrorist attack on Moscow.

Though the inevitable isolation and downfall of the progressor remains intact, Bykov rids his narrative both of the sense of cultural superiority (Katia and Igor' are distinct from the others by their shared love, not by any prominent mental or cultural merits) and of the ensuing Orientalism. Instead of the essentialization of cultural distance, Bykov presents the progressor fantasy as a form of coping with a less and less manageable social reality. The daydream that has been embraced by the technical intelligentsia (both Igor' and Katia belong to this social stratum) acts as a counterweight to social despair and helplessness. Thus, the motif of the progressor's tragic doom, while preserved in *Evakuator*, stems in Bykov's interpretation from the fact that this trope manifests *anything but* the symbolic power and cultural superiority of the intelligentsia. Rather, it compensates for the intelligentsia members' post-Soviet transformation into a new generation of subalterns, manifested by their utter isolation from any means of power and any channels of influence on post-Soviet society. Notably, (post)colonial and (post)imperial overtones are minimized in Bykov's novel: they become increasingly irrelevant as the progressor gives up his mission of enlightenment and modernization, choosing instead to save himself and his loved ones from the impending calamity that he cannot prevent or control.

If all authors discussed above depict the progressor as the embodiment of internal Russian phenomena, two other Russian writers of extreme popularity—Sergei Luk'ianenko and Viktor Pelevin—utilize the trope of the progressor for a science-fictional representation of the West and its relations to Russia. Luk'ianenko, famous for his World of Watches cycle of novels—*Nochnoi dozor* (*Night Watch*, 1998), *Dnevnoi dozor* (*Day Watch*, 2000), *Sumerechnyi dozor* (*Twilight Watch*, 2004), and so on—and for Timur Bekmambetov's screen adaptations of the series' first two entries, is a flaming Russian nationalist.[22] Pelevin is equally critical of Russian conservatives and liberals, but in his Internet postings he consistently defends liberal views on the current events.[23]

Surprisingly, however, the two writers' satirical takes on the progressor device share some basic features. In his novel *Zvezdy—kholodnye igrushki* (*Stars Are Cold Toys*, [1997] 2004), Luk'ianenko openly mocks the Strugatsky brothers' utopian World of the Noon (the motherland of all progressors) with his society of the Geometers. By means of an institution of Mentors, responsible for overseeing the development of each and every individual, the Geometers

---

[22] See his blog pages on LiveJournal under the avatars "doctor-livsy" (http://doctor-livsy.livejournal.com/) and "dr_piliulkin" (http://dr-piliulkin.livejournal.com/).

[23] See his Facebook page at https://www.facebook.com/plvnv.

maintain a civilization of hypocrisy, disguising strict regulation and psychological manipulation as brotherhood and loving care. These twisted principles define the Geometers' relations with extramural cultures as well: their progressors are in fact "regressors," whose goal is to degrade a foreign civilization into inferiority and to allow the Geometers' society to conquer its "savages" by a program of "friendship"—that is, colonialization. Numerous signs (emphasized order, uncanny cleanliness, perpetual smiling, and so on) indicate that Luk'ianenko's pen has scribbled "Geometers" where he means it to write "contemporary Western society," while his protagonist, Petr Khrumov, represents the rebellion of the colonial subaltern against Western cultural and political domination.

Luk'ianenko's novel as a whole represents a blueprint for the breadth of postimperial nationalism—exactly the scheme, in fact, that would be widely adopted by the Russian state media in orchestrating the annexation of Crimea and the conflict in eastern Ukraine. The imperialist methods of Orientalization are pitted against the "West" as an imaginary colonial oppressor. Consequently, the "West" is homogenized and demonized, and in this capacity cast as a symbol of hostile forces against which "all Russia" must unify. Old-fashioned strategies of the Soviet representation of the "capitalist West" merge here with a newfound conceptualization of Russia as a victim of hidden colonial oppression.

Zvezdy can be interpreted as a truly postcolonial work since its narrative patently rejects the progressor's standpoint as repressive and evil. However, a closer look at its protagonist (a mouthpiece for the author) reveals that the "imperial situation" described above remains intact in the novel. Petr is neither a progressor nor a regressor; he is a secret agent, a mole among the Geometers, plotting to uncover their secrets and expose their true intentions. Curiously, while penetrating the Geometers' society, the hero fuses in his body and mind three personae: himself, Petr Khrumov, an Earthling; Nik Rimer, a regressor for the Geometers; and a Kualkua, an amorphous creature who lives in symbiosis with another being. With the conjoined Kualkua's assistance, Petr is able to mimic the real Rimer not only physically but also genetically. At the same time, his somatic partner equips him with supernatural resilience and physical strength. In other words, while remolding progressors and their community into a metaphor of creeping Western colonization of post-Soviet Russian culture, Luk'ianenko depicts his (Russian) protagonist as the synthesis of a colonial subaltern and an imperial regressor, melded by the powers of a perfect transformer-imitator-trickster. This "structure of the subject" suggests that, for the author and his hero, postcolonial posing as a repressed subaltern is really a tactical means to gain power: underneath the sheepskin of the subaltern crouches an aggressor, outfitted with extraordinary mimicry. Simply put, the face of the colonial subject, within the logic of *Zvezdy—kholodnye igrushki*, is but a mask, a cunning diversion in the imperial skirmish for domination.[24]

However much international acclaim Luk'ianenko has amassed, his contemporary Viktor Pelevin enjoys no less, and perhaps more. Many of the volumes in Pelevin's prolific bibliography have become cornerstones of Russian postmodernism. In one of his recent novels, *S.N.U.F.F.* (2012; English translation of 2016 by Andrew Bromfield), the author deconstructs not only the figure of the progressor but also the essentialized image of the West as the alleged cultural and ideological colonizer of Russia. To this end, Pelevin presents a futuristic Earth stratified societally and geographically into two levels: on the planet's surface reside the Orcs, denizens of the nation of Urkaina (derivative of *urki*, professional criminals in Russian prison argot), altogether ordinary people whose agency is limited by a deficit of technological progress and the heavy thumb of an autocratic, oligarchic political regime, reminiscent of Russia (and Ukraine) in the 2000s. Artificial spheres above the surface house the technologically superior society of the Big Biz (Big Business). These spheres are inhabited by "People," whose lives are dictated by an intricate system of social codes, promoting sexual tolerance, feminism, and consumerism, along with other Western liberal values invariably depicted as repressive, hypocritical, and comic.

---

[24] The use of the rhetoric of "repressed minorities" by the Russian government and media to justify the annexation of Crimea and military intervention in eastern Ukraine might serve as a political parallel to Luk'ianenko's sci-fi composition.

The worship of Manity, a fusion of a computer monitor and money, paired with the People's paralyzing dependence on information technologies (in these superterranean quarters, even the landscapes are computer simulations), roundly completes Pelevin's satire of the architecture of Western culture.

S.N.U.F.F.'s protagonist is Damilola Karpov, military pilot and cameraman for CINEWS, a corporation that broadcasts a blend of news and fiction, pertaining predominantly to the world of the Orcs. Damilola is a parodic version of the progressor: with his flying camera/war machine he rescues two young lovers, Khloia and Grym, from the repressive Urkanian regime and evacuates them to the culturally advanced and (supposedly) politically emancipated Big Biz. The novel's parody can be seen first in the fact that overweight Damilola operates his camera-copter from the private space of his apartment, and second in the counterfeit nature of the "rescue," staged as a casus belli for the next "war" between the People and the Orcs.

Pelevin's tale in certain ways exhibits a more complex form of Luk'ianenko's logic. Yet if Luk'ianenko epitomizes postimperial nationalism, Pelevin imagines a new cycle of imperial exploitation, based on the sedative power of spectacles and simulacra rather than the abuse of economic and human resources. In the course of the novel, the reader realizes that the entire Orc civilization is actually a synthetic product of the Big Biz. The primary justification for the existence of Urkaina lies in regular warfare, wherein the People use machines and elaborate cinematic monsters as their proxy, while the Orcs arm themselves with medieval weaponry and dress in colorful, Hollywood-esque outfits. In fact, each new war (waged in the specially designed Circus) is but another gargantuan film production, recorded by scores of flying cameras, though the Orcs shed real blood and die by the thousands. For the "hyperreality of simulacra" epitomized by the Big Biz, the Orc wars serve as an indispensable source of *truth*, or in the Big Biz lingo, *snuffs*: real death and real sex. War provides the background for the production of porno films, used for Manity worship. In short, Urkaina supplies the Big Biz with material for further endless constructions of hyperreality.

One of the novel's plotlines follows the two extracted Orcs, Khloia and Grym, in their acclimation to the Big Biz culture. Khloia easily assimilates and gradually steels her pretty face into a "face of war," while Grym, despite obtaining the enviable position of "content sommelier," responsible for imitating the "rough Orcs' truth," recoils from the constant, ubiquitous simulations and eventually returns to Urkaina. The story of another subaltern, Damilola's sex doll Kaia, plays out as a parallel and supplement to the Orcs' narrative. Highly intellectually advanced, Kaia proves to Damilola that in the hyperreality of contemporary civilization there is no difference between her, a sentient rubber doll, and him, a war pilot and her owner. Their philosophical conversations, along with the Big Biz's depicted "snuff dependence" on its colony of Urkaina, suggest that the dichotomy between the master and subaltern, and between the empire and its colonial possessions, sharply erodes in a society dominated by images rather than substances, by smoke and mirrors rather than scents and flesh—by simulations rather than reality.

The narrative arc bears fruitful evidence to sustain this argument. Kaia, thanks to her vast intellect and emotional complexity, acquires agency (Damilola calls it "bitchiness") and falls in love with Grym. Ultimately, she manages to escape from Damilola's possession and join Grym in the remote reaches of Urkaina. Damilola is ruined both morally and financially (before leaving, Kaia empties all of his accounts, and he still faces an outstanding debt for her purchase). Furthermore, Kaia and Grym's elopement happens at the very moment when the Big Biz's grip over the Urkainian autocracy is shaken and the People's sphere is poised to collapse on Earth's surface. As a result, a new war between the People and the Orcs is dawning—although in this clash the People will have to fight according to the Orcs' rules, spelling the imminent defeat of the "masters."

Both Luk'ianenko and Pelevin transform the progressor into a hypocritical conduit of exploitation and repression, projected onto the relations between Russia and the West. Russia, allegorized by the Conclave alliance of planets (including Earth) in Luk'ianenko's novel and by Urkaina in Pelevin's, becomes the extratextual referent for a collective subaltern squashed by the paralyzing imperial power of the progressors (that is, regressors). Unlike other texts discussed above, *Zvezdy—kholodnye igrushki* and *S.N.U.F.F.* are truly postcolonial: they entail both the dissection of imperial power and its mask of liberal rhetoric, and the exploration of scenarios (illusive hypotheticals, granted) of subalternate emancipation from the specious imperial repression. Nonetheless, in both cases the foundational contrast between the imperial pincers and colonial pinched collapses. Luk'ianenko inadvertently exposes a key covert operation of the postcolonial rhetoric through the power-hunger and potential postimperialism of his protagonist. Pelevin deliberately demonstrates that the empire of the Big Biz, caramelizing in its sophisticated hive of simulation, relinquishes its capability for engaging with reality to its colonized subalterns—or rather, it manufactures subalterns as an inexhaustible fuel source of reality. This dependence loop, in Pelevin's opinion, reduces even imperial domination to just another simulation, which can be undermined when the input—the subalterns, real and substantive—refuses to participate in the social games designed by the empire in its own interest. (Kaia's receipt of agency from her owner exemplifies the logic of such a rebellion.)

Nevertheless, the representation of the progressor in post-Soviet culture, in a devolutionary molt from heroic and self-sacrificial martyr to overweight visual manipulator and evil regressor, proves that this trope in Russian culture of the last fifty years has epitomically expressed power dynamics associated with the ideology of modernization. Changing social and cultural attitudes to various models of modernization produce correspondingly different editions of the progressor. However, despite these variations, the progressor device invariably continues to conceptualize modernization as a colonial procedure, which unavoidably problematizes the process, its goals, its methods, and—most importantly—its price.

The progressor continually emerges as both a model of cultural and symbolic power, justified by a cultural distance from the masses, and a compensatory fantasy of the late-Soviet and post-Soviet intelligentsia, lacking access to actual political clout. This duality explains why the progressor functions as the "switch" between the roles of the master and subaltern, between the postimperial and postcolonial.

Finally, the progressor offers a tenable and symbolically rich example of the formation, deformation, and transformation of Soviet subjectivity, or more specifically, of the peculiar brand of this subjectivity that has been sculpted in the atmosphere of the Thaw, distinguished by enthusiastic dreams of a fusion of Soviet Communism with modernization founded on the ideals of the Enlightenment and humanism. The progressor provides a metaphoric documentation of this idea's historical mutations since the failure of the Thaw era's hopes. In other words, the progressor and its evolution have stood, and continue to stand, as a self-reflexive representation of Soviet liberals—as the mirror into which they stare, eyes straining to detect what has gone so wrong, and why.

Cycles and Continuities in Contemporary Russian Literature

As Boris Gasparov suggested in his article on Pushkin, "History without Teleology," reading the cultural process through the dichotomies of prose vs. poetry, archaists vs. innovators, culture vs. explosion, and so on can be productive despite the common anxiety surrounding binary oppositions, if one would "release these categories from the concept of the progressive historical development, within which they are typically invoked" (2003). Furthermore, according to Gasparov, parallel developments of contrary trends can be identified in any given period. The fact that one of these currents traverses the spotlight, manifesting the tenor of the time, while the other is marginalized and suspended in obscurity, permits the use of these dichotomies as a sensitive analytical tool.

Following this prompt, I will discuss in this article cycles and continuities that connect post-Soviet culture with the cultural phenomena of the Soviet period. I have no ambition of constructing an overarching and universalizing model; I fully realize that contemporary culture—Russian or any other—cannot be reduced to a generalized construct. Rather, I hope that the following might be taken as an intellectual provocation, demonstrating simultaneously the need for historical typologies in the study of the contemporary cultural process and the multiplicity of models that can be applied to it. I am not worried, therefore, over the contradictions that surely await between articulations of the post-Soviet cultural process posited below. Taken separately, each approach would inevitably turn reductive; multiple overlapping angles, however, have a better chance of capturing a three-dimensional image of the present cultural dynamics.

"Simplicity" / "Complexity"

In the early 2000s, talk about the tiredness of overly "complex" forms (i.e., postmodernist, avant-gardist, and modernist experiments) became epidemic in Russian literary criticism. Out of this discourse emerged the notion of "the end of postmodernism," followed by a deluge of manifestos declaring the "new realism" in prose, drama, and even poetry (see, for example, Basinskii 2000, Beliakov 2009, Bol'shakova 2009, Ermolin 2006). The shift from "complex" (sophisticated, self-reflective, fragmentary) forms to "simpler" (transparent, coherent, and democratic) forms is not a new phenomenon in the twentieth-century culture.

Heinrich Wölfflin (1996) was probably the first to propose a dichotomy of styles dominated by either an "open" or a "closed" form. Dmitry Chizhevsky (1952) had argued that literary styles oscillate between two extremes: the pursuit of unity and the pursuit of complexity. While the former quest produces completed forms, the latter generates free-form and even "formless" phenomena. A similar dichotomy is reflected in the typology of "primary" and "secondary" styles developed by Dmitrii Likhachev (1973) and applied to the nineteenth- and twentieth-century literature by Igor' Smirnov (2000). In the 1990s, Georgii Knabe maintained that the development of art is defined by fluctuations within the dichotomy of "culture vs. life" (1993). In his last book, on the theory of genre, Naum Leiderman (2010) divided "grand" styles as gravitating toward the diametric poles of cosmological and chaological strategies in aesthetic world-modeling.

All these dichotomies implicitly presuppose life or reality as something independent of cultural production. Unlike these prominent scholars, I share the belief that "life" *cannot be anything but* a product of "culture." In other words, the "life" situated at the heart of a new "simplified" cultural process is always the remnant of another preceding "complex" period. During each "complex" period, new constructs of the real are introduced and tested; during the ensuing "simple" periods, these new concepts seem congruent with "life," which testifies to their adoption into the culture. Therefore, a fluctuation between "complex" and "simple" forms may be described as a shift between the creation of new, yet incessantly changing, concepts of the real, and the appropriation of already-existing models that are mistaken for actual reality by authors and audiences alike. Thus, it would be more accurate to speak about an ongoing competition of two modalities: one reader-oriented ("simple") and the other author-oriented ("complex"), in the same sense that an utterance can be speaker- or listener-oriented.

Also, unlike the scholars cited above, I doubt that such dichotomies—should they be discernible in the cultural process—necessarily produce new styles or aesthetic systems. These modalities can develop within (or above) any aesthetic language—modernist, postmodernist, or even avant-gardist—without altering its inner structure. For instance, the case of the "simplification" of the avant-garde can be illustrated through the use of avant-garde tropes in posters of the late 1920s and early '30s, or even in Sergei Eisenstein's films of the '30s and '40s (see, for example, Bonnell 1999; Neuberger 2003, 25–135).

The discussion that proceeded in the 2000s about "the end of postmodernism" appears to be quite symptomatic. In my book *Paralogii* (*Paralogies*, 2008), I have argued that attempts to conceptualize contemporary Russian literature in terms of the twilight of postmodernism, post-postmodernism, "new realism," and so on, are misleading. Such trends as New Drama, contemporary poetry, and even the recycling of Socialist Realist tropes in the pop culture of the 2000s still employ postmodernist tactics:[1] the "reality effect" resurges here as a mutable product of language games, and even when binary oppositions seem to be restored, the authors leave

---

1 See "Post-Soc" in this volume.

a handy loophole for their ironic interpretation. The latter device was successfully tested for the first time in Aleksei Balabanov's *Brat 2*, a film that can well be interpreted as a straight-faced expression of xenophobic ideology, yet leaves ajar the door to perceiving it as a postmodernist mockery of post-Soviet nationalism. This opportunity was gladly met by many liberal-minded critics, who scrabbled at the inviting sliver, flung open the door, and heliolatrously lauded this film despite its explicit nationalistic message.

On the topic of postmodernism, it is worth recalling that bridging the gap between highbrow modernist and commonplace popular culture was decreed one of the central goals of Western (and especially American) postmodernism in the late 1960s–70s (Fiedler 1972). For Russian postmodernism, developing in the underground synchronously with its Western counterparts, this task was quite irrelevant. However, in the wake of Viktor Pelevin's *Generation "P"* (1999) and Vladimir Sorokin's *Goluboe salo* (*Blue Fat*, 1999), Russian postmodernism launched a campaign for a broader readership, which, in turn, precipitated easy-to-follow plotlines in place of self-reflective meditation, references to politics of the day and popular culture rather than broad and sophisticated cultural allusions, (quasi-)relatable and recognizable characters rather than metamorphosing narrative masks and multilayered voices, monological narratives rather than polyphonic discourses, coherence rather than fragmentation, and an interest in social and political subjects rather than philosophical inquiry. Another, quite significant, indicator of such a seismic shift in the 2000s can be detected in the transition from the deconstruction of various cultural myths to a new industry of mythmaking; even if these myths are individual, they are still presented by their authors as universal and, typically, enforce binary oppositions. This tendency is exemplified by such works as Sorokin's *Ice Trilogy* (*Led*; *Put' Bro* [*Bro*, 2004]; *23,000* [2005]); by Dmitry Bykov's novels, especially *ZhD*; by the evolution of Evgenii Grishkovets's plays; by Nikita Mikhalkov's films of the 2000s; and by Andrei Khrzhanovsky's much-acclaimed cinematic rendition of the romantic lore surrounding Nobel laureate Joseph Brodsky, *Poltory komnaty* (*A Room and a Half*, 2009).

The turn in the new millennium toward reader- or vieweroriented discourses may be seen as one crest among many waves that first rippled through the entire twentieth century. The Silver Age of Russian modernism, spanning the 1890s–1910s, beheld the radical innovation and complication of poetic discourses. These tandem winds of creative and critical reevaluation extended to the field of prose in the 1920s and converged with a trend toward a breezy oversimplification of artistic language. In the '30s, the latter habit took the upper hand, due not only to the pressure of Socialist Realism: Boris Pasternak's laboring for "unheard-of simplicity" and Anna Akhmatova's affinity for "epic" forms, detectable even in *Rekviem* (*Requiem*, 1940), do not necessarily satisfy the Socialist Realist doctrine, but do resonate with the reader-oriented vector of the period. The 1950s, conversely, witnessed the transmogrification of Socialist Realism into highly codified art, ornate and sometimes nearly baroque in its fantasticality.

Yet a few years later, "the generation of the sixties" was invigorated by a drive toward "sincerity" (to use Vladimir Pomerantsev's catchphrase, from the title of his famous article "Ob iskrennosti v literature" ["On Sincerity in Literature," 1953]). The decade saw emerging a specific kind of social (not socialist!) realism, the so-called "lieutenant" and "youth" prose, as well as a new brand of ideological realism best represented by Solzhenitsyn's novels *V kruge pervom* (*The First Circle*, 1968) and *Rakovyi korpus* (*The Cancer Ward*, 1968), and Vasily Grossman's *Zhizn' i sud'ba* (*Life and Fate*, 1959), which was ironically labeled by Sergei Dovlatov "Socialist Realism with a human face." Along with attention to the details of everyday life, the author's "sincerity," understood as a direct, if naive, reaction to the catastrophic twists of history, was also responsible for the success of the poets Evgenii Evtushenko, Bulat Okudzhava, and Andrei Voznesenskii, as well as that of Aleksandr Volodin's plays. By contrast, "the long seventies" (1968–86) exhibited the surge of "complex" literature and film, not only through the development of underground phenomena belonging to modernist, avant-gardist, and even postmodernist aesthetics but also due to the deeply intricate system of hints, ellipses, and allusions maintained by published Soviet authors (for instance,

Iurii Trifonov) and filmmakers (Andrei Tarkovsky, Kira Muratova, Aleksei German).

Perestroika and the '90s were reminiscent, somewhat, of the '20s: during this late- and post-Soviet period, the simplistic social realism distilled from the Thaw developed alongside postmodernism as it rose from the underground and began to influence the cultural mainstream. These years witnessed more than the parallel dynamic of "simplistic" and "complex" tendencies; they were also characterized by a revival of the so-called returned literature. Texts that had been banned during the Soviet period for political reasons created an unprecedented circumstance when the high modernism of the 1920s–30s, with all its complexity, suddenly acquired a new cultural and political urgency.

Finally, since the late 1990s and throughout the 2000s, we can observe another shift toward "simplicity" as manifested by the spread of the languages of mass culture and myth construction. The rise of Internet-based forms of literature is especially demonstrative of the reader-oriented modality: in blogs, fan fiction, and other forms of net-lit, the reader *is* the writer; the borderline between audience and author is deliberately blurred. That said, it is important to remark that the opposite tendency did not vanish in the 2000s: sophisticated and multilayered high modernist novels,[2] or new films by Kira Muratova, Aleksei German, and Aleksandr Sokurov, all mark the presence of a "complex" countercurrent underneath the "new simplicity" of the 2000s. It would be a stretch to consider this literature as lacking an audience: Mikhail Shishkin's recitation of excerpts from his *Pis'movnik* (*Letter-Book*) was certainly among the most attended events of the Moscow Book Festival in June 2010.

The "complex" undertow can be located in other epochs of "simplicity" as well, and vice versa. Silver Age poetry enjoyed

---

[2] For example, Mikhail Shishkin's *Vziatie Izmaila* (*The Taking of Izmail*, 2000), *Venerin volos* (*Maidenhair*, 2005), and *Pis'movnik* (*Letter-Book*, 2010); the meditative prose of Aleksandr Gol'dshtein's *Pomni o Famaguste* (*Remember Famagusta*, 2004) and *Spokoinye polia* (*Quiet Fields*, 2006); and Andrei Levkin's *Golem, russkaia versiia* (*Golem, Russian Version*, 2000), *Mozgva* (2005), and *Marpl* (2010).

less popularity in the 1900s–1910s than neorealist prose. Andrei Platonov's most complex works, such as *Kotlovan* (*The Foundation Pit*, 1930) and *Schastlivaia Moskva* (*Happy Moscow*, 1933–36), were composed during the "simplistic" '30s. And the aforementioned "returned" modernist masterpieces of Zamiatin and Nabokov were misread during the perestroika period as predominantly political and antitotalitarian statements; that is, their meaning was reduced to a narrow spectrum of simple political ideas.

The Meaning of "Post"

What conclusions can we draw from all these observations? Evidently, transitional periods such as the 1920s and 1990s are marked by a relative, albeit conflictful, balance between reader- and author-oriented tendencies. Phases dominated by author-oriented, "complex" poetics, such as the Silver Age or the long seventies, tend to precede catastrophic or revolutionary historical shifts. But what is the common denominator between the Stalinist thirties, the Thaw, and the 2000s? Is it consumerism? A relief in "traditional values" after typhoons of revolutionary and totalitarian experiment? Not quite; perhaps it would be more productive to seek common tracks not in the features that are inherent in any given decade but in the self-descriptions of each period, which immediately surprise with their similarity. All periods of "simplicity" were regarded from within as following times of trouble, days of havoc and chaos—radical, tectonic shifts and the attendant muddle: in short, traumatic episodes concerning society at large, be it the Revolution and Civil War, the Stalinist terror, or the anarchic nineties. Thus, one might be expected to claim that times culturally marked by the reign of a reader-oriented tendency *imagine themselves as posttraumatic*.

From this premise, I would like to propose another hypothesis: What if "simplistic" and "complex" tendencies in cultural history correlate to two opposing scenarios of digesting traumatic experiences—of acting out and of working through? Of course, any artistic work in some sense "works through" traumas, personal and societal alike. But the resonance between diverse compositions of the same historical hour suggests that certain remedial methods acquire greater urgency and attract more limelight during "complex" moments, while others dominate "simplistic" ones.

The reader-oriented modality arises, perhaps, as an attempt to address and reflect recent traumatic experiences *in a most direct way*. Socialist Realism is not an exception in this context—it only entails a compulsory positive outlook on the traumas of the Revolution and the Civil War, and most importantly, of Stalinist modernization. As to post-Soviet culture of the 2000s, here the concept of trauma is multifold, but consists mainly of two contradictory and overlapping components: the trauma of Soviet history seen in its wholeness, from the Revolution to "developed socialism," and the trauma caused by the collapse of Soviet civilization in the 1990s (see Oushakine 2010a).

Through Dominick LaCapra's interpretation of Freud, one may define such cultural emergency-response measures as the acting out of trauma (frequently mistaken for realism): "Acting-out is related to repetition, and even the repetition compulsion—the tendency to repeat something compulsively [...] [a tendency] to repeat traumatic scenes in a way that is somehow destructive and self-destructive. [...] Acting-out is a process, but a repetitive one. It's a process whereby the past, or the experience of the other, is repeated as if it were fully enacted, fully literalized" (1998, 2, 5). This definition corresponds to many phenomena of recent Russian culture, such as the fascination with (quasi) documentary, a new wave of hypernaturalism as manifest in New Drama (see Beumers and Lipovetsky 2009), and photographic representation (from a minimal distance) of everyday traumatic experiences in present-day nonfiction (including blogs). The repetition impulse can also be detected in the frantic recycling of Socialist Realist tropes endemic to 2000s pop culture, the infatuated revival of Soviet songs (*Starye pesni o glavnom*), regular remakes of popular Soviet films, and the literal and metaphorical recoloring of Soviet "cult" series such as *Semnadtsat' mgnovenii vesny*, as well as in Sergei Ursuliak's miniseries *Isaev* (2009), a prequel to the Shtirlitz spy saga that captivated viewers in 1973.

However, the acting out of trauma has certain intrinsic limitations. These are most evident in the evolution of New Drama: the hypernaturalist poetics of this movement, articulated by various performances of brutality, aspire to act out the trauma of the nineties generation, of those who were too late to quaff the humid euphoria of perestroika but got the full downpour of disappointments, frustrations, and most importantly, violence that accompanied the collapse of the Soviet economy and system in the '90s. Theirs is the generation traumatized by the everyday violence, who immersed themselves in violence as a basic and common language. The isomorphism between trauma and the language of its performance makes for a powerful emotional impact, heaved in the abrasive New Drama productions—although the bruise did not last for more than a few years.

In the plays of New Drama, communication through carnage—and further, the elevation of violence into a language of transcendental pursuit—not only saps all alternative channels of self-identification and self-realization but also leads its speakers to the ultimate self-destruction, or at least reduces them to hueless husks. The semiotic mechanism of New Drama is represented self-reflexively in Kirill Serebrennikov's film *Izobrazhaia zhertvu* (*Playing the Victim*, 2006), based on the Presniakov brothers' play of the same title. Performance (of savagery, of victimization) constructs the protagonist's and other characters' existence solely out of violent interaction. Valia (the protagonist) can find no escape from this "reality" except through the annihilative maw of death: the murder of his entire family, by poison that he administers, functions both as a rebuke for their contentment to live in a false world and as his own logical conclusion to the violent nature of the real. This is where the acting out of trauma reaches its limit, fatally demonstrating that the reproduction of languages of violence as the main source of trauma does not engender any other forms of communication. The traumatic is first presented as an identity-forming device, then aestheticized (and sometimes ritualized), and finally—inexorably—automatized and commercialized. Yet all these operations remain chained to the compulsion to repeat (i.e., they themselves belong to the realm of the traumatic), and more importantly, they fail to produce, in LaCapra's words, the "necessary critical distance" that allows one "to engage in life in the present, to assume responsibility—[which] does not mean that you utterly transcend the past" (1998, 5).

The crisis of New Drama has led to the emigration of many of its playwrights and theater directors to the cinema, and to the translation of New Dramatic aesthetics into cinematic language. This exodus is responsible for some of the key Russian films of recent years.[3] Such films blatantly depart from the orientation toward audience expectations, as testified, for example, by the public scandals associated with *Korotkoe zamykanie* (*Crush*, 2009) or Sergei Loznitsa's *Schast'e moe* (*My Joy*, 2010). In their own ways, these works hint of a renaissance of auteur cinema, with its meditative tempo, sustained long shots, and diminished plot intensity; in other words, they seek a new complexity. These films render the destructive outcomes of communication through violence in a suggestive rather than an explicit way, allowing gaps in the film's texture and forcing viewers to seek their own, emotional rather than rational, justifications of the filmic logic.

Thus, it is not plainly stated why Valia in *Izobrazhaia zhertvu* decides to kill his family; why Pasha in Popogrebskii's *Kak ia provel etim letom* does not immediately tell his boss about the tragedy that has befallen the latter's wife and son; why Proskurina's road movie is entitled *Truce*; and why Loznitsa's travelogue, hopeless and blood saturated (with a similar plot to that of Proskurina's film), bears the title *My Joy*.

I would like to argue that these and similar inner lapses stimulate a critical distance that constitutes the working through of the same traumatic experience that was acted out in New Drama. According to LaCapra, "In the working-through, the person tries to gain critical distance on a problem, to be able to distinguish between past, present, and future" (1998, 2). This distinction, I stress, is

---

[3] For example, Ivan Vyrypaev's *Eiforiia* (*Euphoria*, 2006) and *Kislorod* (*Oxygen*, 2009), Vasilii Sigarev's *Volchok* (*Wolfy*, 2009), Aleksei Popogrebskii's *Kak ia provel etim letom* (*How I Ended This Summer*, 2010), Boris Khlebnikov's *Svobodnoe plavanie* (*Free Floating*, 2006) and *Sumasshedshaia pomoshch'* (*Help Gone Mad*, 2009), Valeriia Gai Germanika's *Vse umrut, a ia ostanus'* (*Everybody Dies but Me*, 2008), Aleksei Mizgirev's *Kremen'* (*The Hard-Hearted*, 2007), Bakur Bakuradze's *Shultes* (2008), Aleksei Fedorchenko's *Ovsianki* (*Silent Souls*, 2010), Svetlana Proskurina's *Peremirie* (*Truce*, 2010), and Sergei Loznitsa's *Schast'e moe* (*My Joy*, 2010).

based on the demonstrated instability of binary oppositions. The working through of trauma, unlike its hastier cousin, tries by all means to avoid the mechanism of scapegoating, which is in turn based on pure binaries between past and present, self and other, and so on.

The Mainstream and Magical Historicism

Such mainstream writers of the 2000s as Boris Akunin, Viktor Pelevin, Dmitry Bykov, Aleksandr Terekhov, Mikhail Elizarov, Liudmila Ulitskaya, and Olga Slavnikova do not pursue an "adequate" imprint of the traumatic experience. Using various forms of modernist and (sometimes) postmodernist defamiliarization, such as grotesque, phantasmagoria, mythmaking, and so on, they instead attempt to whittle a critical distance into the reenactment of traumatic experience, personal and collective alike. Furthermore, these writers are above all concerned with the *mutual connection* between Soviet and post-Soviet traumas—a relationship that the "new realists" failed to recognize. We can see this most palpably drawn in works like Olga Slavnikova's novels *Bessmertnyi* (*The Immortal*, 2001), *2017* (2006), and *Legkaia golova* (*Light-Headed*, 2010); Bykov's *ZhD*; and Akunin's stylized vision of prerevolutionary Russia, permeated by portents of coming historical catastrophes and replete with tongue-in-cheek references to post-Soviet disappointments.

Alexander Etkind has recently introduced an analytical model for gauging this literature's relation to traumatic experience through his concept of magical historicism. In his book *Warped Mourning: Stories of the Undead in the Land of the Unburied* (2013), Etkind isolates the defining principle of this retrospective fancy as the dialectic of reenactment and defamiliarization. The scholar focuses on motifs of the uncanny typical for this mode of literature, including ghosts, vampires, and werewolves, as signs of the returned repressed—first and foremost, in Etkind's view, the repressed memory of the victims of Stalinist repressions. Invoking the Freudian concept of melancholia and Benjamin's ideas on the work of mourning, Etkind argues that in this literature the past is perceived not just as "another country" but as an exotic and unexplored one, still pregnant with unborn alternatives and imminent miracles. [. . .] Possessed by the ghostly past and unable to withdraw from its repetitive contemplation, post-Soviet writers find themselves trapped in a state of melancholia. [. . .] The inability to differentiate oneself from the lost object prevents the individual from living in the present, from love and work. On the political level, the reverse is probably equally important: when there is no choice in the present, the historical past unfolds into an overwhelming narrative that obscures the present rather than explaining it. (2013, 234)

Despite his bitter appraisal, Etkind concludes that "magical historicism does have critical potential," since its propelling minds "are recognizably different from those authors who use realistic techniques to spread their pro-Soviet nostalgia, like Aleksandr Prokhanov or Maksim Kantor" (235) — or, one might add, the "new realists" of the younger generation.

While accepting Etkind's proposal broadly, I would suggest a few amendments. We should not forget that "the inability to differentiate oneself from the lost object" acquires a peculiar form in many mainstream texts. Writers like Bykov, Terekhov, Elizarov, and Slavnikova find unanticipated concurrence in depicting present or future Russian history as a reprise of Soviet patterns. Thus, they *thematicize* the repetition itch. However, in magical historicism it is not the authors (as in "new realism") but their penned personages who undergo the reenactment of trauma, while the scripter observes their perturbation with varying degrees of alienation and sometimes contempt.

These writers more typically nominate the traumatic echo as the "objective" feature of Russian history, as a foundational myth of sorts. In Bykov's *ZhD*, this configuration is materialized through the author's schematic of history driven by the cyclical clash of two forces: Khazars — liberals, Jews, or Westernizers; and Varangians — nationalists, statists, and militarists, repeatedly colonizing and recolonizing Russia. In Slavnikova's *2017*, it is not the pressure of present-day political or social problems — mostly obviated in her novel — but a mere memorial reenactment of the October revolution, performed during the centennial celebrations, that triggers a new quasi-revolutionary eruption.

Most characteristic in this respect is Aleksandr Terekhov's historical crime novel *Kamennyi most* (*The Stone Bridge*, 2009), in which the replication of the traumatic past is internalized by the narrator, a former KGB officer and collector of toy soldiers. On the order of some mystical authority, he leads the inquest into the 1943 murder of Nina Umanskaia, daughter of the Soviet ambassador to the United States, allegedly killed by the son of the aviation industry minister Vladimir Shakhurin. The investigation, the search for meaning in this heinous and legendary crime (the so-called *delo volchat*, "wolfies' affair") is constructed as an exhaustive, more than eight-hundred-page-long Gordian knot of self-repeating interviews and inquiries with witnesses living and dead, all leading practically nowhere (it is one of Mikoian's sons who probably killed Nina—so what?) and testifying only to the hollow core of Stalinist trauma.

Theodor Adorno wrote of the resistance that worn memory poses to a working through of the past: "It tenaciously persists in glorifying the National Socialist era, which fulfilled the collective fantasies of power harbored by those people who, individually, had no power and who indeed could feel any self-worth at all only by virtue of such collective power" (2005). The diagnosis applies well to Terekhov's novel, wherein the narrator finds existential and even metaphysical meaning in his ceaseless, senseless investigation precisely because it affords him the ability, or rather the opportunity, to immerse into communal reveries of power. Power in *Kamennyi most* is represented equilaterally by, on the one hand, the "men of Truth" (*liudi Pravdy*, the sobriquet used by the narrator for the NKVD and KGB henchmen without the lightest touch of irony), whom the narrator impersonates in his metaphysical quest, and, on the other hand, by the Soviet elite—"the Emperor" (as Stalin is exclusively referred to) and his ministers (*pravda zheleznykh liudei*, "men of iron").

Mikhail Elizarov loudest of all proclaims his nostalgia for the Soviet epoch—less in his novels, though, than in his interviews. Among his written works, especially demonstrative is the Booker

Prize-winning *Bibliotekar'* (*The Librarian*, 2008), in which he depicts the restoration of Soviet mythology as a transcendental signified, alleging a meaningful answer while enveloping the characters in the world of enduring violence and trauma. Resultantly, the narrative transforms into a tragicomic ritual of self-destruction for those who seek this promised Truth. Nonetheless, the absorption of power—the symbolic sort, at least—becomes the ultimate objective in Elizarov's reanimations of Soviet discourses.

These writers' efforts to retake Soviet history contralogically testify to the opposite—to the persistent injury of the recent historical experience (the collapse of the USSR and the painful post-Soviet contortions of the former Soviet society) as a source of unremedied historical disorientation. One may conclude that in these works the "critical distance" rent by defamiliarizing turns is *sutured* by the acting out of trauma: grotesquerie and mythologization appear not to be strong enough aesthetic quakes to achieve the effective critical distance that would process the reenactment of trauma into the working through of trauma.

The greater the distance between author and personage, the more obvious is the association between most traumatic phenomena in magical historicism and the inability to sieve the past from the present, dependence on the Soviet historical and rhetorical pattern seeming to dictate the logic of today's events and behavior. This dependence condemns characters, endlessly, inescapably, to revisit and re-incur Soviet catastrophe and to reenact post-Soviet calamities. All the authors of magical historicism conceive of history as an irrational, nightmarish déjà vu, from which one cannot extricate oneself by any effort. Terekhov and Elizarov accept this verdict with almost religious ecstasy; Slavnikova and Ulitskaya psychologize it, and therein, intentionally or not, reconcile with habitual recursion as the norm; while Dmitry Bykov seeks rational algorithms behind the irrational historical turns.

Pelevin represents the most paradoxical expression of this dependence. Beginning with *Omon Ra* (1993), he has essentially rewritten, with varying specifications, the same story: how a man becomes a god, and what doing so means. In Pelevin's earlier texts—plus the plotline of A Huli in *Sviashchennaia kniga oborotnia*

(*The Sacred Book of the Werewolf*, 2003)—this was a tale of achieving ultimate freedom. However, in his output since *Generation "P"* (including the plotline of FSB general Sasha Seryi in *Sviashchennaia kniga*) and with the utmost persistence and even despair in his later works—*Ampir V* (*Empire V*, 2006), *Operatsiia "Burning Bush"* (*Operation "Burning Bush,"* 2010), *S.N.U.F.F.*—he demonstrates how the "ascension" of his hero into a godlike being *changes nothing*, frequently even worsening affairs both for the rookie deity and for the world around them. The deification of the protagonist thus deflates and dissolves into the churning tapioca of déjà vu, historical and ahistorical alike—but always very Russian, despite numerous signs of globalization.

Although Etkind counts Sorokin and Vladimir Sharov among "magical historicists," this title can be bestowed neither on Sorokin's later works nor on Sharov's novels of any period. Sorokin has slipped into the mainstream only once, with his *Ice Trilogy*, in which he invented a metamyth factoring in occultist scholarship of the Silver Age, totalitarian ideologies (Soviet and Nazi alike), and New Age motifs. This myth poeticized the traumatic "eternal return," prohibiting any alternatives to it; no wonder the mortal opponents of the Brotherhood of Ice, in the final movement of the trilogy, actually accepted the truth and the message of their foes, thus becoming their heirs. *Den' oprichnika* (*Day of the Oprichnik*, 2006), *Sakharnyi Kreml'* (*Sugar Kremlin*, 2008), *Metel'* (*Blizzard*, 2010), and *Monoklon* (*Monoclone*, 2011) manifest a different logic: in these texts, Sorokin declares the impossibility of overcoming the traumatic past as Russia's central and sharpest affliction, permitting old wounds to scorbutically split open and ache and precipitating new ones through the self-destructive replication of yesterday's pains. True to his conceptualist schooling, Sorokin in these books focuses on the language—that is, the embodied cultural tradition—that, according to him, is the fountainhead of the compulsive reenactments of trauma in disparate historical settings. These works explore cultural dialects as tongues of trauma; in fact, considering the healthy critical distance they keep from their subjects, languages are essentially promoted to the office of main characters. The deconstruction of cultural linguistic patterns as sources and mechanisms of recurring historical traumas is Sorokin's method of working through trauma and his alternative to the mainstream.

As to Sharov, his mode of operation recalls magical historicism on the surface, while being quite alien to it in deeper layers. Each of his novels could be cursorily read as a reenactment of the catastrophe of the revolution and terror, which his characters invariably interpret as yet another failed attempt of the Second Coming, a missed renewal of the world. However, what seems to be natural and sensible in the process of reading is utterly lost if one attempts to retell his plots. Sharov inserts imperceptible pitfalls of defamiliarization into his diorama of disaster. He methodically enshrouds the reader in catastrophe as an experience of ultimate otherness, resistant to any "external" rationalization. Resultantly, all of his novels inverse the logic of magical historicism: they demonstrate how attempts to reenact (sacred) history perpetually incite further devastation and trauma. All endeavors of his characters to spark the Second Coming typically end in the Gulag or, if one is fortunate, a psychiatric asylum.

Nowadays, however, it is hard not to notice similarities between magical historicism and the cultural simulacra produced by post-Crimea and post-Maidan Russian media. According to Etkind, magical historicism embodies the Freudian logic of the uncanny; it facilitates the "return of the repressed"—repressed memory and historical experience, along with literal victims of political repressions. Thus, fantastic elements, on the one hand, emphasize the alogical and surreal character of Soviet history, and on the other, offer purely aesthetic, fictional links that allow the possibility of restoring the historical continuity between the Soviet and post-Soviet eras, and, most importantly, of connecting them with a simulacra of *teleology* (if negative). Although in many cases such a teleology has been openly ironic (as in Pelevin and Sharov), and in others collapses under its own weight (as in Tolstaya and Terekhov), novels of magical historicism responded to a broad-scale need for historical teleology in Russian society. Furthermore, they normalized the idea that if such a need exists, then anything, any methods and materials, including the openly fantastic, can serve as prosthetics for teleology; here the process is more significant than its results.

This idea has been materialized with impressive coherence by Russian TV since 2014. The quasi-factual mystery play / "geopolitical" soap opera produced by all major TV channels includes all features of magical historicism, with one significant difference: the genre that Etkind considers to be designed for the liberal interpretation of history (the return of repressed Stalinism) has been successfully adopted for imperialist and antiliberal narratives. The entire propaganda discourse of 2014–15 was based on the constant connection—to the point of indiscernibility—of the Soviet past and the post-Soviet present: the Soviet images and rhetorics of victimhood—victims of Nazism, victims of the Holocaust, and even victims of Stalinism—merge with the contemporary demonization of revolutionary Ukraine ("Fascists"), the vile and morally degraded West ("Gayrope" and American imperialism), and, most recently, the anticivilizational hordes of immigrants ("barbarians"). Yet the main purpose of this production is the demonstration of the "eternal" teleology that connects today's Russia with the Stalinist Soviet Union and the prerevolutionary tsarist empire. This is the story of Russia as always victimized by global evil and always representing the last frontier of global good, a Russia that has been humiliated numerous times but has always returned to greatness and glory, despite its enemies' attempts to destroy it forever. Certainly, this binarist grand narrative has nothing to do with postmodernism; yet it requires various conspiracy theories and grotesque horror stories with strong erotic connotations (a crucified boy in Slavyansk, a raped girl in Berlin) that function in ways similar to fantastic motifs in magical historicism. Such a transformation completes the story of this literary genre and transforms it into a set of ideological clichés.

A Doubt in One's Own Utterance

Sorokin's and Sharov's writings of the last two decades, along with the prose of Aleksandr Gol'dshtein, Dmitry Prigov, Mikhail Shishkin, Nikolai Baitov, Andrei Levkin, Nikolai Kononov, and some others, have indeed led the way to the strategies of working through trauma recruited by the "complex" literature of the next generation of writers. However, the turn toward "complexity," as we see it now, began not with prose but with poetry. It was poetry that started to attract and condense diverse phenomena in a common direction. Why poetry? Probably because its artistic discoveries admitted critical distance, the necessary factor for the working through of trauma, into the core of literary discourse.

In short, in the "complex" poetry of the 2000s, a new subject was born. In a programmatic 2001 essay by the title "Postconceptualism," Dmitrii Kuz'min located the shift of subject position in the following: "I know that an individual utterance is exhausted and therefore my own utterance is not individual anymore. But I want to know how to re-individualize it." As the poetic practice of the 2000s demonstrated, each of the new generation's poets sought and secured his or her own solution to this puzzle. Roughly speaking, one may say that the subject of poetic discourse was shaped in the new poetry as the pliable *combinations* of somebody else's borrowed, depersonalized, or authorized voices and positions. The subjective and personal thus appeared to be inseparably conjoined to the Other, and even the most intimate utterance constantly was problematized: Is it I who is speaking? Who is speaking through me? Where am I?

Kuz'min has astutely defined this poetic trend as postconceptualism—certainly, it has emerged on the foundation of poetic discourse, and its understanding was elaborated by Prigov and Rubinshtein. For instance, Prigov repeatedly stressed "the problematization of the personal utterance, its impossibility" (Balabanova 2001, 28) as the central principle of his poetics and ideology. He was also known to define postmodernism by the same formula, but the meaning of this principle is much broader. Speaking about poets of the conceptualist circle, he employed it as the ethical criteria: "We had a principally different premise. It was very relativist and, while criticizing the others' discourses and the Big Soviet discourse, we inadvertently arrived at what characterizes postmodernism—the doubt in one's own utterance. [. . .] In other words, the critique of any discourse naturally leads to the doubt in one's own utterance" (87). By this qualifier, Prigov distinguished other conceptualist literati of his generation and the generation of the 1960s. Elsewhere he discusses Vsevolod Nekrasov, a fellow conceptualist, his discrepancies with whom he explains as follows: "The problem is that he doesn't understand and doesn't presuppose that his language is *his* language. He is convinced that he speaks the universal and *correct* language" (28; author's emphasis).

This "doubt in one's own utterance," and the knowledge that your language is not universal and true—this *ethical* principle supported by Prigov's lifelong project was gratefully embraced by "complex" poets of the new generation, laid as the soil from which critical distance would grow. The fact that the new, postconceptualist poetry is also focused on trauma, while the present remains situated in the climate of continuous trauma, does not require special proofs. Rather, it would be sufficient to cite an acknowledged connoisseur of contemporary poetry, Ilya Kukulin, who wrote, "Today poetry more intensively than prose works out the methods of analysis of historical traumas of contemporary mind and demonstrates the paths of curing these traumas" (2010b). To this I would add mention of such remarkable texts as, for instance (the list is certainly just mine), "Oni opiat' za svoi Afganistan" ("Again They're Off for Their Afghanistan") and "Chernye kostiumy" ("Black Suits") by Elena Fanailova, the Leningrad blockade cycle by Polina Barskova, "Sovetskie zastol'nye pesni" ("Soviet Feasting Songs") by Stanislav L'vovskii, "Proza Ivana Sidorova" ("The Prose of Ivan Sidorov") by Mariia Stepanova, and *Semeinyi arkhiv* (*The Family Archive*) by Boris Khersonskii.

The transmission of this principle into the realm of prose turned out to be quite complicated, necessitating a number of "extensions." By his own route, mainly through adoption of European modernism's experience, Mikhail Shishkin achieved a similar result in his prose. Shishkin's novels *Vziatie Izmaila* (*The Taking of Izmail*, 1999), *Venerin volos* (*Maidenhair*, 2005), and in part *Pis'movnik* (*Letter-Book*, 2010) interweave numerous voices and quotations into a powerful lyrical stream of consciousness. The subject in each book is born before our eyes, absorbing someone else's stories of individual and historical traumas and unifying them by a common *rhythm*, almost forcing on them echoing motifs, correspondences, and rhymes, translating them across languages, and finally convincing the narrator and reader that life always consists of these traumas, and that their cure is found in rhythm, otherwise called love, and that there is no other substance of being apart from this one. To a certain extent, although with important variations, a similar logic can be traced in such significant texts of the recent period as *Gnedich* (2011) by Maria Rybakova, *Kamennye kleny* (*Stone Maples*, 2008) and other novels by Lena Eltang, and *Flaner* (*Flaneur*, 2011) by Nikolai Kononov. The same outlook underlies the prose of the late Aleksandr Gol'dshtein, whose influence on contemporary Russian writing is yet underestimated.

An opposing vector of "complexity" is launched by prose that might be deemed, for lack of a better term, "anthropological." I refer to those works that attempt to penetrate the *other* consciousness and the psychological state always situated amid historical cataclysm. Authors of these works methodically undermine authoritative or, conversely, popular counterauthoritative assessments and beliefs, excavating (or imagining) with the meticulousness of a patient paleontologist all the incredible, unprecedented complexity of the traumatic experience. This profound expedition into *otherness* is founded on a sort of taboo that proscribes any attempts to judge or, for that matter, reward or penalize characters. The aesthetic attitude here is based on Varlam Shalamov's example, with his imperative vision of the writer "as Pluto ascending from hell, as opposed to Orpheus descending into hell" (1998, 4:365). Shalamov's principles fuse with the analytical poetics of the "interim prose" of Lidiia Ginzburg, who taught contemporary writers to seek connections between language and physiology. (Another important influence on this poetics is W. G. Sebald, although only a few of his novels have been translated into Russian.)

It is no wonder that the stories of the Leningrad siege attract today's poets (Polina Barskova, Sergei Zav'ialov) and prosaists alike. Immersion into this dark tempest of Russian cultural memory produced one of the best "anthropological" novels of the last decade: Igor' Vishnevetsky's *Leningrad* (2010), in which the monstrous world of the siege appears as the complex intersection of different layers and languages of culture—stemming from Silver Age, Nazi, and Soviet sources alike—overlapping, interweaving with horrible resonance, and spelling the apocalypse in horrible minutiae. In a different way, through the resurrection of *skaz*, an anthropological prose is crafted by Margarita Khemlin, author of the novels *Klotsvog* (2009), *Krainii* (*The Last One*, 2010), and *Doznavatel'* (*The Investigator*, 2012); and Valerii Votrin in his *Logoped* (*The Speech Therapist*, 2012).

Certainly, lyrical and anthropological renditions of "complex" prose are only the most obvious or tangible avenues taken by the working-through mind-set. I hope that others will appear (or perhaps, have already appeared, though I failed to notice them). It is important to emphasize that "complexity" derives from conditions securing a *critical distance* around historical traumas—conditions created by the inequality of the subject to oneself (and of the author to the protagonist or narrator); by the deconstruction of binary oppositions; by the rejection of expected (i.e., stereotypical) approaches; by limitations self-imposed on those who accept the doubt in their own utterance as the highest aesthetic and ethical principle. Furthermore, the experience of reader-oriented and mainstream literature suggests that the most vital task facing "complex" literature is to detach one's own language from vernaculars of violent communication, including rhetorical and symbolic justifications of violence.

Although the richness of "complex" literature is self-evident, and even evokes a certain Renaissance flavor, the prevailing reception of this literary trend in current Russian criticism is more reminiscent of that met by decadent literature at the turn of the twentieth century. Writers developing such strategies are frequently branded as "anemic" or even "autistic." This field-wide (mis)perception symptomatically mirrors the popularity of the "new realists" and other "reader-oriented" authors. The Russian literary establishment and general readership alike seem to accept violence—beyond the level of representation, on the plane of rhetoric and symbolism—as proof of the literature's vitality. This is why compositions that do not conjure the illusion of a violence-based redistribution of power, or that, however humbly, propose peaceful systems of power, are doomed to dismissal as "decadent"—lifeless, effete, hermetic, designed for a narrow stratum of the "creative class" only. The political consequences of this judgment, sadly, are too obvious to elaborate.

However, today we encounter a scenario where the question of the Other—cultural, ethnic, religious, sexual, social, or ideological—has obtained in contemporary Russia a paramount political weight. These issues stem from historical traumas, not yet worked through, and from the dearth of critical distance before these traumas, Soviet and post-Soviet alike. In the present situation, approaches expounded by "complex" literature have a white-hot opportunity to pass from book pages into streets and squares. Those who have chosen to propel and evolve "complex" pathways of cultural healing will make an unforgivable error if they miss the chance to enrich their "complexity" in the flames of social discontent and protest.

Fleshing/Flashing the Discourse: Sorokin's Master Trope

One of the most famous and most repeated self-commentaries by Vladimir Sorokin sounds as follows: "When they ask me how can you torture people like this, I respond: These are not persons, these are just letters on paper" (Semenova 2002).[1] In another interview, the author tenders something like an apophatic defense of the alleged "immoralism" of his compositions: "On paper one may allow himself to do anything. It will tolerate everything. [. . .] The Word that God had wasn't on paper" (Shapoval 1998, 20).[2] As implied here, his characters and their deeds are merely words and should not be judged on moral or on any extraliterary grounds.

This dictum only partially reflects the actual meaning of Sorokin's texts. It is a half-truth at best, which the writer indirectly admits when he says, "Text is a powerful weapon. It can hypnotize, and sometimes paralyze" (Rasskazova 1992, 121).[3] Note the physiological effects of the text that he highlights—and, most likely,

---

[1] «Когда мне говорят — как можно так издеваться над людьми, я отвечаю: 'Это не люди, это просто буквы на бумаге'».

[2] «На бумаге можно позволить все, что угодно. Она стерпит. . . То самое Слово, что было у Бога, было вовсе не на бумаге».

[3] «Текст — очень мощное оружие. Он гипнотизирует, а иногда — просто парализует».

desires. Sorokin frequently bemoans the lack of attention to material details in Russia's literary heritage, declaring that his own artistic originality blossoms exactly in this field:

> There was no body in Russian literature. There was an excessive amount of spirituality. When one reads Dostoevsky, it's impossible to feel characters' bodies: how Prince Myshkin was built, how Nastas'ia Filippovna's bust looked. I wanted very much to fill Russian literature with corporeality: the smell of sweat, muscle movements, body fluids, sperm, shit. As Artaud once said, "When it smells like shit, it smells like life." (Semenova 2002, 4)[4]

However, this discussion is not simply Sorokin's magnification of the body over the spirit, the soul, and the philosophical and moral themes typical of Russian literary culture. More significant for the present essay is his trademark *transformation* of verbal concepts into corporeal images, or more generally, the translation of discourses and rhetorical constructions into body language. The gesture-phrases of this somatic tongue relate either to the "lower bodily stratum"—eating, defecating, vomiting, copulating (which frequently provokes interpretation through the lens of Bakhtin's "carnivalization")—or to naturalistically depicted violence, graphic representations of the human body in mutilation. In Sorokin's own words,

> I work constantly with liminal zones where the body invades the text. For me, this borderline between literature and corporeality has always been of foremost importance. As a matter of fact, my texts always raise a question of literary corporeality, and I try to resolve the problem of whether literature is corporeal. I take

---

[4] «В русской литературе вообще тела было очень мало. Духа было выше крыши. Когда читаешь Достоевского, не можешь почувствовать тела героев: сложение князя Мышкина или какая грудь была у Настасьи Филипповны. Я же очень хотел наполнить русскую литературу телесностью: запахом пота, движением мышц, естественными отправлениями, спермой, говном. Как сказал Арто: 'Там, где пахнет говном, пахнет жизнью'».

pleasure in the moment when literature becomes corporeal and nonliterary. (Roll 1996, 123–24)[5]

Dirk Uffelmann, in his periodization of Sorokin's oeuvre, defines the writer's first phase as "the *materialization of metaphors*, the second *positivism of emotions* and the third *fantastic substantialism*" (2006, 109; emphasis in the original). I aim to argue that the discursive deployment of bodily gestures, which can be only partially described as the materialization of metaphors, serves as Sorokin's master trope and can be traced across his works from the earliest to the most recent. I would like to call this tactic *carnalization* (from the Latin *carnalis*), not to be confused with "carnivalization" or "canalization," although some parallels are invited. In my view, carnalization represents the core of Sorokin's individual method of deconstruction applied to the authoritative discourses, symbols, and cultural narratives. We might wonder, observing the hygienic operation: How does carnalization acquire deconstructive faculty? What are the symbolic implications of this trope? What is its heuristic potential? Seeking answers to these questions, I will first present an overview of Sorokin's uses of his master trope and then attempt to provide its interpretation.

Direct Carnalization

Sorokin's early works are populated by *direct carnalization*, denoting the materialization of metaphors and idioms. Most exemplary in this respect is probably *Norma* (*The Norm*, 1979–83). In the novel's first part, the idiomatic expression *to eat shit* (*govna nazhrat'sia*) is materialized through scenes depicting various walks of Soviet life, each invariably including the characters' consumption of their daily

---

[5] «Я постоянно работаю с пограничными зонами, где тело вторгается в текст. Для меня всегда была важна эта граница между литературой и телесностью. Собственно, в моих текстах всегда стоит вопрос литературной телесности, и я пытаюсь разрешить проблему, телесна ли литература. Я получаю удовольствие в тот момент, когда литература становится телесной и нелитературной».

norma—a brick of processed children's feces. In the seventh part of *Norma*, which bears the name "Stikhi i pesni" ("Poems and Songs"), Sorokin—or rather, his "substitute author"—invokes direct quotations from Soviet songs and poems in each short narrative. Thus, the trite poetic line about a sailor who leaves his heart with a girl transmutates into the girl's delivery of a jar holding a pulsating heart to the police station. A pair of *zolotye ruki* ("golden hands," an idiom for a jack-of-all-trades), the pride and joy of a boy from flat no. 5, are melted down and exchanged for a foreign-made device that will complete a humongous monument to Lenin atop the Palace of Soviets. The ideologically charged idiom *to breathe one's motherland* (*dyshat' rodinoi*) is sarcastically reconfigured in a scene where, due to a lack of oxygen, members of a submarine crew press a map of the USSR to their faces: "Everyone was pressing to the face a map of his native region and breathing, breathing, breathing . . ." (Sorokin 1998, 1:241).[6] Similar literalizations of metaphoric and idiomatic expressions may be found in *Pervyi subbotnik* (*The First Saturday Workday*, 1979–84; for instance, in "San'kina liubov'") or in *Serdtsa chetyrekh* (*The Hearts of the Four*, 1991), with its memorable materialization of the idiom *ebat' mozgi* ("to fuck the brains," i.e., to bullshit) in the novel's conclusion.

Direct carnalization does not entirely disappear in Sorokin's later output. One might recall the scene in *Moskva* (*Moscow*, 2000) where Lev is tortured with an air pump: Aleksandr Genis (2002, 104–5) was the first to notice that this bit of savagery literalizes the idiom *odin zhulik nadul drugogo*—*one crook cheated* (literally, pumped up) *another*. In *The Ice Trilogy*, the ceremony of the Light brothers is woven around the idioms *voice of the heart* (*golos serdtsa*) and *speak with your heart* (*govori serdtsem*) as carnalized discourse, manifesting the fetishization of ultimate sincerity that commandeered the liberal rhetoric of the perestroika period and the '90s. For instance, the election campaign of 1996 bred the abundant slogan *Golosui serdtsem*, "Vote with your heart."

[6] «Каждый прижимал ко рту карту своей области и дышал, дышал, дышал. . .»

Nariman Skakov noted, during a discussion of this article at the Aarhus conference on Sorokin in 2010, that the nibbling and licking of the titular sugar Kremlin in Sorokin's 2008 collection of short stories responds to the first installment of *Norma* by presenting another new set of variations on the consumption and internalization of repressive rule. However, one may also detect in the imagery a direct materialization of *the sweet taste of power* (*sladost' vlasti*); the same expression is invoked in *Den' oprichnika* when Komiaga debates Mandelstam's line "Power is abject, like a barber's hands."[7] Finally, the entire myth-world of *Metel'*, with its populace of giants and midgets, seems to derive from a cultural idiom vital to nineteenth-century literature: the *malen'kii chelovek* ("insignificant person"), especially relevant to *Metel'* given the numerous stylistic, plot, and characterological references to the works of Pushkin, Tolstoy, and Chekhov.

Usually, these carnalizations have been received as Sorokin's mockery of authoritative idioms and symbols, especially when their relation to Socialist Realism and official Soviet discourse is blatantly obvious. However, as one may notice, even in Sorokin's early works these discursive sources of carnalization are not necessarily marked ideologically. Rather, through carnalization, Sorokin declaratively introduces his overriding theme: the *corporeality of language*, especially, but not exclusively, as represented by various authoritative discourses, cultural and political alike. Using Dirk Uffelmann's apt definition, one may detect in Sorokin's quest "the ontological presupposition [. . .] that nothing exists beyond metaphors (and their materializations) that (textual) reality is creative by (destructive) language" (2006, 109).

From this perspective, Sorokin's plunge into theater and cinema seems not only natural but necessary: these media are able to lay his major theme bare by drawing a *visible* corporeal dimension to the texts. Tellingly, the novelist-turned-scriptwriter highlights the transformation of the textual into the corporeal by using readily

---

[7] «Власть отвратительна как руки брадобрея» (from Mandelstam's poem "Ariost," 1933).

recognizable works of classical literature as the pre-texts of his stage and screen work: Shakespeare's plays for *Dismorfomaniia* (1989); Chekhov's for *Iubilei* (*Anniversary*, 1993) and *Moskva*; Dostoevsky's novels for *Dostoevsky-Trip* (1997); Andersen's "Lykkens Kalosker" ("The Galoshes of Fortune") for *Kopeika* (*Kopeck*, 2001); Tolstoy's *Anna Karenina* for *Mishen'* (*Target*, 2011) . . . Through these allusive intertexts, he underscores the transformation of the *exemplary literariness* of the classical discourses into the contemporary corporeality of filmic representation.

It is hardly surprising that Sorokin's entire oeuvre, from early aperitifs to the present course, is peppered by what may be called *metacarnalization*, representing a body of discourse in a generalized, yet literal, form. For instance, in the short story "Zaplyv" ("Heat"; written in the early '80s, published in 1999's *Goluboe salo*), Sorokin imagines a levitating excerpt from some official documents compiled by torch-wielding military swimmers. Analogously, the entire five-hundred-page breadth of *Roman* (1985–89), stylized as a nineteenth-century Russian novel, may be read as a metacarnalization of the theorized death of the novel (*smert' romana*), a subject of wide debate in the 1950s–70s.

Indirect Carnalization

Sorokin, in addition to these direct carnalizations, intrepidly explores the possibilities of *indirect carnalization*—corporeal imagery that manifests, rather than a familiar idiom, a hidden discursive logic. *Pervyi subbotnik* was probably Sorokin's first exercise of such a technique. The stories in this collection seem to have two faces: one a conventional, middlebrow Soviet narrative, and the other violence, brutal sex, and gibberish: "In the 1980s, I used to make little binary literary bombs consisting of two incompatible parts: a Socialist Realist one and the other built on real physiology; as a result, an explosion followed, and it did fill me as a litterateur with a flash of freedom" (Voznesenskii 2006).[8] The jarring shifts

---

[8] «В 80-е годы я делал бинарные литературные бомбочки, состоящие из

between these tones suggest that the connection between them is not arbitrary but guided by a purposeful inner logic. In the most characteristic examples, a corporeal action appears as the *extension* of a discourse.

For instance, in "Sergei Andreevich," a devoted schoolboy absorbs with admiration all the banalities that his teacher spouts— a discipleship taken to the point of nausea (more or less literally) when the student diligently eats his teacher's feces. In another teacher-student story, "Svobodnyi urok" ("A Vacant Lesson"), a female teacher tames a schoolboy's pubescent energy by manipulating him and exhorting him to "grow up," while schooling the lad in sexuality by forcing him to touch her genitalia. "I am doing this for you, stupid!" (Sorokin 1998, 1:506)[9] she repeats, obviously enjoying the act far more than he. While the studious feasting on an instructor's shit appears to be a profane form of the Eucharist, the other student's rape is matched by the teacher's not-so-secret pleasure. Such motifs appear in these stories as two sibling expressions of didacticism, which many conceptualists (as in Lev Rubinshtein's and Dmitrii Prigov's writings) considered the core of the Russian cultural tradition.

It is noteworthy that in "Sergei Andreevich," as well as in many other stories in this book ("Otkrytie sezona," "Pominal'noe slovo," "Proezdom," "Pervyi subbotnik," and others), the transformation of the intangibly discursive into the corporeal bears a sense of ritual, pointing toward a transcendental meaning. But this meaning is transcendental only because it is situated *beyond* the discourse. This is why Sorokin inserts, along with sex and violence, healthy doses of *zaum'*—nonsensical language—and a rich helping of obscenity, as in *Pervyi subbotnik*, *Norma*, and the play *Russkaia babushka* (*Russian Grandmother*, 1988). Similarly, the dialect of power borders on drivel in *Serdtsa chetyrekh* and the plays *Doverie* (*Confidence*,

---

двух несоединимых частей: соцреалистической и части, построенной на реальной физиологии, а в результате происходил взрыв, и он наполнял меня, как литератора, некой вспышкой свободы».

[9] «Для тебя же стараюсь, балбес!»

1989) and *Zanos* (*Drift*, 2009). I have a suspicion that Sorokin employs Chinese words and expressions for the same purpose, first in *Goluboe salo* and later in *Den' oprichnika, Sakharnyi Kreml'*, and *Mishen'*.[10]

The chain of transformations, from the discursive through the corporeal and into the transcendental, is represented best in *Goluboe salo* (1999). The titular "blue fat," a mystical substance emitted in the act of writing by clones of the great Russian writers, serves as the material equivalent of Russia's famed spirituality. In Aleksandr Genis's words, it is "the Russian Grail, the spirit transformed into flesh" (2003).[11] As the carnalized sacred, the blue fat appears to be equally resonant with the desires of a scientific cosmopolitan society of the future and a retro-utopian nationalist community of *zemleeby* (literally, "earth-fuckers"), as well as an alternative, bloodless totalitarianism in which Stalin and Hitler are allies, and where sexuality and drugs are not repressed but celebrated.

Furthermore, in Sorokin's early and recent texts alike, one may detect relatively stable affinities between the treated discourse and the form its carnalization takes. For instance, the traditionalist, nationalist discourse of love for all things Russian is almost inevitably embodied in ceremonial massacres, where sadistic mass murder is the ultimate expression of Russophilic sentiment. This connection first appears in the third part of *Norma*, in which a Buninesque narrative about returning to a demolished aristocratic household gives way to "Padezh," a story depicting collectivization as an ecstatic festival of accelerating violence and destruction.

The very same linkage appears in *Roman*. Ritualized violence erupts at a provocative moment in the narrative: Roman and Tat'iana's wedding night. The artfully stylized discourse of the Russian classical novel does not leave a place for sexuality. Thus, a scene charged with sexual expectation ruptures that discourse and floods

---

[10] For more on *zaum'* in Sorokin's oeuvre, see Marusenkov (2012, 71–140).

[11] «*русский грааль*: дух, ставший плотью».

it with nondiscursive violence, which resonates simultaneously with the hidden logic of the traditionalist discourse. The fact that Roman's rampage is triggered by two peculiar wedding gifts—an ax and a wooden bell—only bolsters this interpretation: both objects are sexually suggestive and at the same time marked as exotic, as somehow "truly Russian." In short, due to the discursive roadblock set by the Russian classical tradition, Roman (the character and the novel) "makes love" to the Russian people with an ax, in lieu of having sex with Tat'iana. There is nothing irrational, then, in Roman draping the entrails of his victims on icons—these are his sacred gifts of love.

I believe that the same logic also underlies *Den' oprichnika*, with its stylized, quasi-archaic language, and scenes of orgiastic carnage ranging from the oprichniks' assaults on "enemies of the state" to their collective dream shaped as a *bylina* (a traditional Russian epic poem) about the seven-headed dragon who rapes and burns with its purgative fire all of Russia's foes across the globe.

Carnalization in Reverse

An interesting example of indirect carnalization is presented by *Tridtsataia liubov' Mariny* (*Marina's Thirtieth Love*, 1982–84), where the corporeal ceases to function as an appendage of the discursive, obtaining its own agency. On the one hand, Marina's bisexuality serves as a most tangible and glorious manifestation of the free-minded attitude of the 1970s dissident circle. On the other hand, the same sexuality undercuts the dissident discourse that runs through the novel. The first orgasm that Marina experiences with a man, the Solzhenitsyn look-alike *partorg* (the head of the local party organization), not only drastically changes her life but also radically reorients the book's narrative. After that unforgettable night, Marina tosses out all her samizdat and becomes a Socialist Realist poster girl; meanwhile the narrative, which before this juncture balanced Henry Miller and urban women's prose, rapidly transmutes into an unending *Pravda* editorial. *Tridtsataia liubov'* incarnates this discursive logic but also introduces a countercurrent process: the transformation of the corporeal into the discursive, or the *disembodiment* of the corporeal—the female orgasm with a patriarchal figure as a discursive switch. No wonder that Sorokin speaks about this novel as a turning point in his evolution: "This novel in many ways became a turning point for me: I completed my Sots-Art period and began exploring the problem of corporeality in Russian literature" (Shapoval 1998, 17).[12]

The exorcism of discourse from flesh also operates as the driving force of *The Ice Trilogy* (2002–5). The brutal crushing of a victim's chest in order to extract the "voice of the heart" is a common refrain across the triplicate plot. This sacrament bloodily elevates a "meat machine" into a Brother or Sister of Light (or a *pneumaticist*, to adopt the Gnostic terminology), imbued with a spiritual love that encompasses only fellow Light siblings and forsakes everyone else. The amity extended by Brothers and Sisters of Light can envelop only those of their "kind" (by default, "meat machines are excluded") and is emphatically void of any corporeality, being a purely spiritual phenomenon. It is no wonder that Aleksandr Genis defined this novel as "the fairy tale for Gnostics" (2004). The Gnostic code does indeed influence *The Ice Trilogy*: one may detect its traces in the conceptualization of the material world as evil and the human body as a prison for the spirit, in the metaphor of Light as a symbol of "alien" (introduced by the Tungus meteorite) but true life, in the motif of a "true spiritual name," in the quest of the chosen "pneumaticists" who are spiritually equipped for Gnosis, and so on. The dictatorship of this mythology in *The Ice Trilogy* is quite palpable, and therefore the triad's scenes of violence, customary for any reader of Sorokin, do not transcend the discourse but, on the contrary, serve as ritualistic illustration of the Gnostic mythological narrative. Thus, corporeal elements in these novels are transformed into discursive ones, while their vital (wild) energy is "disciplined" by the stern hierarchy of the Gnostic myth.

This is but one analytical jewel of disembodiment in the trilogy. Another can be seen in the tonal transition Sorokin's

---

[12] «Вообще этот роман во многом стал для меня поворотным: я завершил свой соц-артистский период и вышел к проблеме телесности в русской литературе».

narrative undergoes from its first entry (*Led*), the most corporeal, to its last (*23,000*), the most "spiritual" yet equally stereotype laden and lifeless. Elsewhere I have argued that, in drastic spite of his intentions, Sorokin has created in *The Ice Trilogy* a totalitarian metadiscourse, a universal formula for genocide-like "cleansing" in pursuit of a transcendental goal (see Lipovetsky 2008, 625–37). The Brothers of Light fail to overcome the carnage that reigns in the world of "meat machines"; they manage only to elevate it to a new level. Their violence is justified by a sacral discourse, becoming "mythic"—that which, according to Walter Benjamin, serves as empirical proof of the existence of the gods (see Benjamin 1978, esp. 294–95). Sorokin's twenty-three thousand Brothers of Light are these gods, whose existence is confirmed by mythic violence. Sorokin's trilogy authorizes them to purge those incapable of the ascension from "meat machines" to Brothers and Sisters of Light. It is telling that, toward their sacral ends, the Brothers do not hesitate to employ both the Gulag and Nazi death camps.

Considered alongside *Tridtsataia liubov' Mariny*, this novel is hardly anomalous. Rather, it corroborates a recurring pattern in Sorokin's oeuvre, one of which the author may not be entirely cognizant. As these texts affirm, a totalitarian discourse may surface on any basis (see, for instance, ecological totalitarianism in the play *Shchi*), but always emerges from a sort of decarnalization—an unpacking of the physical into the metaphysical, or the discursive, that is, a disembodiment. Thus, in Sorokin's page-world, totalitarianism is reinterpreted as the autocracy of the spiritual—the bodiless and impersonal—over discrete human bodies and concrete lives, of the discursive over the nondiscursive. This formula derives not from the author's ideology but from his immanent aesthetic logic, and therefore may conflict on occasion with his rationally designed themes, as has occurred in *The Ice Trilogy*.

Sorokin in the 2000s

Contrasting Sorokin's works preceding *Goluboe salo* (1999) with those following has become a clichéd practice among Russian and

Western critics alike.[13] The consensus finds that Sorokin "mellowed" in the 2000s, became more reader-oriented, and for this reason jettisoned the most extreme aspects of his style—among them its gore, violence, and obscenities. In the carnalization department, however, Sorokin's works of the new century diverge from his prior, conceptualist writings not in the sheer "quantity" of transgressive gestures but rather in the vector of these transgressions. If in the early period, each of Sorokin's texts is dominated by a particular type of transgressive transformation—usually discourse-to-body— then in the later period, the carnalization of the discursive and the disembodiment of the corporeal *coexist*. The most puissant examples can be found in *Den' oprichnika*, *Sakharnyi Kreml'*, *Metel'*, and *Monoklon*.

In *Den' oprichnika*, the neotraditionalist ideological discourse manifests in scenes of gang rape, social tripping on hallucinogens, group copulation (the "caterpillar"), and finally, mutual torture that consists of power drilling each other's feet—thus presenting a full and resplendent spectrum of carnalizations. It becomes clear that the internal "unity" of the *oprichnina* is fashioned via the same means as its fearsome public authority. Although seemingly reserved for outsiders, violent sex and sadistic bloodshed serve as the cement reifying the "unity" of the brotherhood. At the same time, the gang rape of a boyar's wife is immediately spiritualized when Komiaga preaches about the *oprichnina*'s moral purity: "Just understand, you idiot, we're guards. We have to keep our minds cold and our hearts pure" (Sorokin 2011, 35).[14] The ensuing scene of the *oprichnina* prayer in the Cathedral of Dormition represents the neotraditionalist discourse in a nutshell. Furthermore, the rape and arson depicted in the *oprichnina*'s pogrom of the boyar's household resurge in the next chapter as the constituents of Urusov's crime; what was initially coded as a legitimate ritual of

---

[13] See about this in Uffelmann (2006, 106–8).

[14] «Пойми, дурак, мы же охранная стая. Должны ум держать в холоде, а сердце в чистоте» (Sorokin 2006, 21). An obvious reference to the Cheka motto allegedly authored by Dzerzhinsky makes this statement especially dubious.

the *oprichnina*'s solidarity is refigured as a barbaric crime when undertaken as a private act, situated outside the realm of power and its discursive justifications—an obvious instance of ideological disembodiment.

These multidirectional transitions are typical for Sorokin in the 2000s. Such switches from carnalization to disembodiment appear even in the short texts ("Volny" ["Waves"], "Gubernator" ["The Governor"], and "Tridtsat' pervoe" ["Thirty-First"], for instance). However, the ignition of this device never induces a discursive collapse as in Sorokin's earlier works. The reason for this lies in the nature of the discourses that the writer taps. As the strength of recognizable authoritative discourses was waning in the post-Soviet period, Sorokin relocated his focus to *synthetic quasi-authoritative discourses*, whose functioning is founded in the coexistence of two mutually contradictory operations. While establishing their symbolic power (through the disembodiment of the corporeal), these discourses simultaneously and shamelessly deconstruct their own authority (through the carnalization of ideological constructs in self-gratifying, sexualized violence). One may argue that these synthetic discourses constitute a new *cynical language of power*, reflected by the writer. Notably, from this point of view, Sorokin hardly distinguishes between the neotraditionalist state ideology and its opponents (see "Tridtsat' pervoe," "Underground," and "Kocherga" ["A Poker"]).

Furthermore, Sorokin's later works employ a cluster of recurring motifs that serve as metaphors for the endless reciprocal transformations of the corporeal into the spiritual, and vice versa. Just a few examples:

Food is arguably the ripest example of the *peaceful* fusion of cultural conventions and discourses with physiological needs and reactions. Beginning with *Norma* and *Roman*, Sorokin explored comestible imagery as depicting the *literal* digestion of culture (which is eventually processed into feces). However, in his later works, the writer emphasizes the transgressive potential of food with greater and greater zeal. This nutritional connotation emerges first in the sadistic *Pel'meni* (*Dumplings*, 1986), followed by the cannibalistic Eucharist depicted in *Mesiats v Dakhau* (*A Month in*

Dachau, 1990), which in turn precedes *Goluboe salo* with its fondue of human meat and the collection *Pir* (*The Feast*, 2000), opening with "Nastia," a Buninesque story about the cannibalistic "initiation" of a sixteen-year-old girl. The 1995 play *Shchi* (*Cabbage Soup*) explores the degradation of the culinary art into crime under the regime of ecological totalitarianism. Edible transgression reappears in the script for Il'ia Khrzhanovsky's film *4* (2004), whose climax consists of a revolting old hags' smorgasbord. Food appears here as a field of militant competition (rather than collaboration) between the discursive and the nondiscursive, with the focus carnalizingly shifting from the former to the latter.

Drugs: In a tongue-in-cheek polemic with the dominant perception, since *Goluboe salo* Sorokin has inscribed drugs into a totalitarian, rather than countercultural, context. In his alternative vision of Stalinism, drugs are legal and the image of Stalin toting a syringe is iconic. The same license applies in *Den' oprichnika*, in which certain drugs are not only legal but serve as the foundation of the nation's internal comfort, eternally tendering the masses' illusion of freedom. To invoke Sorokin's self-commentary, "Before the revolution, cocaine was sold in [Russian] pharmacies. In the new Russian state, this is a compensation for the iron curtain. We deprive you of the West, this forbidden fruit, but we are giving you this instead. You don't need any West, go to the pharmacy and buy cocaine. You will be happy. And in the West, all this is forbidden" (Novikova 2008, 14).[15] In the author's logic, as material substances of psychological and even spiritual influence, drugs effect the disembodiment of the corporeal, and are, therefore, essentially totalitarian. Yet the countercurrent, that toward carnalization, is apparent here as well. For instance, in one of his interviews Sorokin directly compares literature with drugs: "I am engaged in literature, because since my childhood I was addicted to this drug. I am

---

[15] «До революции кокаин продавался в аптеках. В новом российском государстве это компенсация за железный занавес. Мы вас лишаем Запада, этого райского плода, но мы вам даем зато вот это. Можете получить удовольствие. Вам не нужен никакой Запад: идите в аптеку, покупайте кокаин. Будете счастливы. А на Западе как раз это запрещено».

a literary addict, like you, but I also can cook these drugs, which not everyone can do" (Kochetkova 2004, 11).

Tellingly, the blue fat of *Goluboe salo*, as the material quiddity of Russian literature, is also advertised as a superdrug, which Stalin eventually injects squarely into his brain. We find a similar analogy between literature and drugs in *Dostoevsky-Trip* and *Metel'* (little pyramids). Much like literature, psychoactive substances allow Sorokin's characters to transcend their physicality, either becoming the Other individually (as in *Metel'*) or merging with the collective Other (*Den' oprichnika, Sakharnyi Kreml'*). As such, even when legalized, drugs accommodate transgression—and, therefore, the dangers of freedom. The latter motif is most obvious in Sorokin's script for the film *Mishen'*: a huge astrophysical aggregate, a relic of the Soviet era, emits a euphoric intoxication, which, in turn, inspires a sense of limitless freedom in the characters. This empowerment is invariably (self-)destructive. Symptomatically, in Sorokin's later texts, drug-induced trips also fashion a new collective body—one that appears to be necessarily *monstrous*, as exemplified by the seven-headed dragon in *Den' oprichnika* and the sleuth of man-eating bears in "Underground."

Ice/snow: According to Sorokin, "Snow is our wealth, like oil and gas. This is what makes Russia herself, even to a larger degree than oil and gas. Snow mystifies life, it, so to speak, conceals the earth's shame" (Rudik 2008).[16] This frigid leitmotif emerges for the first time in *Serdtsa chetyrekh*, where the objective of the protagonists' ordeals is to process their hearts into frozen cubes, marked as dice, which a mechanical gambler rolls onto a field coated with the (also frozen) "liquid mother." Far from merely a macabre metaphor of fate, this scene can be interpreted as a manifestation of the heroic (or transcendentalist) discourse compressed into material form. The frozen matter thus serves as the substance of the transcendental, a liminal zone between discursive and corporeal realities.

---

[16] «Снег — наше богатство, как и нефть, и газ. То, что делает Россию Россией в большей степени, чем нефть и газ. Снег мистифицирует жизнь, он, так сказать, скрывает стыд земли».

The latter suggestion correlates well with *The Ice Trilogy*, where the cosmic ice induces metaphysical transfigurations and serves as the tool for the selection of the Brothers of Light. In *Metel'*, similarly, the snowstorm operates as a metaphor of the resistance of the nondiscursive—that is, the natural, transcendental, or violent elements—to the discourse of modernization. The final, symbolic rape of the modernizer, Dr. Garin, by a ginormous snowman vividly demonstrates the significance of this motif. Another example worth mentioning in this context is the monologue of the therapist Mark in *Moskva*, in which he compares the Russian collective unconscious with *pel'meni*: frozen under the Soviet regime and melted into a formless mess in post-Soviet time. Similarly, in his comments on *Mishen'*, Sorokin mentions that it depicts Russia in a slightly frozen state (*podmorozhennaia Rossiia*; Nuriev 2011). Thus, the ice/snow motif metaphorizes a discourse that has obtained a (murderous) materiality but has not yet become a living body—it remains suspended in a liminal state.

A certain parallel to this theme can be detected in Sorokin's unofficial motif-trilogy of clones, which opens in *Goluboe salo*, then resurges in *Deti Rozentalia* and concludes in *4*. Human clones here represent, like the frost imagery elsewhere, a discourse whose carnalization is incomplete. Due to their liminal status, clones in *Goluboe salo* and *Deti Rozentalia* yield sacred objects as a natural byproduct of their notably brief existence. In *4*, however, a mob of clones that has reached old age assumes the guise of a Boschian carnival, where corporeality is equidistantly severed from justifying discourses and nondiscursive vitality, supplanted by a nightmarish parade of living death.

An Attempt at Interpretation

The radicalism of Sorokin's master trope is far more profound than his critics think. His work does not set out simply to deflate everything lofty and authoritarian, and drive it down to the gutters of obscenity, gore, and gibberish. No; he aims at the very core of the logocentric paradigm.

The ritualistic connotation draped on Sorokin's carnalizations of the discursive highlights the connection between these tropes and the foundational Christian dictum: the incarnation of the Word (Logos) in Christ's flesh:

> In the beginning was the Logos
> The Logos was with God
> And the Logos was God
> He was with God in the beginning
> Through him all things came to be
> Not one thing came into being without him.
> All that came to be had its life (*zoe*) in him
> And that life was the light (*phos*) of men
> A light that shines in the darkness
> A light that darkness did not overcome it.
> [...]
> And the Word became flesh and lived among us and we have seen his glory, the glory as of a father's only son, full of grace and truth.
> (John 1:1–5,14, New International Version)

Situated in this context, Sorokin's carnalizations deeply resonate with a deconstructive reading of the dictum of Word becoming Flesh. Sorokin transforms the corporeal into a radical mockery and critique of the Logos. From this perspective, one could contest that Sorokin's method presents a *kynical* reaction to the cynical manipulations of authoritative discourses in Soviet and post-Soviet—or, generally speaking, of modern and postmodern—culture. In *The Critique of Cynical Reason*, Peter Sloterdijk finds the foundations of kynicism in Diogenes's philosophizing through obscene body gestures. Sloterdijk appraises this strategy as the only viable alternative to modern cynicism: "Cynicism can only be stemmed by kynicism, not by morality. Only a joyful kynicism of ends is never tempted to forget that life has nothing to lose except itself" (1987, 194). Sloterdijk argues additionally that the kynic possesses a particular sort of shamelessness. In the given context, shamelessness implies the rejection of moral taboos surrounding bodily functions, the equation of intellectual and corporeal activities—in short, "existence in resistance, in laughter, in refusal, in the appeal to the whole of nature and a full life" (218).

All of these characteristics perfectly fit Sorokin's carnalizations. In fact, his artistic strategy may be interpreted as one of the most vivid and philosophically provocative examples of neokynicism in all contemporary Russian culture. Where Diogenes lampooned theoretical doctrines with his "philosophic pantomimes," Sorokin mocks the power of authoritative discourses and ideologies through what may be defined as *corporeal charades*, reminiscent of one of the most popular intelligentsia games of the 1980s–2000s. These charades not only lay bare the discursive mechanisms but also strip discourses of their symbolic status. When performed on the level of somatic gestures, a discourse ceases to seem invisible and unnoticeably interiorized, and materializes as a body, that is, as a radical Other. As Jean-Luc Nancy argues, "A body is always ob-jected from the outside, to 'me' or to someone else. Bodies are first and always other—just as others are first and always bodies. [...] *An other is a body* because only *a body is an other*. [...] *Other* is not even the right word, just *body*" (Nancy 2008, 29, 31; author's emphasis). Thus, the carnalization of a discourse leads to the defamiliarization of—and, eventually, to emancipation from—the discourse's hypnotic power. In other words, the process of fleshing out the discourse becomes the scandalous act of *flashing*.

However, this kynical mirroring of the chief logocentric principle in Sorokin's prose produces an unexpected side effect. According to Staten, in John's hyperliteral discourse, Christ's ascent is inseparable from his descent, his journey toward death; and the Eucharist is not much different from cannibalism: "'Unless you eat the flesh of the Son of Man and drink his blood, you have no life in you' (6:53). Bread is meat, water is wine, and wine is blood, and there is no horror in all this if it is understood as the fleshly passion of the Logos and the agapetic action of spirit" (1993, 50). From this perspective, we can argue that while Sorokin's carnalizations deconstruct the discursive pretense of manifesting the universal and eternal truth, they do not entirely divest his own narrative of transcendental meaning. In other words, while deconstructing logocentrism by kynical mirroring, the writer also reproduces certain aspects of the sacramental logic manifested in the incarnation of the Logos into Flesh.

In Sorokin's works, then, the sacred, much in agreement with Julia Kristeva's *Powers of Horror*, is inseparable from the abject, thanks to the externalization of what is typically hidden within the body: "For abjection, when all is said and done, is the other facet of religious, moral, and ideological codes. [. . .] Such codes are abjection's purification and repression. But the return of their repressed make up our 'apocalypse,' and that is why we cannot escape the dramatic convulsions of religious crises" (Kristeva 1982, 209). I would like to suggest that Sorokin presents the sacred in the form of a *discursive apocalypse*, wreaked through the revelation of the discourse's abject (somatic) side. What I have defined as Sorokin's master trope, carnalization, is the essential element of this apocalypse.

As to the meaning of Sorokin's sacred, it can be described as *"the manifestation of the divinity of flesh, of universal lifedeath"* (Staten 1993, 50; author's emphasis)—or *zoe*, bare life—to use once again Staten's treatment of John's Gospel. In Sorokin's oeuvre, this is always the complement of the discursive apocalypse, the potentiality, or the nondiscursive undertow of his texts, secretly countering their rationally articulated "message." The presence of this undercurrent in Sorokin's works reveals a utopian aspiration, akin to that of radical feminism, as, for example, in Luce Irigaray's words, "We have to renew the whole of language. [. . .] To reintroduce the values of desire, pain, joy, the body. Living values. Not discourses of mastery, which are in a way dead discourse, a dead grid imposed upon the living" (as quoted in Mulder 2006, 91). However, citing Sloterdijk's characterization of Diogenes once more, Sorokin's *zoe* philosophy does not go "primarily through the head; he experiences the world as neither tragic nor absurd. There is not the slightest trace of melancholy around him. [. . .] His weapon is not so much analysis as laughter" (Sloterdijk 1987, 160). This is why Sorokin failed in *The Ice Trilogy* when he endeavored to construct a somber mythic discourse around the principally nondiscursive sacred of bare life.

Other Sorokin's texts exhibit positive, albeit tangential, manifestations of this nondiscursive theme of lifedeath. For instance, in the finale of *Ochered'* (*The Queue*, 1983), the celebration of sexuality displaces the abstract and undefinable "transcendental signified" of the queue (and the entire narrative). Other examples include the rapture and eroticism of the characters' self-destruction in *Serdtsa chetyrekh*; the infinity of metamorphoses triggered by the blue fat in *Goluboe salo* (notably, the novel closes on the mention of Easter); the fierce carnivalesque luxury of feasting scenes, from *Roman* to *Den' oprichnika*; the wedding with two brides and one groom at the end of *Moskva*; and the pregnancy of Komiaga's mistress, the only bit of news that he cannot recollect at the end of his long, "almost happy" day. One might assert that the whole procession of events in *4* bears an apocalyptic temper following the death of Zoia (Zoe), one of the four sister-clones (the four apocalyptic riders). From this perspective, it is possible to explain even Sorokin's ire toward his former peers and friends as expressed in the infamous *Den' oprichnika* passage where Komiaga listens to Western radio stations: the author's imaginary oprichniks seem to possess a much greater affinity for *zoe* as the horrifying and exciting sensation of bare life than for cerebral abstractions or post-structuralist obscurities.

Yet most importantly, Sorokin's proclivity for *zoe* manifests itself through his master trope—the carnalization of the discursive, which, as I have tried to demonstrate, methodically forces the discourse to overcome itself in pursuit of the nondiscursive dimension. On this plane, the distinction between the abject and sacred, corporeal and transcendental, vanishes. Sorokin's carnalizations thus correspond to the politicization of bare life, as described by Giorgio Agamben: "Once their fundamental referent becomes bare life, traditional political distinctions (such as those between Right and Left, liberalism and totalitarianism, private and public) lose their clarity and enter the zone of indistinction" (1995, 122).[17]

---

[17] Agamben adds, "The ex-communist ruling classes' unexpected fall into the most extreme racism (as in the Serbian program of 'ethnic cleansing') and the rebirth of new forms of fascism in Europe also have their roots here" (1995, 122).

Prigov used to say that he staged discourses as a theater director manipulates actors. Sorokin does the same, but he also saturates these rhetorical figures with bare life, thus transforming carnalizations into self-sufficient performances. The meaning of these performances is paradoxical: while operating through discursive means, the writer nevertheless creates the illusion of transcending the discourse, if only for a while, into a nondiscursive state of bare life, or *zoe*. As a result, the reader, absorbed by Sorokin's text, effectively finds her- or himself in the position of the *homo sacer*, who stays within bare life and personalizes it—be it as the humiliated victim of the state of exception or the oprichnik whose power stems from this very state. In this respect, Sorokin's performances of discursivity resonate with Agamben's notion that modern society "does not abolish sacred life but rather shatters it and disseminates it into every individual body, making it into what is at stake in political conflict" (1995, 124). Sorokin delivers this comprehension to the level of acute, almost physiological sensation.

PUSSY RIOT AS THE TRICKSTAR

The Pussy Riot performance in the Cathedral of Christ the Savior (hereafter CCS) has been discussed and dissected from a vast panoply of perspectives through literally hundreds, if not thousands, of articles, comments, and blog entries. The members of the punk collective presented themselves as, and indeed were viewed as, heirs to the political dissension of the 1960s–70s and successors to the tradition of holy fools. Their taboo-bursting CCS performance in February 2012 was seen immediately as a challenge to the Putin regime and a protest against the political alliance between the Russian Orthodox Church and the Russian state.[1] Others treated the punk prayer as a revitalization of the avant-garde's political activism and as a wholly valid episode in the postwar history of political and anticlerical performances, worldwide (beginning with the Lettrists' Notre-Dame Affair of 1950) and in Russia specifically.[2]

My approach to Pussy Riot is far less ambitious: I see this group, and its infamous punk prayer, as the cultural return to and rebirth of the trickster,[3] a trope that wielded intense potency in

---

[1] For a review of these approaches, see Willems (2013), Gessen (2014), and Ponomariov (2013).

[2] For a review of these approaches, see Epshtein (2012).

[3] For the mythological functions and features of the trickster see: Kerenyi (1972), Jung (1972), Babcock-Abrahams (1975), Doty and Hynes (1993).

the Soviet period but drastically ebbed in post-Soviet times. Such an interpretation, I believe, situates Pussy Riot in Russian cultural history as a legitimate, yet radically novel, phenomenon.

I argued in my book *Charms of the Cynical Reason: The Trickster's Transformations in Soviet and Post-Soviet Culture* (2011) that the trickster constitutes one of the sturdiest staples of twentieth-century Russian culture. Since the 1920s, this archetype has been upheld by such extremely popular literary characters as Ehrenburg's Julio Jurenito, Babel's Benia Krik, Olesha's Ivan Babichev, Il'f and Petrov's Ostap Bender, Aleksei Tolstoy's Buratino, Bulgakov's Woland with his host of tricksterish demons, Tvardovskii's Vasilii Terkin, Venedikt Erofeev's Venichka and Gurevich, and Iskander's Sandro, to name just a few.

Soviet tricksters became bona fide superstars of Soviet society (in its official and unofficial provinces alike): they served as the cultural justification for dangerous, unheroic, and cynical survival, by elevating this existence through their virtuoso performances to a level of joyful, cheeky, and, most importantly, *free* play. They waved a hand and transformed shameless mimicry into a basically nonpragmatic art of transgressive living. Using Peter Sloterdijk's dichotomy, we might say that these characters validated Soviet cynicism by matching and usurping it with kynicism—instigating the tradition that Vladimir Sorokin would continue with his master trope of carnalization. We remember Sloterdijk's dictum "Cynicism can only be stemmed by kynicism, not by morality" (1987, 194). This, exactly, is what Soviet tricksters managed to do. Thus, they simultaneously legitimized the "self-subversive nature of the Soviet system" (Ledeneva 2002) and offered a viable, and profoundly appealing, alternative to its practical cynicism.

Characteristically, almost all Russo-Soviet tricksters are male. The prevalent absence of female tricksters testifies to the profoundly patriarchal character of Soviet culture, even in its nonconformist spheres. The trickster is simultaneously transgressive and sympathetic—but transgressions that are basically acceptable for men are incompatible with the alleged "proper" woman, and in the context of patriarchy their perpetration inevitably forecloses any empathy with the female transgressor.

Given this dilemma, Pussy Riot's members have revolutionarily introduced to Russian culture a collective incarnation of the *trickstar*—a female trickster, who undermines not only sociopolitical fixtures but, first and foremost, the gender regime of the society, challenging sexism and gender repression. According to Marilyn Jurich, coiner of the term, "The trickstar frequently aspires to self-determination for other than personal reasons; she hopes to expose the hypocrisies and stupidities in the social establishment. [. . .] Tradition, however—that tradition supported by male power—often prefers to see the trickstar as menacing, her tricks as self-serving" (1998, 30, 33).

1.

The cynical countenance of social survival not only refused to fade in the post-Soviet years but in fact became a proud social norm. During this period the trickster trope visibly lost its transgressive and liberating faculty, although the late-Soviet and post-Soviet years have admittedly been marked by the monumental, lifelong trickster act of Dmitrii Aleksandrovich Prigov (1940–2007). A few other winning examples of post-Soviet trickstership have also arisen, most prominently and originally at the hands of such performance artists as Oleg Kulik, Vladislav Mamyshev-Monro, the Blue Noses Group, and collectives like E.T.I. and Voina. Notably, a few female tricksters appeared both in popular culture (Masiana from Oleg Kuvaev's animated films series, and Vika of *Moia prekrasnaia niania* [*My Fair Nanny*, the Russian remake of CBS's *The Nanny*]) and in postmodernist literature (the werewolf A Huli in Pelevin's *Sviashchennaia kniga oborotnia*). Outside of these successes, the tricksters' waning prominence in culture has been (over)compensated for by the surge of tricksteresque figures on the political and social scene, from the ever-popular Vladimir Zhirinovsky to the cinematically lionized Boris Berezovsky and Sergei Mavrodi, to the now-forgotten Dmitry Yakubovsky ("the general Dima"), or Duma deputy Viacheslav Marychev.

The dissipation of the trickster's deconstructive power came about most likely in response to the ulterior, *blat*-based economy and sociality speeding to the forefront of society (see Ledeneva

2002), leaving in their dust the qualities typically associated with tricksterdom to be processed into the normalized, *mainstream* conditions of success and capitalist efficiency—at least in the public consciousness and media representation. Furthermore, the trickster's transgression and liminality presuppose a sturdy conception of societal boundaries and taboo, a demarcation which vanished in the 1990s.

I do not hesitate to concur that the members of Pussy Riot are direct heirs to the trickster lineage in Soviet and post-Soviet culture. The punk prayer was openly ambivalent and therefore provocative; the group members operated as mediators and posed their transgressions as nonpragmatic, artistic gestures, establishing an unorthodox (paradoxical, in fact) relationship with the sacred (see Makarius 1993)—all critical functions of the trickster. Especially illuminating is the acceleration of the balaclava, after Pussy Riot's CCS affair, into a worldwide symbol of cultural protest: with its carnival-like array of face-concealing colors, the balaclava icon not only unifies wearers into a collective trickster body—open for all willing to join—but furthermore designates an internal liminal zone, shared by all participants of the action (which, I believe, explains why members of the group *sans* balaclava are so different, both in manner and discourse, from Pussy Riot as a collective trickster).

It is also no accident that Nadezhda Tolokonnikova considers Dmitrii Prigov to be her entry to the world of contemporary art. The Prigov performance she attended in Noril'sk at age sixteen, by her own acknowledgment, determined the subsequent course of her life, and to one of the court sessions she brought a homemade poster featuring a quotation from Prigov's poetry. In addition, her own writing style, intertwining sophisticated post-structuralist and gender-sociology vernacular with irreverent slang, is strikingly reminiscent of the writings of the fox-trickster from Pelevin's *Sviashchennaia kniga oborotnia*—whose name, A Huli, is no more decent to the Russian ear than Pussy Riot is to the English.

However, since the trickster's business acquires new characteristic forms and new ramifications under each cultural era and in each individual trickster, we must briefly sketch the new cultural significance of the trickstar narrative of Pussy Riot.

Obviously, the punk-protest collective endowed the trickster trope with a renewed deconstructive force, but along with the classic trickster fare they also achieved the unprecedented power of *political* transgression. In Kevin Platt's words, "While response to the open-ended nature of the happening generated at times potentially contradictory significances and alignments, this is surely a symptom of the success of Pussy Riot's strategy" (2012). Mikhail Iampol'skii adds, "Such actions gain meaning only in the context of the reaction that they prompt. One might even say that the reaction is virtually the main component of the action" (2012).

Responses and reactions to Pussy Riot comprised tremendous public debate surrounding both the CCS performance and the subsequent trial of the performers. What aspects of Pussy Riot's cathedral concert triggered such powerful effects, effects that are sometimes artistic, sometimes ideological, sometimes political, but always incredibly explosive?

2.

Seeking the answers to such questions, many sympathetic commentators of the Pussy Riot CCS performance drew on the image of the holy fool.[4] Tolokonnikova herself, in her closing statement, directly invoked this cultural model: "We were searching for real sincerity and simplicity, and we found these qualities in the *yurodstvo* [the holy foolishness] of punk" ("Pussy Riot's Closing Statements" 2012). This is a very curious choice of words, considering that a holy fool is anything but sincere. Conversely, Sergei Ivanov, an eminent expert in holy fools and the author of a cultural-history tome on their significance in Byzantium and beyond (see Ivanov 2005 and 2006), argued that this parallel is inadequate on multiple counts—chiefly because a holy fool's prank necessarily demonstrates a higher truth, next to which all other "truths" and values appear dingy, disposable, fit only for ridicule and utter degradation.[5] In his

---

[4] See, for example, the video recording of the seminar "Pussy Riot i iurodstvo," Volkova (2016), Murav'ev (2012), Satarov (2012), Strel'tsov (2012).

[5] See the video recording of the discussion "Pussy Riot i iurodstvo" at the

book, while noting the kinship between holy fools and mythological tricksters (or "sacred clowns"), Ivanov stresses the difference between the holy fool's work and jest: "A jester is all in a dialogue, a holy fool is monological by the principle; the jester immerses into the holiday time, while the holy fool is outside of time; jest is similar to art, while the holy foolishness is foreign to art" (2005, 16). I would top off this argument with the observation that, although a holy fool is indeed a trickster, his or her act is wholly locked within the religious paradigm.

While Pussy Riot's recital in the Cathedral of Christ the Savior is most certainly not contained by religion, it is also not entirely extramural to this paradigm. After all, the trickstar-rockers did not put icons to the ax, as did Avdei Ter-Oganian in his 1998 performance "The Young Atheist"; they prayed to the Mother of God in the country's main cathedral. On the other hand, their famous music video repeatedly switches registers from Orthodox prayer and pious bowing to punk-rock gyration and riotous singing, with the refrain *Sran' gospodnia* (God's shit) rhythmically replacing the traditional *Halleluiah*. The piece's visual palette paradoxically fuses the hallowed church gilding with the bright colors of the performers' dresses and balaclavas. As Iampol'skii notes, not only are Pussy Riot's outfits reminiscent of the late paintings of Malevich, but the group's entire aesthetics is based on rapid shifts between sacred and profane signifiers, which is quite characteristic of the Russian avant-garde.[6] Mariia Alekhina's and Tolokonnikova's closing statements only enhanced this impression of conscious oscillation between holy and base; held under accusations of blasphemy, they demonstrated deep knowledge of the Gospels.

Thus, the trickstar Pussy Riot staged its transgressive prayer on the borderline between sacred and profane, between church and counterculture, thereby revealing a liminal, ambivalent, and

---

Sakharov Museum in Moscow, June 16, 2012, http://www.sakharov-center.ru/discussions/?id=1663.

[6] Iampol'skii (2012) analyzed numerous deep connections of the Pussy Riot performance with the avant-garde.

explosive region of contemporary Russian society and politics. Boris Grois emphasizes this quality of the CCS concert/recording session in his perceptive commentary:

> And if, for example, Pussy Riot perform an action—and not even really an action, as they are simply gathering material that they use in their video—then it's unclear whether or not they are breaking the law. This is a controversial question related to the law, to boundaries between secular and religious legislation, and so on. In other words, this action exposes a problem that hitherto had not been at the center of attention, and had never been thematized. This action is consistent with the meaning of contemporary art. It has brought out a certain contemporary order of things. A contemporary order of things that is unclear [. . .] Pussy Riot has drawn society's attention to the complicated relationship between the sacred and secular space, between art and religion, and art and the law. They have made this zone visible. Thus society has been riled up and started to discuss it. If they hadn't done it, there would have been no resonance. (Saprykin 2012)

The consequent persecution of the group has only confirmed the ambivalent tether between secular and sacred, political and clerical. The incendiary meaning of this ambivalence became agonizingly obvious when Alekhina, Tolokonnikova, and Ekaterina Samutsevich were charged in criminal court with offending the Christian feelings of believers, while their actual and admitted offense targeted the union between the Orthodox church and Putin's state (and, of course, Putin himself); when the "experts" cited, in their educated conclusions, the rulings of the Laodicean (363 CE) and Trullan (691–92 CE) synods; when the secular court used these arguments to justify the criminal verdict; and so on.

The construction and exposure of various zones of ambivalence and liminality is every trickster's true calling. Considering Pussy Riot from this vantage, one may expand on Grois's analysis and say that the disclosure of vague and ambivalent bonds between the secular state and the Orthodox church, as the events and discussion pursuant to the CCS affair demonstrated, has not been the sole effect of Pussy Riot's trickstar transgression. In fact, their performance achieved such tremendous success because it managed to reveal *multiple layers* of ambivalence and indecision, apparently not limited to the messily intersected grounds of "sacred and secular space, art and religion, art and law."

The venue, naturally, contributed in great measure to this virtual supernova of ambivalence. After all, the CCS is far more than just the symbol of a newfound alliance between the Putinist state and the Orthodox church, or of the Church's corruption and cynical entrepreneurship. Demolished in 1931 and rebuilt from brick one between 1994 and 1997, it epitomizes the overarching post-Soviet project: the restoration of the "national tradition" and traditional values—in other words, *neotraditionalism* (see Sidorov 2000). Since the early 2000s, Boris Dubin and Lev Gudkov have warned that a hazy, yet decidedly conservative, conception of neotraditionalism had effectively united the majority of intelligentsia and *siloviki*:

> "The rebirth of the great power" has become that sole symbolic thesis on which liberal Westernizers, Communist patriots, and crusaders for "holy Orthodox Rus" can come together. Its component elements, the definition of the great power's "majesty," as well as the means for achieving this goal, may vary greatly, but the general programmatic composition is unchanged. (Gudkov 2004, 660)

> Institutions and organizations that could be considered secular and modern spark the population's mistrust and dissatisfaction, while Russians connect a positive orientation and evaluation with the remaining meanings of a realm that is outside of any competition, that is special and that appeals to the past, to traditions, to authority, and particularly to ritualistic and the ceremonial. (Dubin 2011, 255)

If in the 1990s the models for past authoritative traditions were found in pre-Soviet Russia, in the 2000s this fount of neotraditionalism was *supplemented* by a burgeoning nostalgia for Soviet greatness, and with it a longing for the Great Empire across the ages. As Gudkov and Dubin have shown, the neotraditionalism launched by democrats in the 1990s paved the way for nostalgia for the great imperial power and, essentially, for the presiding Putin regime's cultural rhetoric and politics.

From this perspective, the clericalization of Russian politics and its swelling religious fundamentalism are just one side of the neotraditionalist ideology that is the true object of Pussy Riot's CCS engagement. The "indecent" language and behavior brought to the house of God, the inappropriate and "provocative" clothing, the support for gay rights (*gei-praid otpravlen v Sibir' v kandalakh*, "Gay Pride is sent to Siberia in chains"), the sarcastic assault on widespread patriarchal convictions (*chtoby Sviateishego ne oskorbit', zhenshchinam nado rozhat' i liubit'*, "In order not to offend His Holiness, women must give birth and love"), and the explicit appeal to feminism (*Bogoroditsa, Devo, stan' feministkoi, Stan' feministkoi, feministkoi stan'*, "Mother of God, become a feminist!")—all of these were aimed not at Putin's collusion with the clergy per se, but at *neotraditionalist values in general*. These ideals embrace and exacerbate the inclination toward authoritarianism and fundamentalism, toward homophobia and patriarchal repression against women, toward antifeminism— toward the vision of "culture" as an omnibus of the "harmonious" masterpieces of old, and toward the negation of the "ugly" and "immoral" art of today.

Characteristically, many of those Russian celebrities and *intelligenty* who allegedly supported Pussy Riot and expressed their discontent with the trial and the verdict later felt the need to confess that they either were personally offended on religious grounds or found the performance immoral and aesthetically disgusting. Such statements typically partnered or alternated with apologetic remarks, according to which the defense of Pussy Riot members as victims of the system did not annul the despicable aesthetic composition of the performance, which was deemed appalling, talentless, and tasteless. In other words, these supporters of the punk-protest coalition resisted political violence, but silently accepted and sincerely promoted the following neotraditionalist axioms: (a) art and any other form of cultural activity is to be judged by the criteria of morality, while the latter is defined, predominantly if not exclusively, by the religious, that is, Russian Orthodox, standard; (b) nonclassical and especially contemporary art is not art at all, does not belong to the sphere of culture, and must be treated as acts of "petty hooliganism."

Among those liberals who expressed their opposition to the trial of Pussy Riot, Boris Nemtsov, Boris Grebenshchikov, Alfred Kokh, Anastasiia Volochkova, Aleksei Naval'nyi, Andrei Makarevich, and El'dar Riazanov, to name the most famous ones, submitted such opinions. Apparently, while criticizing the system for its political prosecution of Pussy Riot, these liberal "supporters" would not rue the band's (certainly less harsh) social persecution for moral, religious, and aesthetic malfeasance. Religious and aesthetic indignation was also voiced with ardor by other prominent cultural personages of openly conservative persuasion, who, unlike liberals, favored the defendants' harsh persecution—Patriarch Kirill, Nikita Mikhalkov, Stanislav Govorukhin, Valentin Rasputin, Vladimir Krupin, Elena Vaenga, Vladimir Solov'ev, Mikhail Leont'ev, Oleg Gazmanov, Tamara Gverdtsiteli, Sergei Luk'ianenko, Dmitrii Puchkov (Goblin), Iosif Kobzon, Aleksandr Prokhanov, and many others.

Apart from these "minor disagreements," there is a third protuberant problem area in the liberal intelligentsia's perception of Pussy Riot and their actions: the group's feminism. Pussy Riot's members have consistently emphasized the feminist core of their artistic strategy. Yet the feminist component of their musical performance (including the chromosomal resemblance of Pussy Riot to such Western groups as Guerrilla Girls, Bikini Kill, and other Riot Grrrl bands[7]) is typically and unpardonably overlooked in Russia. Even, for instance, by addressing their prayer not to Christ (in whose name the cathedral that hosted the performance is

---

[7] See on this subject Gapova (2012); Akulova (2013). Ekaterina Samutsevich says, "We were just hanging and watching performances, works of the Western feminist artists Guerrilla Girls, Riot Grrrl, etc. We absorbed this all, then started playing with words, and in such a way the name Pussy Riot was conceived. We decided to write songs in the punk style, punk feminism. This is a well-known trend, for instance, in the United States" («Мы просто сидели и смотрели акции, работы западных художниц-феминисток «Гирилья Герлз», «Райот Герл» и т. д. Мы впитывали все это, потом начали играть словами, и так было придумано название Pussy Riot. Решили, что будем писать песни в стиле панк, панк-феминизм. Это хорошо известное направление, например, в Америке»; Sobchak and Sokolova 2012).

consecrated) but to the Mother of God, the group clearly expresses the desire to challenge patriarchal authorities, in secular and religious spheres alike. It is also no accident that the members' visual self-presentation, while clearly feminine, is deprived of anything that could be twisted into the sexist objectification of a woman. Samutsevich says, "Our image is rather androgynous — a creature in a dress and colorful tights. Somebody like a woman but without a woman's hair and face. An androgyn that looks like a cartoon character or superhero" (Sobchak and Sokolova 2012).[8] This fluid, though recognizably female, semblance is that of the trickstar: liminal figure, transgressive mediator, provocateur of ambivalence.

In March 2012, Daniil Dugum aptly remarked that "Pussy Riot is necessary to liberal society as an anti-Putinist project, rather than an antipatriarchal one," a diagnosis that the development of the public discourse on Pussy Riot has unmistakably confirmed. The strongest discursive leitmotif unifying the comments of many liberal "supporters" of Pussy Riot presumed the group's gender-based intellectual inferiority. The artists were treated — first, foremost, and almost universally — as innocuous "silly girls." The degree of intellectual deficiency ascribed to them in statements by fair-weather fans ranged from *durochki* (fools) and *ne ochen' dumaiushchie* (small-minded or "little-thinking") to *debilki* (retards). Aleksei Naval'nyi, one of the leaders of the protest movement, while supporting Pussy Riot politically, articulated his attitude toward their performance in the following terms: "The action in the CCS was idiotic, no argument there. To put it mildly, I wouldn't like it very much if, when I was in church, some crazy girls ran in and started circling around the altar. The indisputable fact is that these are idiots who engaged in petty hooliganism for the sake of publicity" ("Naval'nyi vstupilsia za Pussy Riot" 2012).[9] "Idiotic action," "crazed girls,"

---

[8] «У нас скорее андрогинный образ — некое существо в платье и цветных колготках. Что-то похожее на женщину, но при этом без женского лица, без волос. Андрогин, похожий на героя из мультиков, супергероя».

[9] «Акция их в ХСС — идиотская, и спорить тут нечего. Мне бы, мягко говоря, не понравилось, если в тот момент, когда я в церкви, туда забежали какие-

"idiots," "petty hooliganism for the sake of publicity"—this suite of assessments sounds no kinder than Dmitry Medvedev's famous "I feel like throwing up" (*menia toshnit*) prefacing his plea (the prime minister's plea!) to soften the verdict leveled on Pussy Riot. In truth, such reactions are typical among witnesses to trickstars' movements in patriarchal society: "Trickstars as wise fools rarely occur. Rather, women are generally depicted as simply fool*ish*—ignorant, gullible, incompetent. While they are fooled by tricks, they are not the conscious players of tricks" (Jurich 1998, 38).

Pussy Riot was further qualified repeatedly as *lacking any sense of agency*, operating in actuality as someone's puppet. Curiously, this pattern grouped some liberals near all conservatives. The difference was even rather technical, since liberal blogs and media assigned the role of the "girls' (male) master" either to Petr Verzilov, as their alleged "producer," or to hidden enemies of the Patriarch Kirill, while in conservative circles Pussy Riot was asserted to be manipulated by "the West" or Boris Berezovsky or the leaders of political opposition. Yet even among some liberals, the closing statements of Alekhina, Tolokonnikova, and Samutsevich were met with suspicion: *Who has written the script for these girls?*

The gender terror against Pussy Riot reached its zenith in the promotion of physical punishment over imprisonment. The idea of the preferable, or even merciful, spanking of Pussy Riot's members was advanced by many "supporters," beginning with the known leader of the protest movement, Boris Nemtsov, and seconded by the actor and director (famous by his obscurantism) Ivan Okhlobystin, as well as the Communist leader Gennady Ziuganov—to name a scant few, given that 27 percent of individuals polled by VTsIOM supported this brilliant proposition. No wonder Kirill Kobrin was inspired to make his sardonic commentary: "There's that tone in some Russian liberal quarters—the arrogant, macho disdain for the opposite sex, which posits that woman, by definition, is incapable of conscious action. . . . Here I see a stark disconnect between their

то чокнутые девицы и стали бегать вокруг алтаря. Имеем неоспоримый факт: дуры, совершившие мелкое хулиганство ради паблисити».

democratic, liberal views and the profoundly macho, and, when it comes down to it, profoundly Soviet authoritarian consciousness" (Sharogradskii 2012).[10]

3.

These aftereffects of Pussy Riot's CCS performance have been no less significant than the intended revelation of the state's unwillingness to separate "offense to the King" from "offense to the feelings of believers." The discourse launched by Pussy Riot within the liberal intelligentsia reveals the *hypocrisy* of the liberal opposition, which supported the "girls" only insofar as they served as an irritant to common enemies, while not-so-secretly deriding them as silly, puppeteered pawns who ought to face corporal punishment for their shameful misconduct. Furthermore, these discussions laid bare the *responsibility* of neotraditionalist thinking, shared by many representatives (if not a sheer majority) of the liberal intelligentsia, for the Putin era's ideology and growing Orthodox fundamentalism.

To sum up, the Pussy Riot debate has exposed such flaws in the liberal discourse as the tacit equation of moral values with religious doctrines; hierarchical, essentialist, and, basically, premodern understanding of culture (rejecting contemporary art for its lack of "harmony"); and, most importantly, stalwart allegiance to patriarchal stereotypes. The shared values that are responsible for these flaws appear not so different from the conservatives' rage against "blasphemy" and the assault on national "spiritual ties" (*dukhovnye skrepy*, to use Putin's words), and their aggressive "defense" of "eternal" moral-religious ideals, epitomized by the disgust toward contemporary art. In Mikhail Leont'ev's words, "The targets are chosen quite simply: the church, traditional morality, state

---

[10] «Вот этот тон части русской либеральной общественности — высокомерное мачистское неуважение к другому полу, исходя из которого женщина, по определению, не может произвести сознательного действия [...] Я вижу здесь абсолютное несовпадение их демократических, либеральных убеждений с глубоко мачистским и глубоко, по сути дела, советским авторитарным сознанием». See also Verigina (2012); Rossa (2012).

institutions, political power, and they are covered almost literally in shit, and this is set forth as an act of art" ("[Mikhail] Leont'ev" 2012).[11]

Thus, Pussy Riot has realized the zone of ambivalence not only between the state and church, art and religion, religion and aesthetics, and so on, but also, and most significantly, *between the opposition to the Putin regime and its supporters*. This achievement is soaringly comparable with that of the Soviet tricksters, though in an inverted form. As mentioned above, Soviet tricksters culturally justified via their artistic transgressions a hidden layer of Soviet social and economic reality, proving through their kynical performances that "underground" activities are vital for the survival of the official system. Pussy Riot, willingly or not, has demonstrated the opposite: that the forces that seemingly undermine the authorities in fact share their most fundamental values, coinciding in a basic interpretation of moral, cultural, and gender hierarchies, and differ only in a tactical understanding of political issues. The patriarchal tune uniting critics and supporters of the punk group turns out to be the decisive factor: indeed, in the long run, it validates the autocratic regime better than any political rhetoric.

Marilyn Jurich suggested that the trickstar's strategy characteristically transforms (gender) powerlessness into a trick: "Woman by virtue of gender alone has been marginalized; and the trickstar is a twice-marginal figure. The difference is that the trickstar uses marginality for her advantage, is *intentionally* impertinent and indecent, violating norms in order to invigorate society" (1998, 34). Pussy Riot matches this description to the letter, yet with an important qualification: their trick manifests itself *through* the most blatant acknowledgment of their powerlessness — in the courtroom that has become the spectacle of lawlessness and

---

[11] «Выбираются просто цели: церковь, традиционная мораль, государственные институты, политическая власть и обливаются почти в буквальном смысле говном, причем это выдается как акт искусства».

in the public discourse that has exploded into a similar parade of sexist repression.[12]

Dmitry Bykov wrote in his improvised commentary in verse to the Pussy Riot arrests of March 2012:

> И, куда страшней для всякой гнуси
> Всенародно чаемый итог —
> Чтобы вместо riot of the pussy,
> Тут случился riot of the cock.

> What would be worse that such a strange and fussy
> scandal sparked by performers of punk rock,
> Could only be if a riot of the pussy,
> Were replaced with a riot of the cock[13]

In contrast to this wishful thinking, Pussy Riot has exposed an uncanny symmetry between the authoritarianism of the Putin regime and the patriarchal neotraditionalism of its opponents (and some of Pussy Riot's supposed advocates). In this respect, the "riot of the pussy" appears to be much more radical than a "riot of the cock." It seems that, for contemporary Russia, the trickstar's transgression delves much deeper and produces much more profound effects, than that of the male trickster.[14]

---

[12] Tellingly, even sympathetic and overtly liberal Kseniia Sobchak could not understand how Pussy Riot members in their spare time could discuss such issues as sexism (see Sobchak and Sokolova 2012). See Borenstein's (2012) commentary to Sobchak's symptomatic "cluelessness."

[13] Translated by Eliot Borenstein. See Bykov's reading of this poem, "Grazhdanin poet: Eksprompt Bykova na arest Pussy Riot," March 3, 2012, http://www.youtube.com/watch?v=UikMqS9sA30.

[14] This proposition can be convincingly illustrated by the comparison of Pussy Riot with the subject of analogous discussion in *Slavic Review*: Borat, of Sacha Baron Cohen's feature film. See "Borat: Selves and Others" (2008), especially on Borat as the trickster, and Kononenko and Kukharenko (2008); D. Leiderman (2008).

The Formal Is Political

Seeking a Constructive Principle

The principles of poetic language become most palpable when they are seemingly hidden by ideology, since ideological narratives unwittingly reproduce similar principles. This is especially obvious in today's Russia, where ideology is returning, proving that its apparent departure was itself an artistic device. The formalists have won. At least in today's cultural climate, Bakhtin and even Lotman look much more questionable than Tynianov, Eikhenbaum, and Jakobson. Shklovsky is above any competition.

Although equations of the aesthetic and political are frequently shaky, their very popularity reveals a new tendency distinguishing today's interpretations of formalism from its historical sources. Formalists were careful enough to hide the political meaning of poetics (in exceptional cases—like their articles about Lenin's language—they could speak of the poetic principles of the political). Today, not only theorists but writers as well are fully aware of the political meaning of their poetics. Indeed, the correlation between the author's rejection of rhymed syllabotonic verse and participation in anti-Putin protests, or striving toward the "new realism" and a progovernment position after the annexation of Crimea, is too marked to be ignored. This situation is quite novel, since back in the 1980s, as well as during perestroika and in the 1990s, writers who were close to nonconformist circles or influenced by them preached the superiority of literature that was independent of any kind of political or ideological position. Vladimir Sorokin recalled in 2006, "I was influenced by the Moscow underground, where it was common to be apolitical. This was one of our favorite anecdotes: as German troops marched into Paris, Picasso sat there and drew an apple. That was our attitude—you must just sit there and draw your apple, no matter what happens around you" (279–80). Naturally, this attitude was inseparable from the rejection of Soviet aesthetics, with its ideological dictatorship along with its mirroring by the dissident discourse.[1] The writer and one of the founders of the Russian Internet Sergei Kuznetsov, in a recent lecture for the online Open University, mentioned that Dovlatov's witticism about the mutual mirroring of Soviet and anti-Soviet rhetoric served as the motto for his (my) generation, and that the sense of freedom from politics and ideology rapidly increased after 1991, when allegedly "we"—that is, liberally oriented, anti-Soviet, and antitotalitarian forces—won (2016).

Yet in the mid-2000s and especially after the winter protests of 2011–12, something radically changed, leading to a new attraction of literati to politics. A symptomatic example of an unavoidable politicization of the literary text despite the author's best intentions is Viktor Pelevin's recent novel *The Seer* (*Smotritel'*, 2015). In this book, Pelevin tries to restore the understanding of literature as freed of politics and spectacularly fails. *The Seer*, oddly enough, constitutes a rare case of a modern utopia. Pelevin's heroes—the Russian emperor Paul I and the father of American democracy Benjamin Franklin among them—have managed to create a parallel reality, the Idyllium, which, though woven together from cultural and religious quotations, is nonetheless possessed of an undoubted vitality and, most importantly, enjoys autonomy from the flow of earthly history. The novel's protagonist, Alex, successfully negotiates each of his trials and eventually asserts his power over the Idyllium. Despite his becoming aware of the illusory nature not only of the latter but also of his own personality, Alex never develops the desire to return to the reality of "Old Earth." Insulated

---

[1] See Oushakine (2001).

from history, the Idyllium becomes an ersatz for the universe, an abstraction of all its requisite features. Oriental mysticism is intermingled with European occultism of the eighteenth and early nineteenth centuries, monastic rituals with their masonic counterparts, and Pelevin's brand of Buddhism with mystical interpretations of modern computer software.

Pelevin, who has made his name by writing postmodernist satires about post-Soviet politics, possesses a unique sensitivity to changes in the tenor of the time. Possibly due to a feeling that the meaning of political writing has changed and an understanding that he is unable to reform himself in sync with these changes (or perhaps realizing the risks of such an endeavor), Pelevin attempts to write a novel *without politics.* However, it's precisely this kind of involved utopian fantasy that—perhaps contrary to Pelevin's own wishes—takes on the dimension of a political metaphor in the current social context. The combination of the belief that the "other" is only a reflection (distorted or imperfect) of what is "mine," and, simultaneously, that "my world" encompasses all the diversity of existence—this is, in fact, the formula of imperial consciousness. Replace "Old Earth" with the no less nebulously frightening "West," and the panorama of the Idyllium depicted by Pelevin bears an imprint of the collective imaginary offered up by contemporary Russian politics. Pelevin's Idyllium, therefore, represents an imperial imaginary raised to the level of philosophical utopia. Escape from politics leads only to its "cleansing" of cynicism, villainy and blood. A better filter than metaphysics for such an undertaking would be difficult to find. In other words, Pelevin remains a political writer even as he strives to get away from politics. This time around, however, satire is displaced by utopia. Pelevin has, without realizing it himself, metamorphosed from the most mordant critic of the contemporary cultural-political regime into its promoter.

Pelevin's example better than any other demonstrates that literature's engagement in politics is not a fashion, but a large-scale paradigmatic shift that took about thirty years to develop. An emerging paradigm suggests a new deep connection between the language, or rather *the form* (in the formalist interpretation), of contemporary Russian literature and the political. I would like to argue that even the feminist slogan from the 1960s "The personal is political" (attributed to Carol Hanisch), frequently quoted by one of the most prominent Russian sociologists of culture, Boris Dubin, seems to be too limited for the situation today. Instead, one may claim—with a good helping of wishful thinking—that "the formal is political," or rather suggest that it has always been political. Now this aspect of the literary form has been laid bare. Furthermore, it is a radicalized, estranged form that functions as a political force in today's cultural condition. When political conservatism originates from and finds its greatest support in the cultural mainstream (inherited from the late-Soviet period and creatively adjusted to the post-Soviet condition), any resistance to and subversion of the cultural mainstream obtains political significance. Most likely, it was Pussy Riot's punk prayer that set the example of the new political art (see above), in which the form serves as the explosive vehicle for political subversion; notably, it was not the words of the punk prayer but the "devilish jumping" (*diavol'skoe dryganie*) and punk-rock music that caused the most intense reactions of outrage from conservatives.

However, today many critics of and participants in the cultural process speak about the penetration of postmodernist devices into the government's political discourses and rhetoric. Pussy Riot's Nadezhda Tolokonnikova suggests that today "political actionism loses its strength every day because the state has confidently hijacked the initiative: now it operates as an artist and performs whatever it wants with us. Boris Grois would have said that Putin continues the tradition of the Stalinist total work of art (read his *Gesamtkunstwerk Stalin*), when a whole country is one person's work of art."[2] Does this mean that the postmodernist form has become automatized, that is, absorbed by the mainstream (political and cultural alike) and that more radical estrangements are required? I answer this question elsewhere (see "Post-Soc" in this volume and Lipovetsky 2016), but in a nutshell I believe that postmodernism

---

[2] Facebook post, August 8, 2014, https://www.facebook.com/tolokno/posts/792897714074449:0.

is broad and diverse enough to produce alternatives to those of its forms that have been hijacked and automatized by official culture. Further, I will focus on several such alternatives and discuss their possibilities and limitations.

The Minor Literature

According to Shklovsky and Tynianov, form organizes poetic language by shifts and dislocations palpable only in relation to preexisting cultural languages. The dislocation of language is more visible and more prominent in poetry than in prose, which explains why in the 2000s and 2010s, for the first time since the 1960s, poetry rather than prose took priority in aesthetic innovation.

This happened despite powerful institutional stimulators, such as literary prizes, honorariums, and chain bookstores that predominately support prose rather than poetry, let alone dramaturgy. I mentioned the 1960s, yet today's situation is drastically different from that during the Thaw, since the growth in poetry is not accompanied by liberatory tendencies in the public sphere (quite the contrary), and because the majority of innovative poets belong to what Boris Dubin has defined as the "minor literature." Following Deleuze and Guattari's characterization of the minor literature by "the connection of the individual to a political immediacy" (1986, 18), Dubin wrote in 2009, "This is a marginal culture, a culture of semantic and aesthetic quest. It addresses itself to very narrow circles of the readership, a big part of which is made up of the authors themselves" (278). However, Dubin also believed that such literature strives to achieve "ultimately universal forms and meanings" (279–80) pertaining to existential or even anthropological dimensions of humanity. I find the latter qualifier questionable, yet the definition of experimental and intellectually innovative literature as the "minority within a minority" that is political by default is also novel for post-Soviet literature; in fact, this is a definition of the underground in the 1970s–80s, only transposed into the public space of the Internet, small-run presses, and a few journals, including *Novoe Literaturnoe Obozrenie* (*New Literary Review*) or *Translit*.

The relationships between contemporary Russian "minor literature" and the mainstream paradoxically both agree and disagree with the logic of literary forms' evolution as described by Tynianov in his articles "The Literary Fact" (1924) and "On Literary Evolution" (1927): "Large forms, when getting automatized, emphasize the significance of small forms (and vice versa); an image providing a verbal arabesque or semantic shift, while being automatized, clarifies the meaning of the image [. . .] (and vice versa)" (1977, 262).

The automatization of the large form, its replacement with a "verbal arabesque," "semantic fracture," a fragment, a ruin of the totality testifies to the shift toward a worldview based on the intentional rejection of teleological explanations of history and linear historical narratives. Tynianov, as we all know, demonstrated this shift through the new role acquired by informal and nonliterary genres in the first quarter of the nineteenth century—first and foremost, private letters: "Here, in these letters, we find the most flexible and most needed phenomena that with incredible force highlighted new constructive principles: reticence, fragmentariness, hints. The 'domestic' small form of the letter motivated the introduction of petty detail and stylistic devices as opposed to/in contrast to the 'grandiose' devices of the 18th century" (1977, 265).

If one tries to apply Tynianov's principles to the contemporary literary situation, the result will be self-contradictory. On the one hand, today the automatization of the large form appears inseparable from its mass success. Extremely telling is the story of the novel *Zuleikha otkryvaet glaza* (*Zuleikha Opens Her Eyes*, 2015) by the newcomer Guzel' Yakhina (b. 1977). This novel by a 2015 graduate of the Department for Scriptwriters of the Moscow Film School has become a literary sensation. Awarded the Big Book and Yasnaya Polyana prizes, it was also short-listed both for the Booker and the NOS (*Novaia slovesnost'*; New Literature) prizes, having very strong support in all possible literary circles, conservative and liberal, gravitating to "thick journals" and to the Internet media. Published with a laudatory foreword by Liudmila Ulitskaya, it was also praised by critics from opposing camps, such as Anna

Narinskaya and Pavel Basinsky. What caused such excitement? The novel offers a melodramatic story inhabited by one-dimensional characters and placed against the background of collectivization. Instead of estrangement it offers the reader numerous comfortably recognizable clichés collected from Soviet literature of both liberal and orthodox brands. Close scrutiny reveals that beneath an ostensible multiculturalism focused on a Tatar female peasant, we have a classic case of Orientalism; in the best Socialist Realist fashion, Zuleikha, the female protagonist, leaves behind her national culture, which is represented as repressive, and finds a higher truth in her love for the Russian hero (a Communist and NKVD officer). The post-Soviet author obviously recycles Soviet literature not only thematically but also stylistically. Consider, for example, such a description:

> Ignatov never was a womanizer. Tall, slender, ideologically correct—the women themselves cast flirtatious glances at him, trying to catch his attention. But he didn't rush to attach himself and his soul to anyone. He had just a few women in his life—shame to admit, the fingers of one hand would be enough to count them all. He had no time for them. In 1918, he enrolled in the Red Army—and hadn't stopped fighting since then: first, it was the Civil War, then he mowed down the *basmachi* in Central Asia [...]. He would still have been cutting down enemies, if not for Bakiev. [...] It was he, who returned Ignatov to his native Tataria. Come back, Vanya, he told him, I badly need people I can trust—I can't cope without you. (Yakhina 2015, 119; trans. Irene Masing-Delic and Helen Halva)[3]

---

[3] «Игнатов никогда не был бабником. Статный, видный, идейный — женщины обычно сами приглядывались к нему, старались понравиться. Но он ни с кем сходиться не торопился и душой прикипать тоже. Всего-то и было у него этих баб за жизнь — стыдно признаться — по пальцам одной руки перечесть. Все как-то не до того. Записался в восемнадцатом в Красную армию — и поехало: сначала Гражданская, потом басмачей рубил в Средней Азии [...]. До сих пор бы, наверное, по горам шашкой махал, если бы не Бакиев. [...] Он-то Игнатова и вернул в родную Татарию. Возвращайся, говорит, Ваня, мне свои люди позарез нужны, без тебя — никак».

Generally speaking, such a novel would have perfectly fit in with Soviet literature of the 1960s and could have been written by, say, Chingiz Aitmatov or his imitators (Ulitskaya mentions this similarity as well). Although there are aspects that would have made publication impossible in the 1960s (the detailed portrayal of collectivization and the Gulag), this text today reads as a script for a multiserial tearjerker (which will surely be produced in no time). This novel's success is similar to the hysterical newly discovered fascination of the Moscow and, more broadly, Russian public with Valentin Serov's paintings[4] (although Serov is much more complex than *Zuleikha*): it is driven by the desire to find some simple and clear cultural phenomena that would counterbalance the aforementioned disturbing fusion of nationalist and conservative politics with elements of postmodernist rhetoric.

At the same time, in full agreement with Tynianov's logic, in today's Russian culture social media, such as first LiveJournal and later Facebook, have appropriated a role similar to that of the private letter in formalist theory. One could observe the rise of minor genres, autobiographical notes, vignettes, and anecdotes (in Pushkin's sense) since the late 1980s. Pioneered by Sergei Dovlatov's *Zapisnye knizhki* (*Notebooks*), which formed the cultural idiom of the "last Soviet generation" (Yurchak 2006), this genre flourished in books by Mikhail Gasparov, Aleksandr Zholkovsky, Mikhail Bezrodnyi, Lev Rubinshtein, and Grisha Bruskin, among others. Simultaneously, a powerful tradition of in-between prose (*promezhutochnaia proza*) has been shaped as a radical cultural phenomenon. Epitomized by Lidiia Ginzburg, it absorbed Vasilii Rozanov's *Fallen Leaves*, Kornei Chukovskii's and Mikhail Kuz'min's diaries, on the one hand, as well as Andrei Siniavskii's, Pavel Ulitin's, and Evgenii Kharitonov's works, on the other. Blogging has connected these processes with

---

[4] A recent Serov exhibition in Moscow was attended by a half million people, more than any other art exhibition in post-Soviet history. People stood in line at the Tretyakov Gallery for three to five hours outside in subzero temperatures. See, for example, "Vystavka Serova v Moskve ustanovila rekord poseshchaemosti," BBC, February 5, 2016, http://www.bbc.com/russian/news/2016/02/160205_serov_expo_record.

the intelligentsia's newly discovered means of communication, thus offering a new resonance to the "in-between" genre, or rather *metagenre* of today's minor literature. Aleksandr Il'ianen's recent novel *Pensiia* (*The Pension*, 2015) offers an illuminating example. Il'ianen has been literally writing this novel online, through his VKontakte microblog. Actually, the result was not all that different from his previous works, which fully belong to the in-between prose context. Judging by the resonance of this novel (a special cluster of articles in *NLO*, short-listing for the NOS literary prize), this strategy proved to be quite effective.

The Internet, despite optimistic or pessimistic forecasts, failed to change the nature of literature. We are still reading linearly and not hypertextually. Visuality also has not completely replaced verbal art but rather absorbed it—offering powerful miniseries available on reading devices as the persuasive substitute of serialized novels of the past. Russian Facebook and LiveJournal have proven to be especially suitable for literary experimentation, since these services are less pragmatically oriented than, say, in the United States and less dominated by youngsters. Russian blogs and microblogs represent all generations and do not exclude philosophizing, literary criticism, short essays, or any of the microgenres listed above. They are truly heterotopic in the Foucauldian meaning of the word; by interweaving diverse fragments, uncountable subjects, documents, fakes, intimate confessions, supershort comedies and tragedies, analytical texts and sarcastic (or rude) comments, they create "the disorder in which fragments of a large number of possible orders glitter separately in the dimension without law and geometry" (Foucault 1970, xvii). Unlike TV screens, these media are predominantly verbal. We have here the revanche of literature-centrism, if you wish.

Heterotopias, according to Foucault, "Secretly undermine language, because they make it impossible to name this *and* that, because they destroy 'syntax' in advance, and not only the syntax with which we construct sentences but also that less apparent syntax which causes worlds and things [. . .] to 'hold together'" (1970, xviii). In many ways, this is a perfect characterization of the political meaning of contemporary Russian poetry, which explains why it confidently inhabits Facebook and similar services. Communication between authors and readers through the microblog, where new texts appear almost in a daily regime, has become routine for such prominent poets as Stanislav L'vovskii and Andrei Rodionov, Elena Fanailova and Polina Barskova, Linor Goralik and Boris Khersonskii, Galina Rymbu and Roman Osminkin, Kirill Medvedev and Mariia Stepanova, among others. Similarly, the New Drama as a cultural phenomenon has been shaped by Internet forums and competitions; the docudrama frequently theatricalizes online debates as, for example, in Elena Gremina and Mikhail Ugarov's play *September.doc* (2005).

I am far from the thought that today's Russian poetry and drama are derivative of the Internet. However, I believe that Internet media underscore and "lay bare" those features of poetic and dramaturgic texts that facilitate the political functioning of their form. A poem posted on Facebook sounds different from the same poem on a book page. As a part of the news feed, it is integrated into the process of communication and can be expected to receive direct reactions from readers. This communication also includes a performative element since the poem is contextualized by truly performative gestures that surround it in the news feed, such as political and personal statements, greetings, calls for help, and so on. The online status of a poetic or, more broadly, literary text, by default implies the illusion of authenticity and even "documentality"; the text appears as something that the author has written minutes or hours ago and is sharing with you personally.

This performativity is not a new aspect of Russian poetry; however, it obviously has been becoming more and more important within the last two decades. In minor literature, where Facebook postings and small-size readings acquire the role of major forms of publication, the communicative and performative capacities of poetry are radically enhanced. It would be valid to see in complex poetry and the readers' ability to enjoy it a shibboleth that facilitates belonging to a tight community of the like-minded. At the same time, one can observe the growing influence of Dmitrii Prigov and his method based entirely on performativity, which is perceived within minor literature as a fertile model for new poetry and, more generally, for poetic self-realization. Last but not least, an example set by Dmitri Bykov and Mikhail Efremov's project Citizen Poet proved that performed poetry possesses unforeseen political potential—which, by the way, could not be realized without the Internet. What *is* the relation of performativity and the illusion of authenticity to the emerging constructive principle in contemporary literature, the one that enforces the political meaning of its forms?

Authenticity or Performativity?

Ellen Rutten recently wrote the informative book *Sincerity after Communism* (to be published by Yale University Press), in which she meticulously traces the perturbations and transformations of the chase for authenticity and sincerity in post-Soviet culture. As follows from her analysis, this quest, despite its declarative anti-postmodernist rhetoric, in many cases proves to be a form of postmodernism's self-critique leading to radical innovations, as it was in the case of Prigov's "new sincerity" (1984–86), which resulted in his most brilliant and still underappreciated performance "Appeals to Citizens" (see also Skakov 2016). Sorokin's step in this direction with his *Ice Trilogy* led to his later politicized postmodernism. The desire for authenticity is also responsible for the New Drama theater, which—despite its leaders' claims—belongs to the postmodern cultural paradigm and cannot be reduced to "truth-speaking" of the kind that we had in perestroika aesthetics.

At the same time, Ellen Rutten mentions (although she does not elaborate) that many of those who desired sincerity above all riches ended up in the ultraconservative camp, from Dugin to Prilepin. Indeed, this is an interesting paradox, especially considering that since the 1960s the banner of sincerity served as a euphemism for a liberal worldview. Nowadays, sincerity can mean solidarity with xenophobic, nationalist, imperialist, and similar ideologies. The claim or rather rhetorical signifiers of sincerity seem to release the author from any moral or even logical obligations. For example, consider this text by the famed playwright Evgenii Grishkovets, written and published soon after the annexation of Crimea and Russia's attack on the Ukrainian revolution:

I think that that which took place in Kiev at the end of last year and now is taking place in the whole country has no relation whatsoever to a struggle for freedom. [. . .] The referendum there [in the Crimea] was just, but illegal. [. . .] It was illegal to annex the Crimea. That is what I think. But what else could we have done? I don't know! The annexation was unlawful, but it was done beautifully. Masterfully. [. . .] And I also think that it is fair that the Russian fleet now stands in Sevastopol and does not have to pay. It stands there illegally but justly. It is just that the ships of NATO won't be standing there. They have no right to be there. [. . .] The government of Ukraine is unlawful. I think it lacks independence and is criminal. Criminal in its lack of independence. [. . .] I think that Obama is an untalented and stupid person. He is an ambitious and weak politician. Oversensitive and absurd. [. . .] Europe bears the marks of obvious degeneration, but refuses to see that, continuing to follow old habits and sticking to its old ways and ambitions, like an old man who refuses to acknowledge that he has no strength anymore and is enfeebled, both his brain and his muscles. [. . .] The decision about the embargo of food imports, I think was a really strong move. I saw that myself in Greece.[5]

[5] «Я думаю, то, что происходило в Киеве в конце прошлого года, а теперь происходит во всей стране, никакого отношения к борьбе за свободу не имеет. [...] Референдум там [в Крыму] был справедливый, но незаконный. [. . .] Крым аннексировать было нельзя. Я так думаю! А что было делать? Я не знаю! Аннексировать было нельзя, но аннексировали его красиво. Мастерски. [. . .] И ещё я думаю, что справедливо то, что в Севастополе теперь стоит русский флот без аренды. Незаконно стоит, но справедливо. Справедливо, что корабли НАТО там стоять не будут. Нечего им там делать. [. . .] Руководство Украины незаконно. Думаю, что оно несамостоятельно и преступно. Преступно своей несамостоятельностью. [. . .] Я думаю, что Обама бездарный и глупый человек. Он амбициозный и слабый политик. Обидчивый и нелепый. [. . .] Европа несёт в себе явные признаки вырождения, не желая их замечать и продолжая жить по привычке, с прежними замашками и амбициями, как старик, отказывающийся признать, что силы его покинули и одряхлели, как мозг, так и мышцы. [. . .] Решение с продовольственным эмбарго, я думаю, был сильный ход. Я сам это видел в Греции». First published on Grishkovets's blog at *Ekho Moskvy*, September 4, 2014, http://echo.msk.ru/blog/evgeniy_grishkovetz/1393294-echo/. See also http://odnovremenno.com/archives/4952. Translated by Irene Masing-Delic and Helen Halva.

In the late 1990s, "human documents," masterfully presented by Grishkovets in his one-man show *How I Ate a Dog*, triggered an aesthetic revolution in Russian theater and became the precursors of the New Drama (despite Grishkovets's animosity toward this movement). Grishkovets created a new theatrical discourse based on the "sincerity" of a personal utterance and establishing a new distance between the author/character/actor and the audience.[6] The almost twenty years that have passed since the premiere of his first show transformed Grishkovets's sincerity into an automatized discourse, applicable to various subjects: from love for a woman (*The Planet*) to love for death (*Dreadnoughts*), from exalted love for the motherland (*+1*) to no less exalted love for property (*The House*). The quoted text employs the same technique to express Grishkovets's sincere and authentic love for the government, its new course, coupled with a humble desire to continue milking the Ukrainian audience. After this quasi-individual and therefore self-parodic performance of sincerity that serves as a license to guise or disguise political servility as independence of thought ("*Ia tak dumaiu!*" ["That's my opinion!"]), one can hardly insist on the congruence between authenticity and truth. Authenticity appears as a set of devices (in Grishkovets's palette, these are unfinished sentences, ellipses, an intimate intonation, soft self-irony, and infantilism) that can be attached to any statement, no matter how deindividualized and ideologically engaged it may be.

Unfortunately, Grishkovets is not alone. One of the fathers of the New Drama, producer and director Eduard Boiakov, today produces an exhibition entitled "Orthodox Russia, My History, 20th Century: From the Great Shocks to the Great Victory" in the Moscow Manege and expresses joy about Russia's "rejection of the liberal civilizational paradigm" in these terms: "We have rejected the liberal civilizational paradigm. One can say we shut the door on it. Personally, I feel happy about this. [. . .] We are on the threshold of a new revolution. We can no longer cancel it. We can make it symbolic and mental rather than bloody" (Koval'skaia 2015). Initial

---

[6] See Beumers and Lipovetsky (2009) for more detail.

attachment to sincerity as the weapon against postmodernist perversions served as the marker of the so-called New Realists (Zakhar Prilepin, Sergei Shargunov, Roman Senchin) and their inspiration Eduard Limonov, which perhaps explains why these former rebels so ardently support Putin's course now. An overlap between the cult of sincerity and the new political discourse once again proves that contemporary Russian ideology is not just a pile of formalized dogmatic statements. Unlike in Soviet times, in full correspondence with Slavoj Žižek's concept of ideology (1989, 1–56), it articulates a shared unconscious phantasm rather than certain ideas and programs. In this respect, it is indeed incredibly sincere and therefore radioactively effective.

At the same time, one can hardly fail to notice the surge in interest about documentary forms and genres; documentary theater has become just one of the first symptoms of this wide-scale exponential process. How is an awareness of the illusory and constructed nature of authenticity to be combined with attentiveness to "nonfictional" forms? Typically, the rise of documentary forms serves as an omen of an impending aesthetic revolution. It signifies the moment when all existing cultural languages seem to have become automatized and therefore unusable. Mariia Bashkirtseva's diary, so popular in its time, played no lesser a role in the approximation of the modernist revolution than Chekhov. Rozanov's quasi-documentary prose contained the embryos of the Soviet and émigré modernism of the 1920s–30s. Rozanov's experimentation was passed on by Shklovsky and Ginzburg to today's neo- and postmodernists. There is no need to remind anyone that it was Solzhenitsyn's *Gulag Archipelago*, an "experiment in documentary investigation," that ultimately invalidated Socialist Realism.

Probably, we are today witnessing something similar: dramaturgic and especially poetic forms marked as documentary turn into self-parody when they are presented as vehicles of authentic truth, yet when released from such an ambition, they function as formalized gestures of *rejection of existing cultural languages*. This is exactly what happens in contemporary poetry, which broadly adopts signifiers of authenticity, while at the same time problematizing the category of authenticity. Symptomatically,

Kirill Medvedev, whose poems frequently reproduce the stylistics of a blog, in one of his manifestos declared the dead end of the "new sincerity":

> The new sincerity, or, more precisely, the *new emotionalism*, has rejected the worst aspects of postmodernism. [. . .] But it also rejected its undeniably positive qualities: its irrepressible critical outlook and its intellectual sophistication. [. . .] The new emotionalism reconciles those same market interests with the resurrected figure of the author, bringing forth today's endless stream of ventriloquism (lyrical, essayist, "political," whatever), in which any effort at analysis, any possibilities of differentiating positions and actions simply drown. It's a stream in which it's impossible to separate sincerity from hack work, because one is in the employ of the other: emotions cover up ideological bankruptcy (and the death of rational argument), and ideology in turn excites emotions and captivates the masses. (2012, 237)

In the theater, and especially in docudramas (exemplified by Teatr.doc), theatricality serves as the most powerful tool for the problematization of apparently desired and carefully designed illusions of authenticity. Notably, today's documentary plays, while relying on actual documents, do not avoid using phantasmagorical elements as well—which reflects playwrights' and directors' awareness of authenticity's functioning as a formal rather than semantic element of this dramaturgy. In Teatr.doc signifiers of authenticity initially mark the departure from the perspective of the intelligentsia along with a desire to appropriate a point of view and language of either the marginalized and disenfranchised (migrants, the homeless, prisoners) or, conversely, the new elites (spinmasters, TV producers, oligarchs). Yet recently the situation has changed drastically: the documentary form has stabilized as the marker of confrontation with the government's discourse and actions. In other words, the documentary form has become unequivocally political.

Teatr.doc's most famous productions of recent years deal with trials and the persecuted—the trials of Pussy Riot and of Sergei Magnitsky, or the victims of the Bolotnaia Square clash between the police and demonstrators; these events the theater puts on as its own, performative trial. In some cases, such a trial includes the enactment of the Last Judgment of judges and their henchmen (as in *Chas vosemnadtsat'* [*Hour and Eighteen*] by Elena Gremina); in others, nondisclosed court debates are transposed into the space of the theater, where actors playing witnesses of the prosecution have to defend their positions against the audience (as in *Svoimi glazami* [*With My Own Eyes*] about the Pussy Riot trial).

From this standpoint, one cannot help noticing the kinship between contemporary poetry and contemporary drama, not only because many contemporary poets design their texts for openly theatrical presentations. Along with the aforementioned Citizen Poet, one may here refer to Andrei Rodionov, Psoy Korolenko, and Roman Osminkin, who sing their poems in a highly theatrical manner; Osminkin also makes video performances accompanied by his poems. Many contemporary poems collapse into microperformances of various subjectivities (such as Elena Fanailova's famous long poem *Lena i liudi* [*Lena and People*] or Stanislav L'vovskii's cycles *Chuzhimi slovami* [*Rendered by Alien Words*] and *Sovetskie zastol'nye pesni* [*Soviet Drinking Songs*]) or present lyrical internalization of multifigured theatrical performances (Mariia Stepanova's cycle *Chetyre opery* [*Four Operas*] may serve as an illuminating example). Others "stage" poetic or documentary quotations as dramaturgic pieces, as happens in many of Polina Barskova's poems, most spectacularly in her *Spravochnik leningradskikh poetov-frontovikov, 1941–1945* (*Directory of Leningrad Front Poets, 1941–45*). A deeper correlation between contemporary poetry and drama stems from the combination of a formalized illusion of authenticity with two major aspects of postdramatic theater as defined by Hans-Thies Lehmann: transgression and the focus on a singular, individual, and unreproducible experience (2006, 177–79).

In docudramas transgression is associated with "dangerous" or unspeakable subjects and "obscene" language. In contemporary poetry, the departure from recognizable elements of poetry (rhyme, syllabotonic meters) initially produced a transgressive effect, which has obviously worn off by now; it was replaced by predominantly thematic means. For example, recently, young poets have rediscovered leftist discourse and revolutionary rhetoric as a highly transgressive factor for the readers of Russian poetry. The

St. Petersburg poet Roman Osminkin most playfully employs such transgressions:

> ... на этом месте должен быть припев
> про сильный и организованный пролетариат,
> который исполнит мессианскую роль
> и спасет наше общество от рабства отчуждения,
> но припев натолкнулся на моральную дилемму,
> где найти сегодня такого субъекта
> который пришел бы и сказал бы довольно
> но без разжигания классовой розни.
> (2016, 138)[7]

However, most transgressive in the new poetry is the absence of the postulated unity of the poetic persona and, most importantly, the lack of the author's metaposition. The focus on the personal and singular in this context presupposes not only a departure from grand narratives and impersonal ideologies toward micronarratives that, nevertheless, are frequently inscribed in epic-like frames (as in Faina Grimberg's or Boris Khersonskii's poetry). It goes much further and suggests the rejection of any stable identity and the refusal to find comfort in belonging to any set of group ethics, problematizing it instead:

> Я не считаю себя лучше
>
> Моя претензия круче
> Я считаю себя другим, другой, другими
> Как в кино с таким названьем
> С Николь Кидман в главной роли
> (Fanailova, *Lena i liudi* [2009, 156])[8]

---

[7] "Here there is meant to be a chorus / about a strong and organized proletariat / that will fulfill its messianic role / and save our society from the slavery of alienation / but the chorus stumbled into a moral dilemma / where can such a subject be found today / which would come and say 'enough' / but without inflaming class antagonisms," trans. Jon Platt (Osminkin 2016, 139).

[8] "I don't consider myself better than others. // My claim is tougher than that / I think I'm different—male, female, others / Like in the movie by that name / With Nicole Kidman in the lead" (Fanailova 2009, 156; Eng. trans. Genya Turovskaya and Stephanie Sandler).

Tellingly, after this declaration in her poem *Lena i liudi*, Elena Fanailova presents a scene of the antiritual nonparticipation in the national celebration of the New Year:

> В поезде Москва-Воронеж
> С китайскими рабочими
> У них год крысы наступает в феврале
> И они легли спать в одиннадцать
> И я с ними заснула
> В отличие от привычки
> Засыпать в четыре
> (ibid.)[9]

To be the other means in this context to accept an estranging position of the subaltern, to accept for oneself the status of "foreigner" in one's own country (or elsewhere). The reference to Alejandro Amenábar's *The Others* (2001)—"*Kak v kino s takim nazvan'em / s Nikol' Kidman v glavnoi roli*"—offers a radical metaphor for this gesture of distancing: the central characters in this clever horror movie fight against ghosts inhabiting a spooky Victorian mansion, only to learn (together with the viewer) at the end of the film that they are ghosts themselves.

At the same time, the gesture of detachment from any stable identity, time-honored discursive position, or ideological truth in this poetry produces not a longing for such unity but a new sense of freedom—uncomfortable, painful, but freedom nevertheless; perhaps this sense of freedom is best described as the refusal of nonfreedom, as in this poem by Galina Rymbu:

> ... мы расщепляемся в недрах и все что мы видим
> это не рай не ад это политическая система, суть которой:
>   огонь
> суть которой повтор и неузнавание до смерти,

---

[9] "I spent this New Year's Eve / On a train / From Moscow to Voronezh / With Chinese workers / Their Year of the Rat begins in February / And they went to sleep at eleven / And I fell asleep with them / As opposed to my usual habit / Of staying up until four" (ibid., 157).

повтор, пока жир и ужас не сойдут с наших людей
с наших сограждан [. . .]
они бросили тело мигранта на рельсы
они заживо снимают кожу с наших друзей
они накачали ляжки и приходят убить
они изнасилуют пока ты конспектируешь биографию Лермонтова
они убьют и бросят на рельсы пока ты мечтаешь о карьере физика мечтаешь выкрутиться
пока ты думаешь о пилотируемых полетах к другим галактикам
они закроют флагом смертельным все небо и словно там ничего не было
нет никаких галактик
и ты, может быть, кое-как дописав свой конспект, пойдешь насиловать,
пойдешь заживо снять кожу с мигранта или с бомжа
или крикнешь бизнес — это любовь
потому что они это ты
потому что нет никакого классового врага
только жестокость они
только предательство мы
только молчание я
без любви, без силы, без секса, без времени, без 68-го. . .
(Rymbu 2014a, 57–58)[10]

---

[10] "We uncouple ourselves in the depths and everything that we see / is not paradise not hell it's the political system, the essence of which is: conflagration / the essence of which is repetition and non-recognition until death / repetition, until fat and terror disappear from our people / our fellow citizens. // [. . .] they threw the body of the migrant onto the tracks / they skin our friends alive / they have girded their loins and come to kill / they rape while you make notes reading a Lermontov biography / they will kill you and throw you on the tracks while you are dreaming of the career of a physicist dreaming / to get out of a scrape / while you think of piloted flights to other galaxies / and you too, perhaps, having finished your haphazard notes will go and rape, / will go to skin alive a migrant or tramp / or you will shout out that business — that is love / because they are the same as you / because there is no class enemy / only cruelty is the class enemy / only treachery is us / only silence is I / devoid of love, with no strength, without sex, without time, without 1968 . . ." (trans. Irene Masing-Delic and Helen Halva).

Lehmann argues that the postdramatic theater achieves the ultimate effect of the performative (also characteristic of contemporary art) through a "production of presence" (Gumbrecht 2004) that rejects representation and collapses the distance between the author, viewer, and character. By this means, the postdramatic theater, according to Lehmann, strives "to allude to the somehow nonperformative in the proximity of performance" (2006, 179).

If we project this definition onto new Russian poetry and drama, what can stand for the nonperformative in the proximity of performance? Most likely, affects—strong and isolated psycho-physiological reactions—whose connection to the symbolic seems to be insignificant (at least, at first sight) in comparison with their transferable tangibility. Today's drama and poetry both situate the affect on the place of memory, selfhood, identity, or history. Affects associated with violence (as, for example, in Andrei Rodionov's, Mariia Stepanova's, and Elena Fanailova's poetry) most typically stand for the social, while material objects substitute for the historical (Boris Khersonskii and Stanislav L'vovskii). Yet sexual affects appear to be most important as they simulate (and stimulate) interaction with the reader. Galina Rymbu speaks about this most blatantly when she writes about Faina Grimberg: "Via erotic trust comes the faith in the tellable, for both author and reader. Only when we have slept with the text (the narrator) are we able to believe in the genuineness of his tales. Via sexuality, too, there is a self-affirmation of writing. The desiring body here acts as the cause of the tale, the cause of any conversation" (Rymbu 2014b, 7–8).

Frequently intertwined, these three types of affect make a text performative, since they involve the reader on a somatic, rather than intellectual, level. However, as the affect scholar Eugenie Brinkema emphasizes, "Affect is not the place where something immediate and automatic and resistant takes place outside of language. Turning to affect in the humanities does not obliterate the problem of form and representation [. . .]. We require a return to form precisely because of the turn to affect, to keep its wonderment in revolution, to keep going" (2014, xiv, xvi). This is why the apparently isolated nature of affects reproduces the same principle of fragmentation and multivoicedness that Facebook exemplifies as a cultural phenomenon. Yet "affective management" (to use Serguei Oushakine's joking term[11]), despite fragmentation, is able to create the feel of the entire epoch, as, for example, in Stanislav L'vovskii's poem:

> разговаривать и шептаться между волков, ночь, полустанция гдов
> где неподалёку собак, тут же троица, псков, рублёв триста кусков
> кошка, кот, хлебзавод, рыбзавод, первый отдел, аэродром смуравьёво
> ледяная вода по утрам, самогон, суглинок, неурожай, жэк, газопро́вод. [...]
> полустанция гдов, где ноябрь холодно, голодно, голо.
> менты о пяти головах, о шести лапах местный рублёв
> член союза художников, старожил, богомол
> богомаз, член партии, живописец, болиголов
>
> нам живописует: по дорогам железным ползёт последом броска
> чёрноверхая белая масса: звери, птицы, дети, конвой
> подконвойные, подотчётные, бухгалтера, вертухаи, воры, зэка —
> и не разобрать кто живой тут, кто неживой
>
> полумёртвые мёртвые скачут прямо на нас, прямо в рай из кино сквозь простынное марево слуха раскрываются пазухи лётных полей, волчьих снов, но наружу ползёт ледяная вода, требуха и проруха.
>
> *так мы прикончили первую, а тут остановка. курицу прямо в купе, в окно с перрона суёт глухая старуха.*
> *мы говорим давай сюда, мать, это ж гдов только, нам трястись тут ещё, она берёт деньги, бормочет в ответ.*
> *поезд набирает скорость, в окне, за лесопосадками разгорается солнце, — такой невечерний, осенний свет.*

---

[11] Serguei Oushakine has been most active in introducing the "affective turn" to our field. See, for example, Oushakine 2013a, 2013b, and 2010a.

мы разворачиваем курицу, открываем вторую поллитру
и тут понимаем, что гдов позади, смерти нет.
(L'vovskii 2012, 71–72)[12]

In reference to this poem, the words of the poet and critic Evgeniia Suslova seem to be very fitting: "The catastrophe implies that it is impossible to expect any conventional reactions to what is happening. Therefore, the catastrophe is associated not with the event per se, but rather with the annihilated position of the subject and with the process of its recomposition" (Suslova 2013). The "real" generated by the means of the affect does not restore the wholeness of the authorial subject, who remains fluctuating between multiple subjectivities and fictitious identities. Furthermore, this decentered subject deprived of a metaposition is presented as the performative of an ongoing catastrophe—of constant passing through Gdov, in L'vovskii's words. This cultivation of an unresolved, catastrophic split is deeply political by its logic and results. According to Jacques Rancière, "The essence of politics is the manifestation of *dissensus*,

---

[12] "To talk and whisper amongst wolves, night, the intermediate station of gdov / with dogs nearby, and a trinity too, pskov, rublyov, three hundred bits and pieces / cat, tomcat, breadfactory, fishfactory, first section, the airport gloomish, / ice-cold water in the mornings, moonshine, crop failure, zhek, gas-pipeline / [. . .] the intermediate station of gdov where November, cold, bare. / cops with five heads the local rublyov with six paws / member of the union of artists, a longtime resident, pilgrim / icon painter, member of the party, painter, hemlock / we are offered paintings: along railway tracks following a thrust there crawls / a black-topped white mass: animals, birds, children, a convoy / sub-convoys, subordinates, book-keepers, prison guards, thieves, prisoners— / and it's hard to decide who's alive, who's not alive / the half-dead the dead jump straight at us, right into paradise out of the movie-house / through the sheet haze of hearing there open up the armpits of flight fields, wolf dreams, / but ice water, guts and cuts / [. . .] *so this is the way we finished off the first one, and then there was a stop. a deaf old woman pushes a chicken straight into the compartment through the window from the platform / we tell her, give it here, mother, it is just gdov now, we have yet to shake here in this train, she takes the money, mumbles something in response. / the train speeds up, through the window beyond the newly-planted trees the sun is blazing—such a non-evening autumnal light. // we unwrap the chicken, open the next bottle and then we understand that gdov is behind us, / and there is no death*" (trans. Irene Masing-Delic and Helen Halva).

as the presence of two worlds in one. [. . .] The essence of politics is *dissensus*. Dissensus is not the confrontation between interests or opinions. It is the manifestation of a distance of the sensible from itself" (2001). The contemporary poet internalizes this *dissensus* in the construction of subjectivity and shares it through "postdramatic" performative.

"A constructive principle strives to transcend its customary borders, since, when staying within them, it swiftly becomes automatized," Tynianov warns and emphasizes in italics, "*A constructive principle generated within a given area strives to expand and spread to maximally broad areas*" (1977, 267). "The affective performativity" as a constructive principle has already transcended the borders of New Drama and fertilized New Poetry, while being catalyzed itself by contemporary art (Pussy Riot, Pavlenskii). Not to become automatized, this principle has to invade other areas and genres of literature. We can already detect similar processes in "smaller" prose such as Linor Goralik's ongoing cycle *Koroche* (*Briefly*, 2008–present), as well as in essays included in Polina Barskova's book *Zhivye kartiny* (*Living Pictures / Tableaux Vivants*, 2015). Yet it is not obvious whether this principle is transferable to a novel. (A direction exemplified by Il'ianen's novel *Pensiia* is too idiosyncratic to generate the following.) Nevertheless, I expect the most daring and most provocative texts to be created in this direction. This is where discoveries of contemporary poetry and (docu)drama can fully realize their political potential; this is how contemporary "minor" literature can define its place in the history of Russian letters and make a mark in a broader cultural context. Certainly, we all remember Tynianov's words about the futility of predicting developments in Russian literature: *Ei zakazhut Indiiu, a ona otkroet Ameriku* ("It will be ordered to discover India, but it will find America"; 1977, 166). However, America would have been discovered much later if not for expecting India.

Film

Post-Soc: Transformations of Socialist Realism in the Popular Culture of the Late 1990s—Early 2000s*

Old Songs about the Main Things

In July 2002, *Izvestiia* printed a lengthy front-page article on the Kievan debut of a new comic book based on *Molodaia gvardiia* (*The Young Guard*), Aleksandr Fadeev's famous Socialist Realist novel from 1945, and, indirectly, on the equally famous 1948 film by Sergei Gerasimov. The sponsor of this new graphic adaptation was a thirty-five-year-old Ukrainian liberal parliamentarian and businessman named Viktor Kirillov, who was appalled by the complete disappearance of Fadeev's heroic images from the purview of younger generations. This ambitious legislator hoped to expand the revival project, transitioning from comic books to motion pictures. He even tried to negotiate the production of an animated *Molodaia gvardiia* film with Disney Studios, but due to the insurmountable expense, resorted to Ukrainian producers. Explaining his decision to invest in this project, Kirillov said,

---

* I wrote this article in 2003, which explains dated examples, but, alas, not tendencies. At first, I thought that I needed to update it, but while rereading I realized that the connections and parallels between "Post-Soc" of the late 1990s–early 2000s and today's political and media mainstream are so obvious that they do not require any additional comments or updates.

We conducted a contest among schoolchildren and other youngsters at the Krasnodon Museum of "The Young Guard": they drew pictures of their heroes. When I saw those pictures [*maliunki*], I was flabbergasted: Liuba Shevtsova—a complete sex-bomb, like Marilyn Monroe: breasts like melons, tight clothes, a sheen of sweat, with distinct anatomic detail; Uliana Gromova—a gypsy beauty. Oleg Koshevoi—a slick, high-class dandy, fascists—jocks with biceps. This is how today's children see history. I watched attentively and decided that we shouldn't be scared; instead, we should talk to kids using their own language. Obviously, the majority of them know neither Fadeev nor the history of the Great Patriotic War. So they can learn the truth about the Young Guard from comic books. They don't read Gaidar either, but they have some idea of the Civil War from a cartoon about Mal'shish-Kibal'shish [a hero from Arkadii Gaidar's fairytale]. (Sokolovskaia 2002, 1)

In other words, the new generation of children has no memory of the socialist past, their minds now molded predominantly by Western mass culture and video games. Hence, it becomes a simple (and lucrative) matter to package Socialist Realist plots and images in forms of presentation characteristic to the pop culture of the West. This approach seems to be profitable both commercially and politically—especially in Russia, as evidenced by the interest *Izvestiia* (and other Russian media) paid to the "foreign" initiative.[1]

In fact, one may detect a paradoxical "double encoding" here, to use Charles Jencks's term. For adults, the graphic exploits of Oleg Koshevoi and Liubka Shevtsova will restore the ruined national pride and construct lofty exemplars of heroism and patriotism. Younger readers, meanwhile, will enjoy another set of action sequences, hopefully no less interesting than the business of American cartoons; for them, the *Molodaia gvardiia* comic book will be no more tethered to any kind of reality, past or present, than the X-Men or Spider-Man. The adaptation's organizers understood that this was how their product would be perceived (no wonder

---

[1] A Hollywood-like multi-episode TV remake of *Molodaia gvardiia* was produced by Russia's First Channel in 2015 (dir. Leonid Pliaskin).

they refer to Gaidar's fairy tale as a model). This project, initially motivated by the contemporary youth's allegedly impoverished worldview, would be addressed to *all generations*. According to the article in *Izvestiia*, three versions of the comic were to be launched simultaneously: a "hard" version for the youth, a "moderate" one for the intelligentsia, and a "softer" edition for the older generation who once idolized the "*molodogvardeitsy*."

This double, or rather multiple, encoding can be read as nothing but postmodernist. For this reason, the conservative audience perceives the *Molodaia gvardiia* comic book as blasphemy: "How can one turn something that is dear and sacred to the people into a joke?" asks the indignant pop/folk singer Larisa Chernikova (Sokolovskaia 2002, 10). Yet the postmodernist recycling of Socialist Realist models and myths represents one of the most distinctive trends in Russian mass culture of the late 1990s–early 2000s. The pattern was launched by the show *Starye pesni o glavnom* (*Old Songs about the Main Things*, a 1995 one-off later serialized), in which the day's pop and rock stars playfully—sometimes ironically, but with obvious ardor—perform old Soviet hits. The title of the program (and the entire ironic/nostalgic sentiment attached to it) acquired new significance during the governmental campaign to restore the old Soviet anthem. We might recall, for example, Lev Rubinshtein's astute reaction to these events in his essay "Dym Otechestva ili Gulag s fil'trom" (translated by Joanne Turnbull as "The Smoke of Fatherland, or A Filter Gulag"):

> So then, a filtered Belomor. With the same sickeningly familiar picture on the pack. A new wine in an old wineskin. The appearance of this remake evokes a bright bundle of meaningful metaphors. That his gimmick belongs to the "old-songs-about-the main-thing" class is clear. Perhaps even too clear. What isn't associated today with those ill-fated "songs"? This hackneyed formula seems to have enveloped our entire time and space symbolically. In other words, our space is going through a time of "old songs"—our own inevitably specific and local recension of postmodernism.... Meanwhile, the new and improved Belomor is this: typical socialism with a human face. Or, to put it a bit more crudely: a filtered Gulag. It is like other large and small features of the "velvet" restoration, the same thing as today's Stalinist

anthem without the Stalinist words: the anthem, too, has been fitted with a kind of filter. (Rubinshtein 2001, 143–44)

By no means do I wish to equate the postmodernist wave of Socialist Realist mythologies and structural patterns with the political restoration of totalitarianism. On the contrary, there is an important difference between the deconstruction of Socialist Realism, appearing in the classical forms of Russian postmodernism (conceptualism, sots-art), and the novel attitude toward totalitarian discourses that we could observe in such productions of the late 1990s–early 2000s as *Starye pesni o glavnom* and the *Molodaia gvardiia* comic book, as well as the musical *Nord-Ost* (*North-East*) by Georgii Vasil'ev and Aleksei Ivashchenko (and produced by Aleksandr Tsekalo, known for scripting *Old Songs about the Main Things*), such films as *Brat 2* (*Brother 2*, 2000) and *Voina* (*War*, 2002) by Aleksei Balabanov, *Sibirskii tsiriul'nik* (*The Barber of Siberia*, 1998) by Nikita Mikhalkov, *Zvezda* (*The Star*, 2002) by Nikolai Lebedev, *Ekhali dva shofera* (*A Tale of Two Drivers*, 2001) by Aleksandr Kott, *Oligarkh* (*The Oligarch*, 2002) by Pavel Lungin, and novels such as Pavel Krusanov's *Ukus angela* (*The Angel's Bite*, 1999) and even, to a certain extent, Vladimir Sorokin's *Led* (*Ice*, 2002). Unlike other texts of Russian postmodernism, these films and novels do not try to expose the absurdity or the violence hidden beneath Socialist Realist mythology. Their target audience does not include nostalgic diehards; rather, these works aim to please the middle-aged generation, for whom Socialist Realism is more associated with childhood memories, and they are especially addressed to the first post-Soviet generation, for whom this aesthetic is distant and even exotic.

It is no wonder that the mass culture texts listed above mostly perceive Socialist Realism as an agreeable experience. First of all, Socialist Realism serves as a recognizably "native," and therefore intensely appealing, form of mass culture; second, it is a predominantly *positive* culture, emphasizing optimism and affirmative values over the critical tone, deconstructive tendencies, and *"chernukha"* (dark and grim discourse) of the post-Soviet decade; third, the utopian aspect of totalitarian discourse is reevaluated in the aforementioned texts therapeutically, distracting the viewer or reader from everyday troubles. Irony is present in all these works, but never bites as hard as it did in the works of Prigov or early Sorokin, or even in Sergei Anufriev and Pavel Peppershtein's novel *Mifogennaia liubov' kast* (*The Mythogenious Love of the Castes*, 1999/2002) or the film *Okraina* (*Outskirts*, 1998) by Petr Lutsik. This irony, unlike its fanged cousin, is soft and inviting: it is intended to string postmodernist quotation marks around borrowed aspects of the Socialist Realist system and to smooth the seams between these traditional patches and more recent fabric, represented by contemporary rock and pop stylistics in *Starye pesni o glavnom*, the conventions of the American action movie in *Brat 2*, or fashionable "historiosophic" mysticism in *Ukus angela* or *Led*.

Post-Soc: A Hypothesis

The metamorphosis of Socialist Realist models and myths into ideologically indifferent, yet extremely popular, forms of mass culture invites at least two mutually exclusive interpretations. Both are based on the assumption that in the late 1990s, postmodernism in Russian culture ceased to be a marginal form of artistic experimentation and had become mainstream. In turn, postmodernism as a popular form of expression began to affect mass culture: the commercial success of Pelevin's and Sorokin's novels, and the distinctly postmodernist bent of Boris Akunin's ongoing project of historical fiction, are the handiest evidence of this transformation.

The first interpretation postulates that the merger of post-Soviet mass culture with Socialist Realism's heritage, via postmodernist poetics, eventually decomposes the binary opposition between the post-Soviet present and the Soviet past, the polarity that founded the post-Soviet mentality of the 1990s. The discourse originated in (or rather, shaped by) *Starye pesni o glavnom* has rescued the traditional idioms of Socialist Realism from their totalitarian—and especially, Communist—connotations. New uses have deideologized them, thereby playfully, yet effectively, restoring historical continuity, connecting past and present with an axiologically neutral thread.

If this theory is accurate, then the popularity of recycled Socialist Realism may be attributed to the public need to treat, or at least to cover up, the disturbing trauma of the totalitarian past—the trauma that was not addressed in Russia as methodically and consciously as it was, for example, in post-Nazi Germany. Such a catharsis does not necessarily mean political recuperation: one may interpret this tendency in post-Soviet mass culture as a (remarkably efficient) portal to the postmodernist continuum of posthistory, where neither trauma nor responsibility matter any longer.

The second interpretation is less optimistic—which means more realistic. In essence, it suggests to see in Russian culture of the 2000s a rare case of *postmodernism without postmodernity*. As we know, postmodernist aesthetics in literature and the arts developed in spite of the fact that the late-Soviet and post-Soviet cultures are vastly distant from postmodernity as a type of culture and civilization shared by many a postindustrial society. Roughly speaking, post-Soviet cultural conditions exhibit certain central characteristics of postmodernity while aggressively rejecting others. For example, the post-Soviet cultural landscape, like that of postmodernity, appears "strikingly different from the confined space of its own automatic, purpose-subordinated pursuits. It appears as a space of chaos and chronic *indeterminacy*, a territory subjected to rival and contradictory meaning bestowing claims and hence perpetually *ambivalent*" (Bauman 2001, 178; author's emphasis). On the other hand, such critical postmodern discourses as feminism, multiculturalism, queer studies, and postcolonialism (all focused on the values of the Other) remained underdeveloped and widely abhorred in the Russian cultural mainstream of the 1990s. The term "heterophilia," as opposed to "xenophobic sentiment," is still inapplicable to the post-Soviet cultural and political climate. Postmodernity implies the most radical critique of the premises of modernity, whereas post-Soviet Russia primarily busies itself with modifying the unique Soviet brand of modernity on the basis of democratic, private, and personal values. The controversial and contradictory nature of this process distorts the perception of the cultural patterns of postmodernity in contemporary Russian culture.

Quite predictably, the incomplete modernization of Russian culture causes severe suspicion and aggression toward the habits of "political correctness," which appear in the West as a form of high-wire societal etiquette balancing the postmodernist radical deconstruction of cultural models and stereotypes rooted in the metanarratives of modernity. In the Russian cultural context, "political correctness" is invariably viewed as a "hypocritical" norm of censorship forced on free self-expression.[2] In the Western theater, however, the notorious PC fixation reflects "the *problem* of rules [which] stays in the focus of public agenda and is unlikely to be conclusively resolved. In the absence of 'principal coordination' the negotiation of rules assumes a distinctly *ethical* character: at stake are the principles of non-utilitarian self constraint of autonomous agencies" (Bauman 2001, 186; author's emphasis).

Granted, Russian postmodernism has generated its own mini-postmodernity within the controlled bounds of an underground subculture. The country's postmodernist current faced a substantial challenge upon finding itself in the role of a mainstream form of expression. It could not exist within underground circles any longer: it had to cope with, and appeal to, the tastes of the general public.[3] This necessity has forced some artists to give up their postmodernist complexity, which had proved allergenic to the majority of the population. The need to lean back on something both simple and recognizable to the masses naturally led those Russian postmodernists who desired mass success to the (briefly?) deactivated codes of Socialist Realism. This new cultural turn induced a schism among Russian postmodernists, some deciding to eschew commercial success and instead preserve their artistic and cultural values, others forking over the toll of reductionism and anti-postmodernity in exchange for popularity.

At the present moment, one may only try to isolate this trend's most visible manifestations, across an entire class of applicable works, in order to distill an accurate diagnosis:

---

[2] See, for example, Tatiana Tolstaya's satire "Political Correctness" (2002, 220–43).

[3] For more on this paradox, see Lipovetsky 2002a and 2002b.

1. The plot development issues from a pronounced contrast between "good" and "evil" characters, an unambiguous polarity of light and shadow. The viewer or reader is informed of the "goodness" of the former and the "evil" of the latter at the moment of their first appearance, and these designations are never questioned.

2. This type of plot development usually requires war as its catalyst. This function can be fulfilled by the Great Patriotic War (the official Soviet epithet for World War II); the Chechen War, or various warlike settings, such as the mafia-torn wastelands or the oligarchs' struggle against the Kremlin foes. These incarnations and relatives of war typically involve an extensive arsenal of real and symbolic weapons, assassinations, explosions, threats, spies, and military specialists.

3. The representation of the protagonist stems from *heroic (or epic) archetypes*. The hero appears in the text already "shaped" psychologically, with the subsequent ordeals leading only to the "unfolding" of his character, rather than to any psychological transformations. Social and ethnic attributes clearly supersede other personal features, sometimes to the point of symbolic or literal erasure: he is a certified epic hero, therefore "finding his sublimity in the superpersonal plane, in and through the symbols of universally human values, and not in a plane of individual psychology" (Meletinskii 1975, 229).

4. Generally, romance and female characters play a negligible role and can be subtracted from the plot without consequence. Male friendship or respect for a male superior, however, frequently acquires the status of moral imperative. The majority of these works seem to follow Andrei Platonov's ascetic maxim: "He who desires the truth cannot desire a woman" ("The Future October," 1920).[4]

---

[4] This quotation is borrowed from Eliot Borenstein's book *Men Without Women: Masculinity and Revolution in Russian Fiction, 1917–1929*. His observations on the works of Olesha, Babel, and Platonov show that the gender dynamic of what I suggest to call Post-Soc is deeply rooted in the Soviet cultural tradition. According to Borenstein, "Not only are Babel's and Olesha's heroes physically

5. The mandatory presence of one or more *recognizable* quotations from the Socialist Realist canon constitutes a distinctive hallmark of this trend, encompassing direct citations from Soviet films, Soviet-style songs, or even allusions to the appearance or mannerisms of famous Soviet actors.

6. No less compulsory are references to genre conventions, as well as the telltale bells and whistles of Western mass culture: the representatives of this trend always "compete with" or rather declare their intention to supersede (*"dognat' i peregnat'"*) most kitschy Hollywood directors and TV producers and mark this desire by recognizable, if sophomoric, quotations.

If any future historian should desire to investigate this tendency, the above catalog will not suffice. However, this prospect should not discourage attempts to analyze the most characteristic works of this trend that are presently in stock, which, for the sake of brevity, may be called *Post-Soc*. Studying them, one faces a few essential questions: Is it possible to deideologize the elements of the totalitarian discourse completely? Do these elements retain memories and traces of the totalitarian climate to which they used to belong? Does the postmodernist recycling of Socialist Realism in post-Soviet popular culture deliberately or inadvertently actualize certain aspects of the totalitarian discourse? And if yes, which of these aspects should we expect to see animated anew?

In pursuit of answers, I will examine several films from the early 2000s, and analyze the strategies and results of revitalizing Soviet cultural mythologies in the post-Soviet era, using Balabanov's film *Voina* as a pivotal example.

inferior to the model revolutionaries who surround them, but they are also unable to join in the network of male relationships, the comradeships and pseudo-filial ties, that are formed by revolutionary men. [. . .] Comradeship is the expression of revolutionary male solidarity par excellence; though women can be, and often are, comrades in the literature of the 1920s, the experience of comradeship is based on traditional masculine values. [. . .] The virtues of the comradely bond are extolled by communists and fascists alike, while the public sphere takes priority over the family in both early Soviet ideology and the rhetoric of fascism" (Borenstein 2000, 5, 24, 35).

The Charms of the Uniform

When watching Russian films of this period (up until now, I should add), one cannot help but notice the abundance of military and semimilitary outfits. Uniformed soldiers and officers naturally play prominent roles in war flicks like Balabanov's *Voina* and Lebedev's *Zvezda*, but comparable costumes adorn the screen even in present-day pictures like Govorukhin's *Voroshilovskii strelok*. In the idyllic *Ekhali dva shofera*—set, as its jacket informs us, in the "glorious postvictory days"—a young truck driver receives a pilot's uniform and wears it with pride. If we also recall the numerous TV series about men in uniform (*Agent natsional'noi bezopasnosti* [*The National Security Agent*], *Muzhskaia rabota* [*Men's Work*], *Spetsnaz* [*Special Army Unit*], *Uboinaia sila* [*The Killing Power*], *Granitsa/Taezhnyi roman* [*The Border/The Taiga Romance*]), which almost entirely supplanted Latin American soap operas during prime time, then the strange infatuation of the post-Communist culture with military dress codes becomes all the more apparent.

Even in films that apparently confront their Post-Soc proclivity, such as *Kukushka* (*The Cuckoo*, 2002) by Aleksandr Rogozhkin, *Nezhnyi vozrast* (*Tender Age*, 2000) by Sergei Solov'ev, or *Liubovnik* (*The Lover*, 2002) by Valery Todorovsky, the military past of the characters plays a key part in the plot development—as do the uniforms that signify this past. Military attire appears to serve in these films as a quasi identity, accidentally assumed by or forcibly impressed on the hero, which he struggles to shirk. In *Kukushka*, the World War II confrontation between Finnish and Soviet soldiers is rendered meaningless by the comedic plot. In *Nezhnyi vozrast* the protagonist Ivan (Dmitrii Solov'ev, also the movie's scriptwriter) finds himself embroiled in the Chechen War in search of a distraction from his turbulent love life, much like the protagonists of the Russian classics. At the climactic moment, however, he apprehends the gap between his expected military function and his personality: responding to a radio signal, he screams, "What goddamn 'arrow'? I'm not an arrow, I'm Gromov!" (*Kakaia ia tebe na khren strelochka! Ia Gromov!*). In *Liubovnik*, a retired military officer (Sergei Garmash), contrary to popular stereotypy of career officers as thick-skinned bores, turns out to be a far more sensitive and tragic soul than his rival, a professor of linguistics (Oleg Iankovskii) who failed to notice his late wife's infidelity and double life.

Contrastingly, in the films of Balabanov, Lebedev, Govorukhin, and Kott, the heroes' uniform is *equivalent* to their personal identity. *Voina*'s Ivan remains a soldier, taking up arms against the Chechens even after his demobilization. The fact that he is prosecuted for the murder of "citizens of the Russian Federation," having almost single-handedly eliminated an entire platoon of Chechens and released their hostages, is presented as unjust and hypocritical. According to the film's logic, Ivan fulfills his duty as a soldier, even if he is not affiliated with a standing military unit—how could anyone call him a murderer? In Lebedev's *Zvezda*, a reconnaissance squad's brand-new uniforms (appearing despite the setting of 1944, when anything brand-new was rather scarce) dramatically dissolve the members' personal and social differences by molding them all into a single organism. In *Voroshilovskii strelok*, Ivan Fedorovich's (Mikhail Ul'ianov) military shirt, vaguely military cap, and weathered old jacket, bedecked with veteran's medals, visually underscore the gravity of his intentions; his mission statement follows suit: "It's war. I just can't figure out who's fighting whom" (*Voina, ne poimu ia tol'ko, kto s kem voiuet*). Tellingly, the vengeful protagonist defines his foes—the New Russian rapists and corrupt authorities—as "occupiers" and "blood-suckers," or, in other words, as aggressive and undesirable Others. His most pointed, poison-tipped question is "Where did they come from?" (*Otkuda oni berutsia?*). In *Ekhali dva shofera*, the pilot's uniform endowed to Kol'ka (Pavel Derevianko) almost automatically places him in competition with an actual pilot for the affection of a beautiful woman: paradoxically, the masculinized heroine's love for Kol'ka proves that he is in fact a real pilot (much like the *nastoiashchii polkovnik*—"the real colonel"—from Alla Pugacheva's popular song), though he commands a rundown truck instead of an airplane.

Hence, the military uniform aids the authors of these films in performing a significant displacement: a *problem* of personal identity is silenced by a *statement* of collective identity. The haziness of "self," quite natural for a period of drastic historical changes, is swapped for the triumphal emergence of "we," the euphoria of "belonging" to an aggregate body. Uniform is cinematically enlisted as a (however unconsciously) recognizable signifier of Soviet military discourse, with its characteristic mixture of class and patriotic rhetoric and its master myth of the "heroic struggle of the Soviet people" against *whomever*. In the words of Evgenii Dobrenko,

> Military discourse is the cultural equivalent of the totalitarian regime (in agreement with Orwell's classic formula: "Peace is war"). [. . .] Those qualities of Soviet mentality and Soviet culture that defined the "face of the Soviet man" for the future half-century were forged in the crucible of war. [. . .] In a totalitarian culture, much like in a system of war, "a part," by definition, should cease being the whole, should die as an individual, and must enter the "unity of a lower order" (a sort of "ant-hill"). [. . .] The cultural model formed by Socialist Realism, in its main parameters, is certainly that of a *war machine*. (Dobrenko 1993, 210, 214, 215; author's emphasis)

Another tried and true Socialist Realist trope further augments the ethos of deindividualization in Post-Soc films: synecdoche between characters and their tools or instruments. Given this analytical scent to follow, the scenes of passionate firearm selection in both *Voina* and *Voroshilovskii strelok*, and the thoughtful adjustment of weaponry and camouflage before the raid in *Zvezda*, are pungent indeed. In *Ekhali dva shofera*, the contest between Kol'ka's ramshackle truck and Raika's (Irina Rakhmanova) pristine "Ford," with interference from a postal airplane, reproduces the human love triangle on a vehicular scale, while simultaneously displaying the totemic ties between each character and their "tool." It is no wonder that Kol'ka proposes marriage to Raika not after dating or even kissing her but after helping her with a spot of car trouble and being allowed to drive her truck as a reward. Since these characters act as appendages to their automobiles, professional cooperation serves as a legitimate substitute for intimacy: Raika gladly accepts his proposal. The film critic Natal'ia Sirivlia astutely described this situation:

The "attachment" of all the characters to their labor tools and means of production is all the more striking due to the complete absence of any industrial plot in the film. Neither socialist competition, nor a struggle for the best results, neither heroic battle with nature, nor the fulfillment of civil duty [. . .] Everything that constituted the dramatic backbone in Soviet movies about truck and tractor drivers, construction workers, etc., is totally eliminated from this film as superfluous details. Only that which can be amusing today remains intact—namely, the naive love and suffering of charming human cogs, the side dish that was traditionally served for the "warming" of an industrial plot. As a result, the film's action finds itself in a dead end. It can develop neither according to the logic of the psychological film, nor according to the mythological models of Socialist Realism. (Sirivlia 2002a, 48)

Despite the absence of Socialist Realist ideology, Kott inadvertently breathes new life into the forgotten and happily buried "conflictlessness" of postwar cinema and literature: in his film, there are no "bad people," only "nice guys," as Kol'ka puts it. The struggle between "good and better" as depicted in this 2002 feature is not, however, as toothless as it appears at first glance. Supported by the stylized setting, reproducing not an actual Soviet province of the late 1940s but rather a Socialist Realist mirage of provincial life, the movie delivers a deeply nostalgic wallop. Even the artificiality of the film's plot is presented as a reminiscence on the lost naiveté and purity supposedly basic to postwar mores. In complete accordance with the logic of "restoration nostalgia," *Ekhali dva shofera* "builds on the sense of loss of community and cohesion and offers a comforting collective script for individual longing" (Boym 2001, 43).

However, another aspect of this "restoration nostalgia" is largely based on various conspiracy theories: "The mechanism of this kind of conspiracy theory is based on the inversion of cause and effect and personal pronouns. 'We' (the conspiracy theorists) for whatever reason feel insecure in the modern world and find a scapegoat for our misfortunes, somebody different from us, whom we don't like. [. . .] 'They' conspire against 'our' homecoming, since we have to conspire against 'them' in order to substitute for the conspiracy itself" (Boym 2001, 43). This worldview *necessarily* engages the discourse of war; Kott's film, in truth, declares war on the implied present, which is "immoral" and "corrupt." The covert strategy of his picture becomes overt in the majority of Post-Soc films addressing different kinds of war: it is always war against the present (present chaos, disgrace, degeneration, etc.).

Applying Boym's definition of nostalgic conspirology to the works of Balabanov, Govorukhin, Lebedev, and Lungin, we must also define the supplementary concept of "homecoming" in Post-Soc: I would like to argue that "homecoming" refers here not to a territorial or temporal loss but, first and foremost, to the lost *collective identity*. The paradox of Post-Soc is thus found in the juxtaposition of two opposing modalities: the affirmation of the missing collective identity (through various spigots of military discourse) combined with an aching nostalgia for it. Of course, in this viscous thematic stew, the heroic declaration of belonging to some communal body (a "we") cannot aspire to more than a postmodernist simulacrum—the meaning of "we," today, happens to be annulled. This explains the Post-Soc affair with the military uniform: the outfit is a sheer simulacrum, a pure sham, a surface charade of joint identity that shifts the focus away from personal identity and masks the disheartening dearth of a collective to which the hero could proudly adhere—a costume, indeed.

Nevertheless, this nostalgic yen constitutes the raison d'être for the heated warfare of Post-Soc. First, because war itself, as the Soviet historical experience proves, can efficiently forge a collective identity: in his review of *Zvezda*, Iurii Gladil'shchikov maintains that "war again emerges as the single unifying idea for the film's characters and the film's audience, that which allows them to feel that 'we are of one blood.' [. . .] We lack another unifying idea. [. . .] Unable to find another way to attract viewers to domestic film, Russian cinematography inevitably returned to war" (Gladil'shchikov 2002a). And second, because war is one of the few phenomena able to sculpt a monolithic identity, as opposed to the kaleidoscopic and transient nature of postmodern (as well as postrevolutionary) identities.[5] In war, the identification problem is drastically simplified: "we" have a common enemy, the enemy is our common denominator; hence, "we" are not "they." As Susan Buck-Morss writes, "To define the enemy is, simultaneously, to define the collective. Indeed: *defining the enemy is the act that brings the collective into being*" (2000, 9; author's emphasis). This principle of totalitarian identification is wholeheartedly adopted by the Post-Soc aesthetic. Fulfillment reaches the Post-Soc character only when he learns to recognize "the enemy." Moreover, he becomes a hero only when he proves able to *act like the enemy*: paradoxically, he obtains—or rather, fashions—his share in the collective identity (since his personal identity remains invariably diminished) after his actions become indistinguishable from the actions of the enemy— that is, criminal, by definition. War acquires a new function here: an ultimate justification for this equation. "John, it's war. No think at war," says Ivan, in broken English, in Balabanov's *Voina*; the line is probably the most blatant exemplification of the inner mechanisms of the Post-Soc wars for identity.

Voina: The War for Identity

The plot of Balabanov's *Voina* (2003) is quite straightforward: a Russian sergeant named Ivan (Aleksei Chadov) is held in Chechen captivity and treated as a slave. He meets his fellow hostages— Captain Medvedev (Sergei Bodrov Jr.), paralyzed as a result of a concussive head injury, and two English actors kidnapped during

---

[5] "In our postmodern times [. . .] the boundaries which tend to be simultaneously most strongly desired and most acutely messed are those of *identity*: of a rightful and secure position in the society, of a space unquestionably one's own, where one can plan one's life with the minimum of interference, play one's role in a game in which the rules do not change overnight and without notice, act reasonably and hope for the better. As we have seen, it is the characteristic of contemporary men and women in our society that they live perpetually with the 'identity problem' unresolved. They suffer, one might say, from a chronic absence of resources with which they could build a truly solid and lasting identity, anchor it or stop from drifting" (Bauman 2001, 208–9).

a trip to Tbilisi, John (Ian Kelly) and his fiancée, Margaret (Ingeborga Dapkunaite). The leader of the Chechen captors, Aslan (Georgii Gurguliia), releases Ivan because no one is able or willing to pay his ransom. Concurrently, he frees John while keeping Margaret, on the condition that John will gather a ransom of two thousand British pounds and return for her. In England, John manages to collect only part of this sum, a significant portion of which constitutes an advance received from a TV station in payment for filming his visit to Chechnya. He fails to obtain any support whatsoever from the authorities—the British and Russian bureaucrats alike heartlessly reject his pleas for help.

Understanding that he is unable to negotiate with Aslan or travel to Chechnya by himself, John hurries to Tobol'sk—the hometown of his former prison mate Ivan. The sergeant has already been discharged, and we find him rather downcast in his return to civilian "peace": many of his friends have been killed in gang wars, his Chechen tenure numbs the meaning of any prospective job, and he does not know what to do with his life and freedom. When John arrives to beg for his help, Ivan lends it—not because he is lured by the Briton's promise of an honorarium but because he wants to rescue Captain Medvedev, who trilled Ivan's heartstrings as a true "father-commander": "Nobody can break or twist him. If only all the commanders were like him!"

Ivan and John travel to Moscow, where they secure military equipment and weapons with the Englishman's funds. When their Vladikavkaz "contact" from the FSB (Federal Security Service, the heir to the KGB) turns out to be a crook, scheming after John's wallet, Ivan assumes command. His first decree is to pay Aslan an unexpected visit. In a mountainside ambush, the duo captures an arms jeep belonging to the Chechens by killing its "passengers" (including, we should note, a woman). Later, Ivan takes a Chechen shepherd named Ruslan (E. Kurdizis) as a hostage, abusing and mistreating him, controlling him with beatings and threatening to murder his family. John is startled by Ivan's cruelty, but the sergeant authoritatively explains that *they* understand only *this* language—that is, the language of terror and violence—and John's discomfort is quelled.

With the shepherd's aid, Ivan and John assault Aslan's village. Ivan manages not only to suppress all resistance, killing the guards along with bystanders (an old man and a child), but also to take the unit commander himself prisoner. Defeated, Aslan praises his table-turning ex-captive: "You acted like a real mountain man!" Congratulations are cut short, however, when John discovers that Margaret has been gang-raped despite Aslan's vow. Thrust into a state of uncontrollable rage, he shoots Aslan, thereby wasting the sole bargaining chip by which the heroes could have made their safe exit from the mountains.

Ivan, John, and Margaret, under the leadership of the immobile Medvedev, build a raft to carry them within the reach of Russian choppers. The generous and noble Ivan releases Ruslan with a compensation of two thousand pounds. The rest of his honorarium he donates to Medvedev, who needs the money to treat his injured spine. However, in the denouement Ivan is not rewarded but punished. The footage shot by John incriminates the demobilized Ivan, and he is arrested and held in the Russian prison from which he has been narrating his odyssey to a visiting journalist. Ruslan testifies against him in court, and his sons, apparently illiterate in Russian, are admitted to Moscow University in exchange for bribes. Margaret, who has fallen in love with Medvedev in captivity, breaks up with John. Medvedev returns to his wife and daughter and is the only one who continues to fight for Ivan's release.

According to the film's logical schema, Ivan—as his folkloric name suggests—is a symbolic representation of Russia. As such, he equivalently opposes West and East. The latter is embodied by Aslan and his tribal morals: he remembers the names of his seven ancestors, and inherits their toils in his own struggle with the Russians. (The same morality is represented by Ruslan, for whom Aslan is a blood enemy after centuries of interfamilial feuding.) The West, of course, is epitomized by the English tourist: with his Western humanistic values, John is portrayed as *weakness incarnate*. His tantrums about "human rights" sound unbearably irrelevant against the backdrop of the cold-blooded beheading of captive Russian soldiers; of the ceaseless beating of the "slaves" (also captive Russian soldiers) by virtually everyone, including children; and of the severed fingers of a Jewish businessman tortured "according to the laws of *shariat*." John's beliefs seem to make him, in a sense, impotent; no wonder Margaret prefers Medvedev, who retains his machismo even while paralyzed. By contrast, on Aslan's side stands crude force, real and murderous power based on fear and blood. Ivan unambiguously chooses Aslan's "truth"—and with it, defeats Aslan. As Natal'ia Sirivlia remarks in her review of the film, "Ivan's 'art of war' is borrowed from the Chechens. His force is a mirror reflection of their barbaric power. This is not a conflict of two civilizations, rather a demonstration of their mutual similitude" (2002b, 212). True, it is amazing how nimbly Ivan, not long ago a slave himself, assumes the "master" role, and how much he enjoys thrashing and threatening his new slave, the shepherd.

However, the ease of this transformation can be explained by the fact that the absolutization of power and brute force similarly dominates under "peaceful" conditions—that is, the life Ivan knew before and knows after the war (as critics including Sirivlia, Bykov, and Slatina have observed). The strategy of control through terror is not foreign to his childhood friends, who have grown into mafia "muscle," nor to the Moscow bosses, indifferent to others' suffering, nor to the corrupt FSB officers, nor to Ivan's father, who extols war from his deathbed—"I'd stand up and go to the war" (*Schas by vstal i na voinu!*), nor to any of the other transient characters in the film. Even Ivan's affection for Medvedev—basically unmotivated—claims this justification: in the captain, Ivan senses a commanding force, and elevates it as the "rightful" power. Symptomatically, Margaret's fate is immaterial not only to Ivan but to the filmmakers as well—this part, played by one of the brightest stars of the post-Soviet cinema, is virtually *wordless*! There is only one answer for this absence of both interest and articulation: because Margaret is "weak," she can be only a victim and therefore must have nothing to say.

There is nothing novel or extraordinary in the "truth" of terror; it constitutes the norm of post-Soviet life. This is what, according to *Voina*, favorably differentiates Russia and Russians from the West and Westerners, who are seen as enfeebled by political correctness and other unnecessary restraints. Therefore, Ivan's seemingly *free* choice is not in fact very free—it is predetermined by the cultural logic of the post-Soviet lifestyle.

Ivan's opposition to John and Aslan, despite its "geopolitical" coloring, distinctly reflects the disposition of social forces *within* post-Soviet Russia. Aslan, the anti-Russia militant, mentions that he owns two restaurants in Moscow and that he "milks Russians like goats." Any obvious arguments in support of Chechen separatism—for example, the struggle for national independence—are never used by him. The film wants us to believe that Aslan and his ilk are not actually striving for independence, that they really do belong to, or rather *own*, Russia's politics and economics. Thus, Aslan is not depicted as a separatist, but as a new master of Russia—a "new Russian," so to speak—who has used terror and violence to hijack real power in the country.

In contrast, John is presented despite his "foreignness" as a typical (or rather, stereotypical) Soviet, and especially as a post-Soviet *intelligent*, able to mumble lofty locutions but radically unable to acclimate to coarse living conditions that do not match his culture-founded expectations. Symptomatically, he is victimized without end, helpless and hapless. It is quite illuminating how the Englishman collects his lover's ransom: we might imagine that, as an actor and a man of public reputation, he would first organize a fundraiser or at least apply for bank loans and humanitarian grants. This would be the strategy of a person with Western experience. Instead, John acts exactly as a Russian *intelligent* would: he pleads for government support, and when the officials withhold it, he sells his own property and tries to borrow money from friends and relatives.

Squarely between Aslan and John—the new master and the old intellectual—the film places Ivan, an iteration of the "simple man," another archetypal figure of Russian/Soviet cultural mythology. This archaic role is revitalized by Balabanov, as well as some other authors of the recent period, in the capacity of the *ultimate victim* of the post-Communist redistribution of power. The intelligentsia can incur only contempt from the perspective of the "simple man," who remembers how the *intelligenty* strove to undo the "stagnant" but comfortable order of late-Soviet life, and as a result lost all their own privileges and social status. The new masters of life, on the other hand, generate a mixed sensation of hatred and envy: the New Russians' dominion over the "simple man" is not secured by state or ideology and more resembles the looting of a cunning thief and impostor who has managed to plunder the last penny before the others even arrive. Their rule is regarded as accidental and definitely illegal—though it surpasses that of the old Soviet elite considerably.

This triad—the simple man, the New Russian, and the *intelligent*—does not replace but rather overlaps the symbolic opposition of Ivan (Russia) to both Aslan (the East) and John (the West). Each of these juxtapositions is rather worn and stereotypical, but their combination in *Voina* produces a handful of unexpected results.

The transformation of the ternary correlation (Russia—East—West) into a rigid polarity of terrorist power and weakness seems incompatible with postmodernist relativism and ambivalence. Instead, it appears to restore much more traditionalist and even, as Natal'ia Sirivlia suggests, precultural or at least pre-Christian paradigms. It is true that, in the Russian cultural tradition, war was never regarded as a justification for immorality. Following Tolstoy, until the best literary works of the former World War II "lieutenants" emerged in the 1960–70s, the conditions of war were treated as experimentation on the limits of humanity, with the conclusion that human transgression inevitably leads to human failure. In official Soviet literature, however, untempered cruelty toward enemies—external and internal alike—became a vital criterion for the hero's integration into the collective body of the Soviet people: "The villain [in Socialist Realism] is a symbolic victim who must be purged in order for the microcosm to be purified. But this is not a complete explanation of the function of villainy. The tale of villainy is subordinated primarily not to the aim of social cohesion but to the initiation ritual" (Clark 2000, 186). The notorious concepts of "proletarian humanism" (as opposed to "abstract humanism") and "class morality" (which justifies the physical elimination of class opponents, women and children included) were coined by the ideologues of the 1920s and '30s specifically to validate terror.

No wonder the war with the Chechens shown in *Voina* acquires the meaning of *class warfare*. Dmitry Bykov rightfully noted that "in terms of contents and aesthetics, ideology and morality, etc., Balabanov's film is a clone of Govorukhin's *Voroshilovskii strelok*" (Bykov 2002);[6] the latter directly depicts class warfare by antagonizing an old proletarian with a New Russian, a decadent intellectual, and a web of corrupt officials, along with their children, who are responsible for the rape of his angelic granddaughter (no doubt, another symbol of Russia). Hence *Voina* is not entirely "savage" in its "morality" — one may detect here the firm reinstitution of Socialist Realist models. Although the concrete meaning of the totalitarian ideology is drained, its "pure" logic of terror (preserved by the "memory" of forms, "memory" of discursive models) is resurrected intact.

However, in the Soviet tradition, warfare can be *either* class, against a resident threat, *or* patriotic, against external invaders. It cannot be both, since each type requires its own rhetoric: class warfare is justified with "proletarian internationalism" that is alleged to compensate for the destruction of traditional bonds (families, communities, and the entire society), while the patriotic war accentuates nationalism and even authorizes the rehabilitation of former class enemies, so long as they prove themselves true patriots. By combining these two models, Balabanov induces their mutual annihilation, observable in the inadvertently ambivalent position of Ivan, the hero, who, in agreement with epic archetypes, abhors ambivalence. The film consistently stresses his *similarity to the enemy*, Aslan (symbolizing Ivan's unsentimental force), and his *contradistinction from his ally*, John (symbolizing Ivan's rejection of moral reflections). Aslan, as previously mentioned, even applauds Ivan as a "mountain man" (*gorets*) — as one of his, Aslan's, crowd — while John is debased and humiliated, first driven to abandon his humanistic convictions and murder the unarmed Aslan, and then made responsible for Ivan's imprisonment because of his "honest" documentary.

---

[6] This parallel is also analyzed in Sitkovskii (2002, 31).

The mutual annihilation of opposite models, both rooted equally in Socialist Realism, accounts for Ivan's ultimate *emptiness*. Natal'ia Sirivlia argues that "Ivan does not have a world of his own. [. . .] It is no accident that the ideal Captain Medvedev has a broken spine. The hero's father is also broken—he drinks, and doesn't have any interest in life. [. . .] The only thing that remains for the hero is war, and in war he follows Aslan's lessons. It is amazing how easily he absorbs the enemy's wisdom" (2002b, 212–13). Dmitry Bykov interprets Ivan's intellectual vacancy as a product of the "ideological vacuum" of the 1990s. Tat'iana Moskvina's view is similar to Bykov's; however, she suggests a psychological rather than sociological interpretation for both Ivan's emptiness and his involvement in the war:

> What moves Ivan? Is he seeking profits? Not at all! He is driven by a far mightier engine—the absolute lack of knowledge about what to do with his life. [. . .] He needs nothing. He acts not "for the sake of," there is nothing addictive in his behavior, only emptiness, cold, power, a lone man, by his free will eliminating an "enemy." By the rules and without hatred. Calmly. With cold pleasure. (Moskvina 2002, 25)

Ivan holds neither convictions nor lasting interests. He hates the Chechens, but without zeal: if not for John's proposal, he would never return to Chechnya, not even for the captain, let alone for Margaret. In Balabanov's *Brat* diptych, the hero was driven by a "quasi-filial" sentiment based on the revisited "Great Family" concept. Only now, the Great Family is bonded not by common ideology but by the connotatively vague adhesive of "brotherhood"— semiracist, semi-gang-like (see Sirivlia 2002b). According to Susan Larsen, "Balabanov's stubbornly loyal brothers [. . .] offer images of heroes whose cultural authority and sexual magnetism derives from their allegiance to a masculine moral code that equates patriotism with filial and fraternal loyalty" (2003, 511). Next to these films, *Voina* is shocking for the happenstance nature of Ivan's motives. Balabanov certainly could have invoked some grand, lofty—or, in fact, worldly and pragmatic—ideology for Ivan, be it nationalism (Russians vs. Chechens), neocolonialism (culture vs. savagery), or, say, patriotism (the state vs. the separatists). Yet the director did not bundle Ivan's emptiness into any of the available ideological banners; apparently, he preferred to present Ivan's "way of the sword" as a paradoxical "nonideological" ideology—one that does not require rational justification or even snappy sloganeering, being attractive merely "by performance."

Ivan displays a *simulacrum of a hero*, and his identity transitions into a *simulative identity*. This transformation explains Ivan's allure and, so to speak, his innocence: nothing breaches him; nothing inspires him, with the exception of all scenarios of domination, battle, and violence, as the unswerving expressions of his nonideological vitality. Yet the same transformation invalidates the objective of the war for identity: the identity of the hero, forcefully composed through violence, is completely erased by this method—nothing is left, and we are invited to applaud and to pity . . . the victorious Zero!

Ivan's simulative identity, by the same token, revalidates the role of violence in the film. Bloodshed breaks through all the oppositions erected by Balabanov: Ivan mimics the Chechens who enslaved and abused him; John mimics Ivan, as well as the Chechens who raped Margaret. The film intentionally obstructs the factor of Russian imperialist aggression (the devastation of Grozny, the concentration camps, the "cleansing" operations, and so on) that triggered this process of violent "mimetic desire." Yet even this substitution—not obvious to the unprepared, including foreign audiences—does not alter the general impression that *Voina* imparts. The movie drives the viewer to a point where the main measure of distinction between Ivan, John, and Aslan becomes quantitative rather than qualitative: the number of people each has killed. Violence becomes the common denominator, uniting all the "members" of the contradictory "geopolitical" as well as "class" oppositions. Mutual butchery serves as the sole viable basis for a collective identity, an identity that necessarily implies the endless metamorphoses of victim into victimizer and vice versa, as René Girard suggests. A joint identity founded on aggression obliterates all the constitutive differences between East and West as well as those between the "man of culture" (John), the "man of power"

(Aslan), and the "simple man" (Ivan). Thus, the entire film proffers itself as a self-sufficient *ritual of violence*, striving to involve the viewer in its sacral carnage.[7]

This is war, Balabanov's fans would argue; but there is a great difference between war as a human tragedy and war as ritualized and poeticized violence. Despite the naturalism in its presentation of killing and torture, *Voina* leans toward the latter denotation—because the authors do not even attempt to seek an alternative to war, because war is presented as a social norm and, moreover, as a norm of socialization.

It is easy to argue that the poetry of violence in *Voina* is derivative of the models of Socialist Realism, which apparently preserve totalitarian impressions despite "deideologization." However, analysis of the picture reveals that, paradoxically, the accentuated binaries originating in these models in fact further enshroud the "fuzzy logic" of the film. The moral righteousness of the protagonist is undermined by his affect of hollowness and simulation. The hero's unshaken certainty thornily intertwines with the moral ambivalence of his actions. His infallibility counters the radical absence of any graspable objective. Underneath, the "truth" harbors naked violence, presented as supreme, if divine, "force."

---

[7] This, probably, explains Balabanov's enthrallment with the force, violence, and pathos of war as "a true man's work," as mentioned in several reviews of the film. For example, "You die today, and I'll die tomorrow. You play by the rules, and I won't. I can do everything, and you can do nothing. The one who has the power is the right one (hence, might makes right, and vice versa). This simple criminal code is absorbed by everyone during their teenage years. Alexei Balabanov and all his characters serve as mouthpieces for these so-called ethics. There is no need to confuse them with patriotism, war, and other policies. [. . .] [Balabanov's heroes] kill because they enjoy killing and don't enjoy anything else. They enjoy other people's fear and their own power" (Bykov 2003a). Also, "If in the earlier films Balabanov declared that 'the force is in the truth,' now he believes that 'war makes a man out of a boy, and man (*muzhik*) is power.' [. . .] So, is there truth in war? Aleksei Balabanov is a true artist, almost impeccable from a professional standpoint; he plays on popular xenophobia, provokes the viewer. [. . .] Balabanov's cinema is alarming, because the director abhors pacifism, his films push the viewer not to save a friend, but to kill a foe" (Slatina 2002, 73).

These metamorphoses hark back to the notion of postmodernist deconstruction, defined by its progenitor as "the whole theory of the structural necessity of abyss" (Derrida 1990). In actuality, *Voina* reveals vacuity, chaos, and disorder beneath all the structures of order, opposition, and organization it engages, be they geopolitical opposition or the post-Soviet social triangle, class competition, or patriotic warfare.

Yet this deconstruction of the neototalitarian premise occurs unwittingly—*despite* the author's best intentions! Perhaps it happens exactly because the film's creators, aiming to attract the widest congregation of viewers, have cast their nets in all directions and appropriated as many traditional cultural models as possible, Socialist Realist as well as classical. Each of these models, taken individually, invokes heroic archetypes, elevating the hero and humiliating his enemies; all together, they produce mutual annihilation.

It is important to emphasize, though, that the effect of the inadvertent deconstruction that *Voina* and other Post-Soc films undertake is not necessarily ripe for direct emotional perception and can be revealed only in the light of thorough analysis. The furtive and involuntary nature of the dissection separates Post-Soc from postmodernism. More specifically, none of these works implies any desire to question the protagonist's, let alone the author's, "truth." Post-Soc, in fact, *simulates* postmodernism by imposing postmodernist stylization, and even nostalgia, on the viewer, while demonstratively rejecting the postmodernist critique of authoritative discourses and "truth" of any kind.

Paradoxically, the place of Post-Soc between Socialist Realism and postmodernism, without actually belonging to either of these models, happens to be quite comfortable and profitable for those who aligned their careers with this trend. It is much harder, I would say, to be a hard-core conservative (like Prokhanov) abhorred by all the liberals, or a radical experimentalist (like Sorokin) scorned by all the conservatives. Post-Soc appeals to the intellectual public with its professionalism and its ability to employ select up-to-date postmodernist devices and, simultaneously, to the mass public, touched by the reminiscences of totalitarian—more generally, traditionalist—aesthetics.

To some extent, the phenomenon of Post-Soc serves as a microcosmic metaphor for the whole cultural situation in Putin's Russia, whose chief dilemma is not the blending of modern and postmodern flavors, but the fact that this mixture is not introspectively addressed, let alone interpreted as such. The lack of reflection in this case justifies intellectual cynicism when the opposite strategies (modern or postmodern) are used on demand— defined, in turn, by the rationale of commercial or political needs.

WAR AS THE FAMILY VALUE: *MY STEPBROTHER FRANKENSTEIN* BY VALERY TODOROVSKY

The symbiosis of the theme of war with the representation of fatherhood in Soviet and post-Soviet culture is persistent but not logically self-evident. In the wake of such films of the 1960s as *Sud'ba cheloveka* (*Destiny of a Man*, 1959, dir. Sergei Bondarchuk), *Kogda derev'ia byli bol'shimi* (*When the Trees Were Tall*, 1961, dir. Lev Kulidzhanov), *Mir vkhodiashchemu* (*Peace to Him Who Enters*, 1961, dir. Aleksandr Alov and Vladimir Naumov), and *Otets soldata* (*Father of a Soldier*, 1965, dir. Rezo Chkheidze), the understanding of the Great Patriotic War as a backdrop in which to beatify the father figure was solidified in Soviet culture. All these and many similar movies and books arose during the period of the Thaw, which had, on the one hand, deposed the supreme patriarchal authority of Stalin and commenced the task of scouring its cultural vestiges, yet, on the other hand, affirmed the nation's victory in World War II as the most important if not the sole legitimization of the Soviet regime. Invoking the valorous war as the cornerstone of paternalistic authority, feature film directors of the sixties strove to replace the crumpled and debunked father figure of Stalin with a markedly less godlike image of the nuclear father and thus, in the same stroke, marshaled the totalitarian mythology of the war into a more democratic and humane mythology of the collective national suffering that was instigated by the war.

Although the war significantly depleted the Soviet male population and inevitably transferred to women the principal responsibility for familial well-being, war films of the 1960s unanimously neglected to undermine or even to question patriarchal authority, and, moreover, rarely ventured to examine the correlation between the war and women's changing social roles.[1] It is well known that the core of totalitarian culture was shaped by the prioritization of society's interests over the interests of the nuclear family as well as by the mandatory sacrifice of individual values for the sake of collectivist ideologies. In contrast, the sixties' reorientation from societal "fathers" to private father-child relationships reflected the comprehensive problematization of the entire system of Soviet values, a problematization that was generally indicative of the Thaw-era culture. Yet despite the anti-Stalinist ideology of the aforementioned films, the connection drawn in them between the war and its culture of violence and suffering with the symbolic capital of the father(ing) was merely a manner of rewriting Stalinist totalitarian mythologies. As Aleksandr Prokhorov argues, "The Thaw culture has inherited from Stalinism a family trope—as a symbolic image of the Soviet society, and a war trope—as the symbolic image of this society's main form of existence" (2007, 152). In Thaw-era cinema, the elementary structure of the totalitarian Great Family was preserved in the realm of the nuclear family—it was domesticated and divested of imperial grandeur, but it at least maintained, and arguably increased, its sacredness.

Thus, the war theme tilled a unique discursive field in the culture of the 1960s–80s, one in which the official state and alternative liberal discourses frequently merged, or at least tolerated one another. The mythos of the war—invariably held as the triumphal equinox of patriotism in which the interests of the state were no different

---

[1] Symptomatically, the texts that demonstrate how the war undermined and problematized the father's role in the family and society—for instance, Andrei Platonov's magnificent short story "Vozvrashchenie" ("The Return," 1946)—were consistently marginalized. Among these marginalized exceptions, the films *Kryl'ia* (*Wings*, 1966, dir. Larisa Shepit'ko) and *Dikii med* (*Wild Honey*, 1966, dir. Vladimir Chebotarev; based on the eponymous novel by Leonid Aiskii) should also be mentioned.

from the interests of an individual or a single family—allowed the perpetuation of a balance, however fragile, between society and the individual of post-Stalinist Soviet culture. Moreover, the association of war themes with the father figure, or more precisely with the idealization of patriarchal values and corresponding models of social order, constituted the foundation of this poise.

The mythology of the Great Patriotic War not only retained its symbolic currency into the post-Soviet period but has been richly reinforced during the years of Vladimir Putin's presidency. Cultural historian and sociologist Lev Gudkov, having analyzed numerous poll data from VTsIOM (the All-Russia Center for the Study of Public Opinion), argues that since 1995 and up to the present, "An extremely structured social attitude towards the war is incarnated and consolidated in the main symbol that integrates the nation: victory in the war, victory in the Great Patriotic War. In the opinion of Russia's inhabitants, this is the most important event in their history; it is the basic image of national consciousness. No other event compares with it" (Gudkov 2005, 4). Gudkov convincingly suggests that the post-Soviet perception of the war, notwithstanding the newfound access to a wealth of formerly banned historical sources, still respires all the key features of the Soviet myth of the Great Patriotic War:

- the virtual repression of all traumatic aspects of the war and postwar experience (i.e., the Holocaust, the coercive labor, the chronic hunger and poverty, the ethnic repressions, etc.), combined with an emphasis on ecstatic victory celebrations;

- xenophobic overtones in the war mythos—victory in the war serves as proof of the superiority of Russia and Russians over the entire world: "Russians are not willing to share their triumph with anyone else in the world. Sixty-seventy percent of those surveyed [in 2003] believe that the USSR could have won the war even without the help of the allies. Moreover, as Russian nationalism is intensifying and the war is receding further into the past, it has gradually begun to be integrated into the traditional idea of Russia's 'mission' and its 'rivalry with the West'" (Gudkov 2005, 7);

- "a number of unpleasant facts [. . .] repressed from mass consciousness: the aggressive nature of Soviet regime, Communist militarism and expansionism [. . .] the fact that World War II began with a joint attack of Hitler's Germany and the Soviet Union; the human, social, economic, and metaphysical cost of war . . ." (ibid., 8);
- the justification of an extremely low valuation of human life: "The idea that mass losses were inevitable and that millions of victims somehow 'are unavoidable' are a constituent element of the general semantic complex of national exploits and general heroism. [. . .] Russians' mass consciousness is unable to imagine a war where the military leaders would aim to save the lives of their subordinates at any cost" (ibid., 10);
- the legitimization of "people's view of themselves as victims of aggression" (ibid., 9), which, Gudkov further notes, "was also expressed in a readiness to justify (but not to support!) any aggressive or repressive state police against other countries or territories withstanding the USSR or Russia" (ibid.), ranging from Hungary in 1956 and Czechoslovakia in 1968 to Afghanistan in 1979 and Chechnya in the '90s and 2000s.

Bolstered by lavish jubilee celebrations of the victory in 2000 and particularly in 2005, and, moreover, fueled by the ceaseless media bashing of the Baltic countries and former Soviet satellites (Poland especially) that allegedly overslaughed the memory of Soviet "liberators" for the glorification of the Nazis, the Great Patriotic War myth in the twenty-first century, as Gudkov demonstrates, serves as the main basis for negative self-identification ("we" vs. "them"), which, in turn, emerges as the formative impetus for the mainstream of post-Soviet culture: "This confidence [in being constantly victimized by 'enemies'] was routinized in an extramoral, socially primitive, archaic, almost tribal distinction between 'our people' and 'not our people' as a basis for social solidarity" (2005, 9). It naturally follows that today "the repression of the war [myth] keeps spawning state-sponsored aggression—the Chechen war and the restoration of the repressive regime" (11). Furthermore, the potency of the war myth elevates the wartime condition of normalized violence to "a norm of symbolic self-identity" (10): of present-day Russian citizens, 77 percent share the conviction that "Russians display their national character and mental qualities at the fullest in times of crisis, trial, and war [. . .] rather than in calm and happy times" (ibid.). These phenomena certainly help to illustrate the ties between Great Patriotic War mythology and the father figure as the symbolic reification of the "very principle of a 'vertical' construction of society, a mobilization, command-hierarchical model of social order" (11).

In this context, exceptional significance befalls the engagements of contemporary Russian culture that problematize and deconstruct the symbiosis between the war myth and the myth of the patriarchal authority. *Moi svodnyi brat Frankenshtein* (*My Stepbrother Frankenstein*, 2004)[2] by Valery Todorovsky (b. 1962) exemplifies the cinematic breed of this rare species.[3] Todorovsky's film won three honors, including the Grand Prix, at the Kinotavr film festival in Sochi, was recognized as the best film of the Russian program at the Moscow Film Festival, and received the FIPRESCI award at Karlovy Vary

[2] Produced by Prior-Film and Rekun TV, producer Leonid Iarmol'nik, director of photography Sergei Mikhal'chuk, production designer Vladimir Gudlin, music by Aleksei Aigi.

[3] Another important example is *Svoi* (*Our Own*, 2004) by the director Dmitrii Meskhiev and the famed screenwriter Valentin Chernykh. In this film, which is situated in the first months of the war, the opposition between "us" and "them" emerges as constantly lingering and problematic. The complex relationships between the newcomers and their host, a father figure, reveal the dialectics of the kinship and warlike hostility between the members of the "social" family. The father in Meskhiev's film manages to save his family and create social solidarity between those who are "ours" by subverting the very foundations of the stereotypical Soviet requirements for "our man": the father turns out to be a former kulak, who supposedly returned illegally to his native village from exile, and is the German-appointed *starosta* (elder) of the village. However, the film does not entirely deconstruct the Soviet myth of the "war father"; rather, *Svoi* releases it from Soviet stereotypes while preserving the mechanism of elevating the "vertical" patriarchal authority in the war setting. The father, though he embodies the antipode of the Soviet father figure, preserves a similar authority to distinguish between right and wrong, to define who is "ours" and who is the "enemy," although his worldview has nothing to do with Soviet ideological or even nationalist systems. If *Svoi* inverts the Soviet myth of "father vis-à-vis war," Todorovsky's film presents a radical deconstruction of this foundational archetype.

as well as several other prizes at various European film festivals (Rotterdam, Honfleur, Lecce). The movie's originality is especially conspicuous against the backdrop of such reincarnations of Socialist Realist representation of the war as Nikolai Lebedev's *Zvezda* (*Star*, 2000) and also particularly striking in contrast to popular portrayals of the war mythology's defense of nationalist and neo-imperialist ideologies such as Aleksei Balabanov's *Voina* (*War*, 2002) and Fedor Bondarchuk's *Deviataia rota* (*The Ninth Company*, 2005). Todorovsky's film, based on an original screenplay by Gennadii Ostrovskii (b. 1960), depicts the invasion of a physically and emotionally maimed Chechen War veteran, Pavlik Zakharov (Daniil Spivakovskii), into the family of his alleged father, former Moscow physicist Iulik Krymov (Leonid Iarmol'nik, also the producer of the film), who previously had not known of his son's existence.

As follows from the picture's title (and numerous textual signals), Todorovsky proposes a subversion of the Dr. Frankenstein story; it is not by accident that Todorovsky directly quotes the 1931 classic *Frankenstein*, directed by James Whale and with Boris Karloff as the Monster. *Moi svodnyi brat* seems to place responsibility for the monstrosity—in this case a paranoid yet goodwilled and forgiving son—only on the father's shoulders and, in a broader sense, on the conscience of the contemporary liberal intelligentsia, who have safely separated themselves from the violence and terror of the post-Soviet period. According to Todorovsky's own description, there is more than one guilty party here:

> This is a story that has no way out. Everybody in it is right and guilty at the same time. This is a story about father and son, as well as about society, and the desperate situation that we are all in. It's a story about the war. Not any particular war, but war in general. The war that's around us. (Khoroshilova 2004)

However, despite the political angle, *Moi svodnyi brat Frankenshtein* escapes definition as a political film since it does not offer any clear answers to political questions and, moreover, avoids laying solitary and conclusive blame, whether it be on the intelligentsia, the authorities, soldiers, officers, or any other isolated group. On the contrary, the movie unfolds in an atmosphere of permanent problematization, in which any assumption or interpretation that the viewer might take for granted is reversed in the next scene. This ambiance of uncertainty is conjured by the nervous musical score by Aleksei Aigi as well as by the style of acting—psychologically precise, yet devoid of the melodramatic theatricality so typical of Russian actors. Furthermore, one can argue that Todorovsky's film transmediates to the screen the multivoiced, meditative, and at the same time intellectually charged and historically explosive intonation of Iurii Trifonov's prose. The most important intelligentsia writer of the so-called stagnation period of the 1970s and early '80s, Trifonov relentlessly inquired in his novels about the hidden underpinnings and the historical and moral *uncanny* (*Unheimlich*)—associated with Stalinist terror—of the comfortable intelligentsia's life during the period of stagnation. In *Moi svodnyi brat Frankenshtein*, Todorovsky reopens this investigation in the context of the present, post-Soviet stagnation.

To a cushy Moscow home arrives an abandoned son, dressed in tattered clothing, his face disfigured by terrible scars and an ominous black patch over his missing eye. He is the foreboding shadow of a war that the majority prefer to forget, at least as long as it does not affect their lives. Daniil Spivakovskii's stunning portrayal of this all-but-orphaned son, Pavlik Zakharov, is perhaps one of the strongest examples of the post-Soviet uncanny. It is the war, or in other words, normalized and routinized violence, that epitomizes the ultimate uncanny of contemporary Russia, and especially of the Muscovite lifestyle. Pavlik's jarring appearance in the life of the Krymovs tears down the barrier that keeps war at a distance from the comfortable "stabilization" of the 2000s. Pavlik naturally brings destabilization and eventually death into his newly adopted family. In the film's finale, he takes his relatives hostage, sincerely believing that by doing so he is saving them from pervasive, invisible peril; during the subsequent police "rescue" operation, he is killed.

In Freud's interpretation, the "uncanny is in reality nothing new or alien, but something which is familiar and old-established in the mind and which has become alienated from it only through the process of repression" (Freud 1955, 241). Specifying the most typical meanings of the "repressed familiar," Freud mentions various manifestations of death (including motifs of the double, the automaton, and the mask), as well as fear of castration (frequently associated with images of animated severed limbs and heads). All these themes are recognizable in the representation of Pavlik and are augmented by the parallels with Mary Shelley's monster. Julia Kristeva argues that Freud's vision of the uncanny "teaches us to detect foreignness in ourselves": while it "creeps into the tranquility of reason itself and, without being restricted to madness, beauty, or faith anymore than to ethnicity or race, irrigates our very speaking being. [. . .] Henceforth, we know that we are foreigners to ourselves, and it is with the help of that sole support that we can attempt to live with others" (1991, 170). Thus, any textual presence of the uncanny inadvertently reflects the divisions and doublings of cultural/societal identity and, therefore, undermines the dominant societal/cultural mythos, usually promoting global and centripetal, rather than local and decentering, patterns of identity. The detection of the uncanny in the war-sanctioned father-son relationship defines the novelty of *Moi svodnyi brat Frankenshtein* and not only indicates the split within the identity of the intelligentsia but also undermines both the patriarchal mythology and the resurrected social mythology of the war as "a norm of symbolic self-identity" (Gudkov 2005, 9).

War and Peace: The Mimicry of Othering

Moi svodnyi brat Frankenshtein is reminiscent of numerous films, mostly American, that examine the posttraumatic stress suffered by Vietnam veterans—films such as *The Deer Hunter* (1978, dir. Michael Cimino) or even *Rambo: First Blood* (1982, dir. Ted Kotcheff). In Todorovsky's picture we can easily behold society's indifference to the needs of a physically and emotionally disfigured veteran. An official from the Ministry of Defense utterly refuses to accept any responsibility for Pavlik's wounds, declaring him "healthy" so long as he does not wet his bed. Even the empathetic doctor at the military hospital says that she has a queue of maimed veterans just like Pavlik that could stretch from the hospital to the defense ministry, and only to the tune of $20,000 can she treat Pavlik earlier than scheduled.

The film's posttraumatic discourse is further manifested in the immense gap between the Krymovs' peaceful middle-class lifestyle and Pavlik's horrific and agitated perception of reality through the prism of his nightmarish war experience. As Iulik laments, "For him, everybody is the enemy." Pavlik's own actions corroborate his father's observation: he is on permanent alert, constantly standing guard, scanning for "spooks," and not thinking twice before attacking "suspects." "They think that we are all dead, but there are three of us left," he confesses to his former commander, Timur Kurbatovich (brilliantly played by Sergei Garmash). "They" are the "spooks," or *dukhi* (ghosts, spirits)—the army argot first used in the Afghanistan campaign for "dushmans" or mujahideen, which also refers to first-year recruits in the Russian army. The way Pavlik uses this epithet makes it obvious that he almost automatically presumes the hidden enemy to appear in the ethnic Other: in one scene he nervously and at length eyes a non-Slavic fruit seller; in another, he beats up a "black-assed" stranger so brutally that he is arrested by the police, albeit only for a short while; and throughout the film, he suspects the neighbor's boyfriend of being a spook and even mistrusts the Krymovs' best friends when they come to a dinner party ("They could have poisoned your drink!").[4]

[4] The "posttraumatic" interpretation is supported by such sophisticated viewers of the film as the critic and film director Oleg Kovalov and the writer Tatiana Tolstaya: "Not raising his voice and rendering a somewhat 'private' story, Todorovsky demonstrates how the hypocritical and indifferent society betrays its children—at first transforming them into physical and moral freaks, and then contemptuously turning away from them. [. . .] This film is akin to Polish films of 'moral anxiety,' which are usually based on the seemingly impassive depiction of 'family chronicles.' The most conscientious and courageous socially engaged statement in the cinema of the recent years . . ." (Kovalov in "*Seansu* otvechaiut. . ." 2005). "Neither a good and decent Moscow bourgeois family, their circle, nor even society want to take responsibility for boys whom they themselves send every year to learn how to kill—for our security, what else for? You are the warrior, sonny, be proud of it. You are all covered in blood, freak, don't dare to approach us. The elder son [Pavlik] is a top graduate of this school, an inhabitant of the world of shadows, who had elevated to the state of absurdity a natural archaic logic of

We might relate all these demented suspicions and paranoias to Pavlik's dream of obtaining a diamond eye to replace his lost organ, which ultimately becomes a symbol for the distorted optics that haunt him. Pavlik himself, however, believes his point of view to be far from distorted—superior, in fact, or even transcendental. A definitive military etiology of this phantasmal perception may be inferred from the fact that only his war commander can share his dream, while Iulik and his wife Rita (Elena Iakovleva) simply shrug in embarrassment.[5]

However, unlike the Vietnam veterans depicted in American film of the 1970s, Pavlik does not feel alienated upon his return. Quite the opposite, when he joins Iulik's other son Egor (Artem Shalimov) to watch *Frankenstein*—which Egor rented as a joke at the expense of his long-lost stepbrother—Pavlik apparently does not recognize himself in the Monster, "kind but unloved," and, moreover, does not sense the hint of compassion directed at Karloff's tragic fiend, and by extension at Pavlik. "Who could love such a guy!" he exclaims with poise. Rather than feeling estranged and reviled, Pavlik firmly believes that once he has secured his diamond eye, all women will fall irretrievably in love with him. Never lost or disoriented in his composure, he operates coolly and calmly on the faith that he alone knows the truth and, therefore, must protect his newfound family from dangers they are unable to perceive.

It is worth noting that several critics have detected in Todorovsky's film a polemical response to Aleksei Balabanov's depiction of another war veteran: the xenophobic and nationalist icon of the post-Soviet generation, Danila Bagrov (Sergei Bodrov Jr.) of *Brat* (*Brother*, 1997) and especially *Brat 2* (*Brother 2*, 2000). As Iurii

---

any society: ours are good, aliens are bad. Defend your own kind until your last breath; kill the others until they will kill you. A defender crazed in his defense..." (Tolstaya, ibid.).

[5] This motif can be also interpreted as an indirect reference to the Monster from Whale's *Frankenstein*. As Rick Worland vividly recounts in his analysis of the film, "A drawing of the monster's eyes radiating beams of light as clawlike hands stretch toward the viewer dissolves into a field of slowly circling eyes, suggesting at once the Monster's menace as well as its own terror of the existence it beholds" (2007, 162).

Gladil'shchikov argues, "In my view, *Moi svodnyi brat Frankenshtein* can be adequately understood only as an intentional polemics with Aleksei Balabanov's film *Brat*, according to which the Chechnya war generates its own heroes who are invisible to the world, superfluous in it, but because of this no less real" (*"Seansu* otvechaiut. . ." 2005). "In fact, *Moi svodnyi brat Frankenshtein* refurbishes the plot of *Brat*, and revamps its ideology," claims Andrei Plakhov, adding, "On the material of the war in the Caucasus Balabanov creates something like a tragic Western with a lone hero. Todorovsky, on the contrary, transforms the patriotic myth of the country, of brothers and sisters, into a farce" (ibid.). Balabanov presents his war veteran as the nation's defender from the insults and offenses of various Others, ranging from Chechens to Americans, and paints his hero as the prophet of "Russian truth" and the living proof of Russian (spiritual!) superiority over the world. Todorovsky's Pavlik, by contrast, emerges not as a hero of our time but rather as its ultimate victim; and the film portrays his aggression toward the universal Other not as a mission, but as a symptom of clinical paranoia.

Nonetheless, there is method in Pavlik's madness. While perceiving the bulk of humanity as hostile and conspiratorial Others, he exempts from this roster of suspects those whom he designates as "his own." This circle of relief includes not only former comrades-in-arms such as Kurbatovich and the emotionally disturbed lieutenant housed at the military mental institution, to whom Pavlik gives helpful advice based on their comparable hallucinations, but also the members of his new family. Considering Pavlik's paranoia, it is surprising how readily he forgives his father, not only for his inceptive abandonment but also after fresh betrayals. For instance, at the train station Iulik pretends not to recognize his son; he does not invite him into his home until Rita, seeing that the soldier has been waiting by their door, goads her husband to bring the boy inside; he continually refuses to acknowledge their kinship; and finally (following his wife's demand that he get rid of the "monster"), he drives Pavlik out into the middle of nowhere and deserts him like an unwanted dog. Conceivably, Pavlik interprets his father's various slights as tests of loyalty, or perhaps he subconsciously censors the notion of possible *dis*loyalty from his "kin." In the same vein, when Pavlik is attacked by Egor's friends at Egor's behest, he perceives the assault as a provocation dealt by the Others, not as isolated bullying instigated by his brother: "They wanted to set me against you [*Menia na tebia razvesti khoteli*]. But I'm not who they think I am. . . . I'll cover for you."

The critic Viktor Matizen reminds us that the name of Todorovsky's protagonist is associated "not only with Saul/Paul but also with the three cult heroes of Soviet culture: Pavlik Morozov, Pavel Vlasov, and Pavel Korchagin" ("*Seansu* otvechaiut. . ." 2005). The parallels with, or counterpoints to, Pavlik Morozov and Pavel Korchagin are especially telling. For one, Todorovsky's Pavlik vividly contrasts with Morozov, the thirteen-year-old who garnered Soviet adulation after betraying his father for the sake of the "Great Family": in *Moi svodnyi brat*, Pavlik Zakharov considers blood kinship an absolute value, and his every action is explicitly committed for the safety of his father's family (as he understands it, of course). Meanwhile, the likenesses between the movie's hero and Pavel Korchagin are not limited to the former's loss of an eye in the war and the latter's mutilation and blinding as a result of his dedicated service to the Revolution: the Soviet cult of Korchagin, as a modern martyr cementing the self-sacrificial ethics of the Great Family, laid the foundation for the Stalinist cultural concept of "chosen sons," who, in recognition of their extraordinary service, were admitted to the "higher order of reality" (Clark 2000, 126–55). Thus, in a way, Pavlik Zakharov tries to mold his nuclear (if estranged) kin into a Great Family and attempts to restructure society into a circle of "proven [blood-related or war-tested] ours," thereby marrying the Soviet utopia to post-Soviet xenophobia.

It is significant that Pavlik includes in his Great Family his war buddy Vasia Tobolkin, for whom he patiently waits at the railway station, having repressed the friend's martyr-like death before his own eyes. This detail demonstrates that Pavlik's utopia can be built only in proximity to the land of death, since it necessitates a war with the entire world of the Others. It is quite logical, then, that when Pavlik approaches the realization of his utopia in the film's finale, his master plan finds its ultimate fulfillment in the abduction of his newfound brother and sister, which, in turn, leads to a hostage situation ending in Pavlik's own death.

If the war trauma is to be held responsible for Pavlik's distorted worldview, then the essential question arises: Why do his reactions so often and hauntingly mimic the attitudes of the so-called peaceful Muscovites? For instance, the cop who arrests Pavlik for assaulting a non-Slav cheerfully releases him to Iulik and assures the father, despite the victim's protests, that no charges will be filed against Pavlik: "Your son did right. Should fuckin' beat them. But by the book, right? [*Syn u tebia molodets. Voobshche-to pizdit' ikh nado. No po zakonu.*]"

The mirroring between Pavlik and other characters in the film becomes especially obvious in the sequence that begins with Pavlik leering intently at the "suspicious" fruit vendor. Immediately following is the ambush organized by Egor and carried out by his friends, who between blows quite literally voice the same aggressive formulas of intolerance—"Hey, freak! Get out of here! We're warning you: Don't you ever come here again! Move out of here!"—that are typically used against ethnic Others, not unlike the fruit man in the preceding scene. At the same time, Spivakovskii's physical acting during the melee somewhat imitates Boris Karloff's performance as the Monster, and Pavlik's hysterical feat of turning the tables, with strings of saliva dripping from his mouth onto the faces of his frightened and battered assailants, makes the supposed hero look really rather horrifying. This sequence, along with other scenes in *Moi svodnyi brat Frankenshtein*, suggests that, while the Krymov family and friends are appalled and alarmed by Pavlik and his actions, these representatives of the allegedly refined and liberal intelligentsia nonetheless abide by the same principle of othering, thereby making the "prodigal son" a *true* monster. If anything, they are only differentiated from Pavlik by their lack of consistency.

Two firm, antithetical attitudes toward Pavlik are embodied in the Krymovs' children, Egor and Ania. Ania (Marianna Il'ina) immediately embraces the scarred veteran as her brother, and everything about him that others perceive as strange and forbidding she finds marvelous. Even Pavlik's phantom diamond eye occupies a place in her wonder-tale narrative about a brother who never sleeps at night. She is not in the least afraid of Pavlik, as is evident in the scene where her parents frantically search for her at the railway station, fearing that she has been abducted by her stepbrother, but discover her cheerfully hopping around Pavlik and discussing the comparative features of different prosthetic eyes; the contrast between their panic and her playfulness is tremendously puissant.

Contrarily, Egor—whose name alludes to Igor, the hunchback and the Monster's only friend in *Son of Frankenstein* (1939, dir. Rowland V. Lee), the second sequel to Whale's classic, and later in Mel Brooks's spoof *Young Frankenstein* (1974)—immediately snubs Pavlik as an Other. Following Dr. Astrov's principle that "everything in a man should be beautiful," which he ironically quotes during the film's opening scene, the fifteen-year-old boy detests his disfigured, provincial, and menacing stepbrother so greatly that he invites his friends to watch the *Frankenstein* movie and make fun of the Monster's real-life double. Furthermore, he lobbies his father to "make Pavlik go away," and when his plea is ignored, demands that Pavlik be beaten, thereby, ironically, actualizing Pavlik's paranoid fears. Notably, it is Egor's perspective that is reflected in the film's title, which suggests that this position is representative not for his character alone but for the entire future generation as well (and, perhaps, the viewers too).

The parents, Iulik and Rita, vacillate between these two stances of rejection and acceptance. Iulik, at first striving to deny Pavlik's presence, gradually develops a sense of responsibility for his abandoned son as the film progresses. The acme of his attachment to the boy is hit during the scene set in the mental institution to which Iulik, prompted by Rita, attempts to have Pavlik admitted; at the last moment, he cannot bring himself to leave his son in such a "house of grief." Yet Iulik's sense of paternal duty and pity for Pavlik is affixed to his concurrent desire to permanently sever his life from that of his socially and emotionally errant child, which accounts for the father's repeated abandonment of Pavlik—most notably in the sequence on the isolated roadside, where, without explanation, he hands the bewildered youth a few rubles and drives off. Of course, Pavlik reappears in no time at all, as the uncanny always does.

A reverse trajectory marks Rita's response to her stepson's "invasion." At the outset, Rita shows Pavlik more compassion than does her husband. It is she who persuades (that is, forces) Iulik to allow the boy into their house, she who urges Iulik to care for him. She becomes "maternal," in a sense, but that maternal affection is challenged when she beholds the danger to her biological children, posed by a child who "belongs" to another woman and for whom she can act only as a surrogate mother. Rita's shift from amity to fear is dramatically colored by her dream, in which she watches Pavlik tearing apart Egor's eye. When she realizes the depth of Pavlik's trauma, she herself develops a paranoid dread of him as the Other who can and inevitably will hurt her children.

Rita's change of heart concerning Pavlik is noteworthy in several respects. First, despite the fact that the very organization of the Krymovs' family (a typical post-Soviet post-intelligentsia family) presents a striking inversion of the patriarchal family roles, Pavlik's appearance in the Krymovs' household reinstates patriarchal stereotypes not only by emasculating Iulik but also by forcing Rita back into "maternal" and "domestic" roles: with Pavlik around, Rita cannot help but invest all her energy in protecting her children from the invader, paying only minimal and rather mechanical mind to running her real-estate business.

Second, while performing these traditional gender roles, Rita is nevertheless forced to break with the supreme value of the patriarchal family: a wife's respect for and subordination to her husband. Her blood maternity (and blood is a hot-button issue in the film) masculinizes her; a threat to her own children galvanizes Rita into the tough head-of-household woman who commands her husband to eject Pavlik—again, a fascinating blend of "issuing orders" to the male yet being unable to act on them herself. Following the party scene, Rita directly and aggressively, with physical and verbal violence, assaults Iulik's budding devotion to his newly recovered son. In the post-party spat, Rita undermines Iulik as a father ("You cannot protect your own family!") and jeers at his social and professional failure ("Cannot write even a miserable article! Some great scientist!"). Iulik cannot defend himself rationally and employs the language of violence, hitting and shoving Rita in response to her attack. Although in the next scene the heroes are reconciled—apparently united by something more important than patriarchal values—the scandalous squabble does not wane in significance. It illuminates that patriarchal gender roles, summoned by the "habitus" of war (epitomized, in turn, by Pavlik), can only conflict with each other, thus demonstrating the incompatibility of patriarchal models with the complexity of the present—indicative of the entire post-Soviet society as a "post-patriarchal" social family.

It is significant that the film's optics largely favor Iulik and his family's perception of Pavlik rather than explore and divulge Pavlik's vision of the world. From the soldier's arrival at the railway station, he is consistently rendered by the camera as a monstrosity—that is, as the Other. His forbidding visage encourages us as bystanders to align either with Rita's hostility or with Iulik's hesitation. By this means, the movie raises a powerful provocation: since its logic reveals the mirroring of Pavlik's xenophobia in the Krymovs' perception of him as Other, the ultimate effect of the film lies in the viewers' recognition of the fact that we also desire to insulate ourselves from "my stepbrother Frankenstein," who manifests *our* uncanny.

In keeping with Kristeva's contention that the uncanny "teaches us to detect foreignness in ourselves," Pavlik's presence reveals xenophobic and paranoid attitudes toward the Other as the "foreignness" hidden deep inside the mind-set of the polite and caring intelligentsia. Veiled and inconsistent at first, this foreignness increasingly turns vigorous, aggravated by stressful conditions, until these othering predilections finally envelop not only the Krymovs but also us, the audience.

What Is to Be Done? The Inversion of Fathering and the Language of Violence

"Pavlik says that he always knew that you'd find him," Rita tells Iulik. The irony of her statement is double layered. To begin with, this is a neatly excavated quote from Mikhail Sholokhov's *Sud'ba cheloveka* (and also from the film of the same title by Sergei

Bondarchuk). In the original, the words are spoken by the orphan Vaniushka when Andrei Sokolov, a Great Patriotic War veteran who has lost his family, identifies him as his son. In Todorovsky's film, however, the line resurrects this father-war narrative only to subvert it: first, it is the son, not the father, who is deformed by war scars; and second, Iulik never searched for his son, was not even aware of the boy's existence, and later argues that "according to the theory of probability," the odds of his being Pavlik's father are nil.

This "inside-outing" of the classic Soviet narrative reflects the inversion of father-son roles in the relationship between Pavlik and Iulik.[6] Tellingly, Iulik and Pavlik, father and son, are bonded through the assonant echo of their names' diminutive forms, which suggests their similarity rather than hierarchical relations of adult and youngster.

From the outset Iulik is depicted as a weak, or at least weakened, father figure. Seemingly an authoritative and caring dad, he, like many post-Soviet intelligentsia representatives, has irrevocably lost his social status during the preceding decade. A former physicist whose talent once augured a brilliant future, he is now virtually unemployed, eking out articles about great scientists of the past for popular magazines ("Or, for instance, Boyle Mariotte. Tell us about his life." "They're two different people." "See, that's already interesting!"). Rita, on the other hand, is a true breadwinner, and the Krymovs' wealthy lifestyle relies entirely on her real-estate business. Though the patriarchal model of the father's authority is clearly subverted, both Iulik and Rita maintain the appearance of its preservation. As the film critic Elena Stishova observes of Rita, "She is the leader, the head, the breadwinner, but she remembers to demonstrate her woman's weakness, fragility, and fictitious dependence on what He will say and how He will behave" (2004). Pavlik's unexpected arrival gives Iulik an opportunity to restore his authority. To the surfaced son, his father's every word is sacred: the

---

[6] The same is true for some other films—such as *Ivanovo detstvo* (*Ivan's Childhood,* 1962) by Andrei Tarkovsky or *Koktebel'* (2003) by Boris Khlebnikov and Aleksei Popogrebskii—in which the son is marked or aged by traumatic experience and therefore assumes the paternal function by default.

boy admires everything about Iulik, down to his silly poems and his fictitious scientific discoveries—simply because he is the father.

However, it is Pavlik, despite his overengorged respect for Iulik as the paternal liege, who fathers Iulik; he only pretends to be the "obedient son," much as Rita pretends to be the "obedient wife" (the mirroring effect, once again). The true nature of the father-son relationship becomes apparent in their first conversation, when Iulik tries to conceal under quasi-scientific jargon his fear of taking responsibility for this gruesome new addition to his family, while Pavlik calmly dismisses his father's petty efforts with the simple reassurance, "Dad, don't think about it, okay? Don't worry. You have a lot of other things to deal with: your house, family, work. Everything's fine [*Vse normal'no*]." The image of Iulik dozing on his son's shoulder, as Pavlik remains awake, alert, and "on guard," becomes a visual hieroglyphic of the inversion they perform—this very image was used for the film's poster.

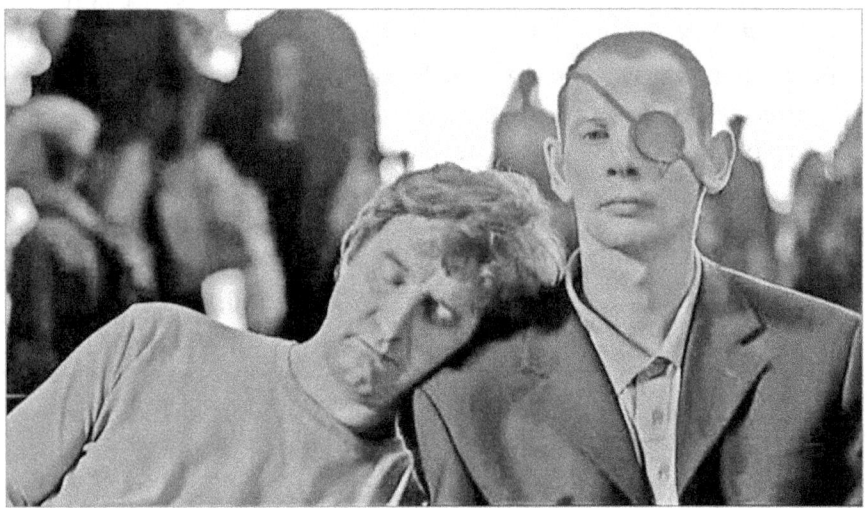

Fig. 1. Iulik and Pavlik

Pavlik's fatherly authority stems from the war myth, a myth in which war experience stands for true, transcendental knowledge about life. Iulik, untouched by war, can meanwhile only assume the role of a child, who follows the veteran's wise leadership, gratefully accepting his protection. According to this paradigm, it is Major Timur Kurbatovich—the former battlefield superior whom Pavlik saved from death—who fathered Pavlik during his army tenure. His war experience outweighs the boy's, so he not only can relate to Pavlik's traumas but also can serve as the youth's father figure, which is why Iulik and Rita place such high hopes on the major's influence over Pavlik. Yet according to their interests, this "alternative father" utterly flops: not only does he accompany Pavlik during his stakeout of "spooks" allegedly occupying the adjacent fifth-floor apartment, but in the final act, Timur gives the paranoid young man a pistol with two cartridges, despite having sensibly noted that the weapon is for war and not for "normal life."

The failure of this surrogate, trauma-bonded father figure as the magnified manifestation of Pavlik's paternalistic role ultimately exposes the false-bottom reality of the war myth as the basis of symbolic authority, especially when applied to the Chechen War and its veterans. In the post-Soviet mindscape, this conflict, unlike the mythologized Great Patriotic War, is not sanctified by victory, and its soldiers definitely do not match the archetype of victims of imperialistic aggression. Moreover, the traumatization that is regularly glossed over in the mythos of the Great Patriotic War is all too tangible in the figures of Pavlik, Timur, or any other Chechnya vet who appears in the film (such as the shell-shocked lieutenant in the mental institution). Deprived of these symbolic modifiers, the myth of war in *Moi svodnyi brat Frankenshtein* dwindles to its fundamental elements (as outlined by Gudkov) of xenophobia and the language of violence.

Pavlik is truly conversant in the language of violence. "Can you bash somebody's mug in? [*V mordu mozhesh' komu-nibud' dvinut'?*]" he asks his stepbrother genially during their first exchange. Egor, obviously taken aback, responds, "What for?" "Just for kicks," explains Pavlik. "Whose face?" Egor asks, still confused. "Anyone's. Mine, for instance."

Especially indicative of communication through violence is the scene in the public bathhouse, where Iulik takes his long-lost son for a ritual of male bonding. At first they gab about boxing, and we learn that Iulik was once a champion in the sport, revealing a talent of which Pavlik is especially enamored since his dislocated shoulder prevents him from participating in such activities. Following this conversation, Iulik discovers that another man, remarkably tall and thick, has surreptitiously appropriated their birch bunches (*veniki*). With a civil strategy of words, Iulik tries to make the thief confess his crime, only to be condescendingly ignored. When Pavlik enters the exchange, he instantly resorts to action: seizing a metal bowl, he unhesitatingly slams it down on the pilfering head until the stranger collapses. Pavlik's violent course proves to be more effective than Iulik's polite attempts at persuasion; though embarrassed by his son's interference (they hurriedly depart the bathhouse), Iulik is undeniably impressed and influenced by Pavlik's diatribe of violence.

This influence immediately manifests itself in the following scene, the dinner party at the Krymovs'. This is one of the crucial scenes in *Moi svodnyi brat*, largely because during this soirée, Pavlik, for the first and last time in the film, shares his memories of the war:

> "Then they [spooks] ran into the village. Vasia and I chased them in the armored car. There were local folks there, running and shouting: don't kill us, please don't do this, what are you doing, we're your own folk [*my svoi*]. We wiped out the whole village [*My davai eto selo utiuzhit'*]."
>
> "Who? Civilians?"
>
> "Who can tell one from the other? It was dark and scary.... We crushed about twenty of them with our vehicle [*Shtuk dvadtsat' tochno podavili*]. Vasia got a leave then.... And I was washing the blood off the wheels for three days."

The recollection is so shocking that the Krymovs' guests—all their close friends—are left speechless, despite having just before greeted Pavlik with standard salutations and praises habitual for the war myth ("We respect you very, very much," "We are proud of you," etc.). Iulik himself attempts to deploy this rhetoric, standing up for Pavlik to his friend Edik (Sergei Gazarov): "[He] risked his life for you and me, for the children." Needless to say, this rhetoric is painfully inappropriate: stampeding and devastating an entire village with an armored vehicle hardly corresponds to the image of a defender, nor to the image of a victim of aggression. Yet Edik's definition of Pavlik as an "utter fascist" (*zakonchennyi fashist*) is no better, belonging to the same mythological discourse of the Patriotic War—if to its negative, rather than positive, verbal repertory. Having failed to find adequate words to defend Pavlik and his war experience, Iulik starts a scuffle with his best friend ("I'll smash your light out!") and then with Rita, thereby setting into action what he learned from his son at the bathhouse.

His education is further applied the next morning, when Iulik drives Pavlik away to desert him. The violence of this act is confirmed by Ania's reaction to the news of it. She begins crying desperately when, after the safe "removal" of Pavlik, her father offers to buy her the puppy she has long dreamed of; Ania clearly recognizes a sinister intention in the bribe and intuitively refuses this procedure of othering, which means to equate her brother with a pet that can be bought at the market and thrown out at will.

The tension, however, appears to lie much deeper than Iulik's personal failure to communicate with Pavlik. Pavlik's monologue at the dinner bash describes an experience that cannot be accommodated by any binary structure at all, let alone by the one suggested by the war myth. In fact, his claim that one could not tell, in such bedlam, the difference between civilians and soldiers markedly erases binaries. Fear and panic fuse in Pavlik's discourse with blind hatred and indifference to human life, self-defense with bloodthirsty aggression, victimization with the seat of a mass murderer—this primal, hungry tar pit of dark feelings is the well that spouts the language of violence. What can Iulik or anyone else invoke to challenge its smoke and spray? The old and inadequate rhetoric of the Great Patriotic War? Or silence, quasi communication, as typified by Egor's or Rita's conversations with Pavel? It is no wonder that after failing to secure any discursive counterresponse to Pavlik's violence, Iulik unconsciously learns from and emulates his son—thus confirming Pavlik's role as father in their relationship. Especially worth noting is the attic scene, in which Iulik tries to convince Pavlik that the "spooks", who he suspects lay hidden there, are only figments of his sick imagination.

Pavlik does indeed find and startle a man (who turns out to be just a bum), whom Iulik seizes; a fight begins, and Iulik beats the squatter so savagely that Pavlik has to intervene: "Stop, Dad, stop. . . . You really got going, Dad. [*Vse, batia, vse. . . . Nu ty daesh', bat'.*]"

Pavlik's language of violence inexorably overcomes all discursive attempts at rebuttal, not only because of the strength culled from its idolization of force but also because it is situated outside of any discursive field. It is completely performative and therefore immune to any rhetorical intercessions, oppositions, or resistance. Pavlik's symbolic power, his paternal role, becomes most evident in the climactic passage when he abducts Egor and Ania and, through this act, establishes total control over Iulik and Rita as well. The orchestration and outcome of his hostage takeover compellingly invoke media and cinematic representations of terrorism. Although Pavlik, by his actions, demonstrates his unwavering care for his new family and his genuine desire to harbor them from the dangers of the world—crucial duties of the patriarchal father figure—such authority based on the logic of war can be nothing but an act of terror.

Furthermore, Pavlik's policy of violent communication not only fails to protect "his own" but instead *produces* Others, engenders enemies, and thereby transforms phantoms of posttraumatic stress into deadly corporealities: almost immediately after locking himself and the Krymovs in their dacha, Pavlik finds himself surrounded by the police, whom he takes for the "spooks." Spooks or no spooks, their determination to eliminate the deranged captor places them in a position from which they might easily hurt the Krymovs—that is, they literally threaten Pavlik with his own nightmare. When Rita screams in desperation to the police, "Don't shoot! There are children here!" Pavlik responds, "Kids or no kids—they don't care [*dlia nikh tut detei net*], like I didn't back then. Period." This judgment is not as senseless as it may seem, because Pavlik "back then" (i.e., in Chechnya) and the police "here" are both doing the same "job"— "fighting terrorism."

This dearth of effective dialogue via the language of violence, justified by the myth of war, underlines a profound problem in contemporary Russian culture: the crises of the liberal intelligentsia who tried but ultimately failed to develop enlightened discourses of modernization that were opposed both to the Soviet rhetoric of power and to the post-Soviet performances of bloodshed. Boris Dubin describes this miscarriage as derivative of the post-Soviet intelligentsia's "distancing from the present, conservation of cultural models, and the adoption of xenophobia as a defense mechanism. [...] Today's Russian intelligentsia and its representatives, who pretend to leading positions, merely react to the situation, which they have no control of and no effect on, as it were" (Dubin 2001, 338). Lack of touch with the present, the sense of the intelligentsia's isolation, in Dubin's opinion, is behind a purely negative identification of post-Soviet intelligentsia: not unlike other social groups, the intelligentsia "identifies itself through negation and becomes consolidated around 'the image of the enemy.' Its own incapacity for self-realization, its suspiciousness and aggressiveness are projected onto the interpretation of the enemy and extrapolated to its imaginary constructed figure" (339).

This sociocultural collapse of the intelligentsia is exposed by Iulik's failure as a father figure: he is symbolically bankrupt, and Pavlik and his war-sanctioned language of violence only make this bankruptcy agonizingly transparent. From this perspective, it becomes clear why Todorovsky's film does not really promote the parallel between Iulik and Dr. Frankenstein, who of course, in Shelley's novel is responsible for the *purposeful* and *knowing* creation of the Monster. Paradoxically, Iulik bears responsibility because he *does not know* and, moreover, does not *want* to know about the existence of Pavlik, and therefore tries to insulate himself and his family from Pavlik's barbaric and demented world. In doing so, Iulik subjects Pavlik to the same procedures of othering and enemy-production that normally appall him, as they do other liberal post-Soviet intellectuals of his ilk.

After the Krymovs escape from the surrounded house, Pavlik vanishes; though it is implied that the police kill him, we do not see him die, nor is his body presented to the viewers. The anticlimactic nature of the finale is further underscored by the complete lack of any dialogue between the surviving family members or with the police. The silence—the muting of discourse by white noise—

signifies a repeated cycle of repression of the uncanny, which would best be forgotten along with the traumas that produced it. The film ends on a long and high shot of the police force congratulating themselves and then of Iulik embracing his family. The image expresses yet another stifling of the uncanny. If one invokes, once more, Kristeva's observation that the uncanny kindles the knowledge "that we are foreigners to ourselves, and it is with the help of that sole support that we can attempt to live with others" (1991, 170), then this tender, seemingly peace-restorative embrace signifies quite the opposite: the revealed and repressed vision of mutual foreignness among the members of the nuclear family unit. By extension this image can be interpreted as a powerful metaphor of a social family, the post-Soviet society, that tries desperately to deny its own unconscious, its Otherness, thus choosing repression over any forms of negotiation. Only the faint sound of military drums is perceptible in the background during this closing scene, and its beat provides a powerful herald of the uncanny that has just reared its perversely familiar mug, only to be once again wrestled into the darkness of nonrecognition.

The Soviet myth of the Great Patriotic War that was adopted by the post-Soviet rhetoric of national identity exemplifies the repression of the historical experience of terror as the source of the societal uncanny. However, it must be underscored that it is the son (a representative of the future generation, albeit in the paternal role) and not the father (normally representative of the past) who embodies the uncanny in Todorovsky's film. This inversion suggests that not only the past but also the present and, moreover, the future are persistently repressed in the contemporary Russian mindscape. Thus, under the analytic eye of the film's authors, the "stabilization" of the 2000s reveals its cultural fabric's ticking bombs that will explode in the next decade—the 2010s.

A Road of Violence:
My Joy by Sergei Loznitsa

After the Russian Ministry of Culture refused to finance the famed documentary director Sergei Loznitsa's (b. 1964) debut feature film, it was realized under the coproduction of Germany, the Netherlands, and Ukraine. *Schast'e moe* (*My Joy*, 2010) went on to receive the Best Director Prize and the award of the Film Critics' Guild at the Kinotavr festival in Sochi and became the first-ever Ukrainian competitor in the Cannes festival program. Based on Loznitsa's original script and filmed by Oleg Mutu, who shot Palme d'Or-winner *4 Months, 3 Weeks and 2 Days* (2007), among other headliners of the Romanian New Wave, *Schast'e moe* was exuberantly praised for its sophisticated cinematic texture in the *New York Times* and other Western media.

In Russia, the film predictably caused a rift in opinions: some placed it among the supreme achievements of the new Russian cinema for its attention to the dark underside of the post-Soviet world (see Gulin 2011, Dolin 2010, Gusev 2011), while others like Karen Shakhnazarov, head of Mosfilm and chair of the 2010 Kinotavr jury, have defined it as an openly anti-Russian film and summarized its message as "everyone living in Russia should be shot" (*nado perestreliat' vsekh zhivushchikh v Rossii*; Liashchenko 2011). Shakhnazarov's indignation was seconded by Elena Iampol'skaia, editor in chief of the newspaper *Kul'tura* and a vehement adversary of all that does not fit the present iteration of the Orthodoxyautocracy-folksiness triumvirate. She has accused Loznitsa of no less than political treason: "Considering the fact that the film is sponsored predominantly by Germans, it is amazingly harmonious. For the complete picture, Loznitsa would have to be delivered to the Moscow premiere of his film by a sealed train coach. Unfortunately, there will be no Moscow premiere" (Iampol'skaia).

The film follows a truck driver called Georgy (Viktor Nemets) and his passage through a provincial territory (the film was shot in the Chernigov region of Ukraine), during which he encounters different, but predominantly vile, locals. First come corrupt road cops and an old man (Vladimir Golovin) who has lived in hiding since 1945 (his story constitutes the first World War II flashback in the movie); then an underage prostitute, whom the driver tries to help but is rebuffed with hostility; and finally village goons, who set sights on Georgy's cargo, clunk him over the head with a log, and leave empty-handed when they find the truck to be loaded with flour.

After a second World War II flashback, defined by the director as the film's turning point, "the film's structure changes: in the film's first half we have one day and the corresponding temporality. In the second half, the time moves with a different pace—we have fragments with long intervals between them" (Shakina 2010). In the second part of the movie, a different Georgy emerges: bearded, mute, and probably amnesic, he is hardly recognizable and has taken up residence with a Roma woman and her son. A substantial period of time seems to have elapsed since his traumatic confrontation with the thugs, as the setting has shifted from summertime to cold, gray winter. Tellingly, the direction of motion has changed as well: where in the first part the camera replicated Georgy's gaze, with the world unfolding in front of him, in the second part either his eyes are closed or he is driven with his back turned to the road ahead. Eventually, his trajectory comes full circle in his return to one of the opening locations—the roadside police station.

In the second part, the Roma woman uses Georgy's senseless body for sex and loots his flour to sell at the market. Eventually, pressed by police, she sells his truck and disappears, abandoning him without company or property. Arrested at the market and then left to freeze by the road, Georgy is rescued by the old man from the first World War II flashback—the one he met at the film's beginning. In the next scene two soldiers, trying in vain to deliver a serviceman's corpse to his mother, stumble on the old man's reclusive hut somewhere deep in the woods. The ensuing conversation between the old man and one courier is a fandango of misunderstanding: the soldier asks whether the hermit will sign papers confirming that the dead body was delivered to its destination, while the old man apparently thinks that they have come to arrest him for the murder he committed in 1945. Georgy arrives to find his host covered in blood, dead, with a pistol in his hands. He takes the gun and goes to the highway, where he stops a truck and hitches a ride to the police station featured in the beginning of the movie. There, cops are beating a cuffed driver—a police major from Moscow who refused to cope with their harassment. Dragged to the station as a supposed witness of the victim's "resistance to authorities," Georgy shoots first the cops, then the major and his wife, and finally the truck driver who also witnesses this scene. This done, he vanishes into the dark.

This rough plot summary certainly falls short of justice to the film's complicated narrative design, which, as I will try to demonstrate, is essential to an adequate understanding of *Schast'e moe*. Even on a superficial level, the film's plot resonates with the New Drama. In our book *Performing Violence: Literary and Theatrical Experiments of New Russian Drama* (2009), Birgit Beumers and I argued that the central discovery of New Drama is associated with the focus on various forms of social violence that in the post-Soviet period assumed the role of a social metalanguage, which has gradually replaced all other, insufficient and disintegrated languages inherited from the Soviet period.

Schast'e moe is shot in a quasi-documentary manner—an aspect resonating with New Drama's interest in verbatim and theatrical "nonfiction." This effect in Loznitsa's film is emphasized by numerous nonprofessional extras. (Especially impressive in this respect is the scene at the village marketplace where Georgy, in the *New York Times* reviewer's words, is "almost engulfed in a sea of coarse faces and bodies" [Dargis 2011].) The film overwhelms the viewer with various languages of everyday violence: obscenities spat zealously by thugs, old ladies, and youngsters; ubiquitous criminal songs (*shanson*) reproducing the prison subculture as normative; and, of course, incessant beatings and rapes (both figurative and literal), constituting "communication" both between authorities (cops) and the public and among ordinary people. Notably, the film begins with an "epigraph" in which the half-naked body of a man in a penitentiary uniform is lugged by two other inmates into a pit and then smothered with cement: references to Andrei Platonov's *Kotlovan* (*The Foundation Pit*) aside, the normalized prison-style violence appears as the cemented foundation of the current condition (no pun intended). No wonder Georgy's journey commences at the site of the first, "foundational," murder.

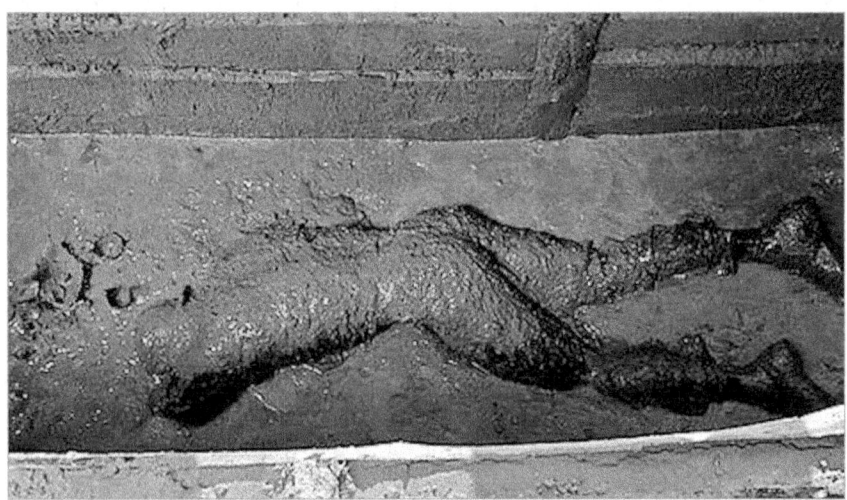

Fig. 2. The murder with which the film begins

Thus, one might perceive *Schast'e moe* as a cinematic version of the Bildungsroman, in the course of which Georgy is instructed in the language of violence, with each episode of the film a lesson. Bakhtin argued in his analysis of the Bildungsroman that this genre, while situating at the center stage the figure of the changing, "becoming" person, at the same time radically departs from the cyclical representation of time that was typical for the premodern depiction of human growth and transformation (see Bakhtin 1996). Contrarily, Loznitsa in his filmic gauntlet paradoxically adjoins the logic of the Bildingsroman with the emphatically circular model of time. One might even argue that time becomes cyclical as a result of the protagonist's *successful* education in the school of violence.

The accumulation of violence logically culminates in the catastrophic finale, when Georgy indiscriminately kills both sadistic cops and their victims. This scene can be read as the ironic result of Georgy's "education" in the process of his journey: if in the beginning he appears as a friendly and generous person, who avoids obscenities, lends a hand to underage prostitutes (tries to, at least), and trusts cunning thugs, in the second part we see a broken old man, a former subject, stripped of his memory, identity, and speech by a devastatingly intimate encounter with normalized brutality. The reformed Georgy can express his agency and his relationships to others only through violence. For the protagonist crippled by savagery and simultaneously infused with it, the climactic massacre stands both for his protest against the cops' terror and his solidarity with its victims. In the director's words, "I intentionally supercharge the situation in order to reach the finale with a very simple message: the society designed in such way is doomed to self-destruction" (Shakina 2010).

Obviously, for Loznitsa, much like for New Drama authors, violence serves as the basis of social fabrics, thus weaving a metalanguage. Yet, it seems, Loznitsa finds that this metalanguage isolates rather than connects, oppresses rather than expresses, thus becoming an *antilanguage*. It is noteworthy that after the life-changing assault of the thugs, Georgy becomes silent for the rest of the film, and more noteworthy that he is not alone in his silence: another mute victim of social violence is one of the thugs, who apparently lost his speech in childhood when his father was killed—this scene constitutes the content of the second World War II flashback. This commonality is quite significant as it reveals the aspect of *Schast'e moe* that places the film beyond the context of New Drama.

According to the New Drama playwrights, the elevation of violence as the universal metalanguage results from the collapse of Soviet metanarratives and social norms. In other words, for them the language of violence belongs exclusively to the post-Soviet domain, articulating both the cause and the effect of the historical trauma wreaked in the downfall of the Soviet social order. On the contrary, Loznitsa does not confirm the ascension of violence to the status of all-purpose metalanguage (or antilanguage); he inserts into his narrative two historical episodes that present the contemporary normalization of violence as a direct outcome of the entire Soviet experience. For him, social communication through violence is not a post-Soviet phenomenon but the product of Soviet history, concealed behind Soviet ideological myths and exposed when these screens collapsed.

The first of such episodes is inserted just after Georgy's opening encounter with corrupt traffic cops. An old man, appearing in his cab from nowhere (and afterwards vanishing into thin air), tells the driver about an experience that has changed his life: when he, as a young lieutenant, was returning from Germany in 1945, a military patrol officer cunningly robbed him of his modest "trophies," consisting of a red dress for his bride and a Leika photo camera for his future career. In response, the lieutenant shot the officer and fled from the world, socially died off, forgetting his name and living since then as a ghost. At first sight, this scene only superficially connects to the present, with the greedy patrol officer in 1945 prototyping today's dirty cops—much like him, they are eager to shake down passing drivers, taking anything from money to sex and never hesitating to use violence to make their request irrefutable.

On the other hand, this ghoulish raconteur, in the greater scope of the film, appears as the embodiment of an important, and costly, life strategy: one may resist social violence by violent means at the expense of one's personal identity. Paradoxically, in the realm of normalized violence, personal dignity can be defended only on the basis of personal anonymity. Furthermore, Loznitsa himself interprets this ominous encounter as foreshadowing the protagonist's future: Georgy, too, will lose his name and identity. However, in comparison with "reformed Georgy" as he appears in the second half of the film, the old veteran looks every bit the winner: until his very end, he remains in control of any given situation and maintains his humanity. And it is he, we remember, who saves helpless Georgy when all others either cynically abuse or ferociously shun him.

Yet even the composed hermit is eventually subsumed in the swell of violent death. The uncertainty surrounding his demise—it remains unclear whether he slew himself or was killed by the soldiers—is essential to the presented vision of history. In the second half of the movie, the filmic time not only becomes fragmented but also begins to incorporate surreal elements. First, a lieutenant, one of the two officers accompanying the soldier's corpse, sights a hangman on a tall tree in the woods—apparently a hallucination, as his subordinate can spot nothing of the like. Later, the lieutenant falls into delirium and recognizes the executioner in the old man. Even earlier in the movie, a wizened wanderer appears and maniacally assails the military truck with a stick, mumbling that he had "killed them all," "put all those bitches in one grave," and "fulfilled the general's order." Both the hangman and the meandering madman can be read as projections or spectral "flash-forwards" of Georgy beyond his shooting spree. Obviously, this interpretation presumes the temporal confusion of cause and effect, of events preceding and following the action, which becomes an important attribute of Loznitsa's vision of history.

At the same time, these corporeal vagaries also function as ghosts of the past, who, in accordance with Etkind's concept of magical historicism, manifest the unrecognized and repressed traumas of history. Loznitsa represents the scars of normalized violence not by references to the Great Terror but through imagery of the Great Patriotic War, which is much more radical, since this war has been glorified in late-Soviet and post-Soviet culture as the golden age of valor and the crowning heroic achievement in all of Russian history. In Loznitsa's understanding (also informing his 2013 film *V tumane* [*In the Fog*], based on Vasil' Bykov's novella), this very glorification solidifies and obfuscates the normalization of violence.

Through this lens, we can see why the old veteran confuses contemporary soldiers with agents of the state terror seeking to arraign him for a murder that happened sixty-five years ago. He mistakes them for ghosts of the past, and every eerie atom of the movie's atmosphere justifies his mistake. Furthermore, his error is absolutely logical, as it follows both from his own phantasmal being and from the ghost-like condition into which Georgy is thrust by present-day violence. Yet the inevitability of his misperception undermines the old man's strategic defense of his dignity by the sacrifice of his identity. He might have succeeded if his ghostly existence were exceptional, but it is not. In the surreal historical time, when the traumatic past melds with the equally traumatic present and when cause and effect are indistinguishably fused, everyday violence *normally* turns people into ghosts; the old man's position, then, is both vulnerable and unstable.

The status of the aged lieutenant is counterweighted by the equally, if not more, vulnerable position of the teacher in the second World War II flashback, which, as mentioned above, Loznitsa considers to be the crux of the filmic narrative. In this sequence, two retreating soldiers find shelter at the house of a teacher and his son. The teacher feeds them and invites them to spend the night under his roof. During the dinner, he admits that he works as an educator under the Germans, as he worked under the Soviets, and that he does not view the Soviet regime as preferable to German occupation, calling Germany a "civilized nation" (*tsivilizovannaia natsiia*). Most importantly, the teacher proclaims, "I can't teach killing. I can teach love only." His guests receive this confession as proof of his treason. In the morning they drag the sleeping teacher from the bed that he shares with his little son to a shed where they execute him. Then they rob the house and depart, leaving a scared child in a white nightshirt standing alone on the steps in silence.

This episode can be traced directly to the film's present-day characters: the traumatized child, we may guess, will become the mute thug in the gang that sticks up and log-wallops Georgy, which feeds into his consecutive connection with the mauled and muted truck driver. Moreover, the creed of the teacher appears to be the most radical response to the normalization of violence as presented in *Schast'e moe*: he chooses love over carnage, and by this dooms himself to ineludible victimization. The Christian overtones of his stance are obvious (the Teacher). However, this parallel has been overlooked by the most rabidly Orthodox critics, probably blinded by the teacher's reference to Germans as a "civilized nation." For example, the aforementioned Elena Iampol'skaia writes about this episode, "A treacherous pacifist does not cease being a traitor. In general, to maintain that paralyzed pacifism is better than crazed aggression is the same as to declare the advantages of an impotent before a sexual maniac. The impotent is harmless, but he is also deprived of any perspective" (2011). The critic obviously fails the test that Loznitsa proctors with his film: commendation of German society implies a direct reference to innumerable Soviet films and books where such approval served as an unquestionable warrant for one's denunciation as a traitor, deserving a violent or lethal penalty. Those viewers whose reaction to the teacher's Nazi praise in *Schast'e* is dictated by a cultural reflex are intangibly swallowed into the domain of the film, becoming accomplices to the murder of the peaceable Teacher.

Loznitsa seems to maintain here that if you are prepared to justify the killing of a peaceful person because his principles do not match the Soviet stereotype of an agreeable character, then you too are implicated in the normalization of violence, in the past and present alike. In one interview, the director offers a similar interpretation of this episode:

> When in the film we see such a situation [the episode with the teacher and soldiers], according to the laws of the genre we feel the need to identify with either this side or the opposite, although this is not necessary. In the process of watching, we are forced to switch sides, leaving the side of the hospitable host and taking the other—the side of people who are offended by their compatriot's holding out for the enemy. We always identify with "ours." [. . .] When the viewer is watching this scene, it works as a lance that separates the human features from those inserted into our heads by the ideology. The side of the soldiers—criminals, murderers—can't be accepted, but the camera mercilessly places the viewer into their position. The camera could have been located elsewhere, but it adopts their perspective, and this is why this episode is so provocative. (Tuula 2011)

This artistic provocation emphasizes the theme of culpability for violence that permeates the entire composition of *Schast'e moe*. Between two radical responses to societal violence, as represented by the unrepentant old man and the pacifist teacher, Loznitsa erects several variations on the theme of noninterference—observing without acting in situations in which others are violated—as a means of self-protection. As the filmmaker stresses in the same interview, "'Do not interfere'—it's not just a defense, it's a contemporary ideology, a widespread concept of the world order" (Shakina 2010). However, the film's dialogic structure fledges full motivic correlations between the similar episodes in the first and second halves of the movie. These linkages serve a methodical undermining of faith in the protective power of noninterference. Basically, the scenes of the first part deliver the "lessons" of noninterference, while those of the second part ironically subvert these lessons by mirroring the tutorial scenario and twisting the "didactic" message into its opposite.

In the film's beginning, Georgy takes his documents and leaves the police station unnoticed. Yet in the final episode, the police major, buoyed by his rank, tries to do the same and falls victim to his colleagues' wrath. In the first part Georgy gets a hands-on education in noninterference from the underage prostitute who is appalled by his attempt to help her. But in the second half of the movie, he himself becomes essentially a prostitute for his hostess. This dialogic pattern is represented in the most concentrated form in the final sequence, which begins with the truck driver from whom Georgy hitches a ride preaching about the imperative of noninterference and ends with the same driver's desperate attempt to aid the shackled major, his scuffle with cops, and his death from Georgy's bullet.

Loznitsa obviously abhors didacticism as another, intellectual, form of violence. This is why a carefully balanced construction of the filmic narrative in *Schast'e moe* (small surprise that Loznitsa is a mathematician by training) is emphatically antididactic. As one can see, it intentionally undercuts any attempt to distill a focused moral lesson from the film, to erect a binary opposition of any kind. At the same time, the film's structure functions as a circular story arc, in which the execution of the teacher echoes through the murder of a prisoner in the movie's epigraph—which may also be read as a possible portent of Georgy's future. From this perspective, even the enigmatic episode at the beginning of the film, depicting Georgy's departure on his fateful journey while his wife (we assume) appears to be in mourning and oblivious to his presence, could be interpreted as retroactive proof of his ghostliness.

Thus, the road transforms into a circuital stream of historical-cum-everyday violence. Through the Soviet past and post-Soviet present, this cyclical movement envelops "lessons" of noninterference and their demonstrative deconstructions. From this standpoint, *Schast'e moe* could be viewed as a reproduction of a typical New Drama discourse on violence, yet on a metalevel, as a self-mythologizing and self-reflexive narrative.

However, what ultimately contradicts this notion is the fact that Loznitsa does not explicitly show the circularity of the narrative. Why does he prefer presenting it only potentially, through the film's structure? He could have easily returned at the end to the prelude, having us recognize Georgy in a poor prisoner's body. In so doing, he would have openly validated his narrative as a myth unifying Soviet and post-Soviet violence. However, he chose a different strategy. In my view, this comes about precisely because *Schast'e moe* not only tenders a concentrated edition of New Drama but also aspires to transcend its limits and its symbolic tautologies, achieving this by a *structural* rather than representational effect of the narrative.

While inspiring the sensation of a self-repetitive and self-reflexive cyclical motion without expressly depicting it, the movie attempts to unleash this whirlwind of social self-destruction into the viewer's imagination. If such an effect is indeed achieved by *Schast'e moe*, it would inevitably engender the viewer's acute emotional yearning to depart from this circular road movie and to seek alternatives to the life force founded on violence and feeding on noninterference into others' violent business. This emotional outcome, it seems, is more important to Loznitsa than a straightforward mythologization of violence.

IN DENIAL: *THE GEOGRAPHER DRANK HIS GLOBE AWAY* BY ALEKSANDR VELEDINSKY*

Before 2013, Aleksandr Veledinsky (b. 1959) was best known for his films *Russkoe* (*The Russian*, 2004) and *Zhivoi* (*Alive*, 2006), and for his scriptwriter credit on the famed miniseries *Brigada* (2002, dir. Aleksei Sidorov). His 2013 work *Geograf globus propil* (*The Geographer Drank His Globe Away*) superseded the success of all his previous projects: the film not only won the Grand Prix at the Kinotavr film festival (additional awards included Best Actor and Best Music) but also generated laudatory, almost ecstatic responses among viewers and the majority of critics. While audiences raved over the rehabilitation of the intelligentsia and the arrival of a "normal" and "humane" movie "about us," critics declared *Geograf* the best film of the year, ranking Konstantin Khabenskii's leading performance among the peak achievements of his career. Since its release in November 2013, the movie grossed $4 million (with an overall budget of $2.5 million) and half a million viewers in Russian theaters alone, figures that testify to the profound resonance that *Geograf* struck with the educated public's cultural expectations.

The film is based on Aleksei Ivanov's 1995 novel and is set (and was shot) in Perm', a city that in preceding years became the petri dish for a massive experiment in radical cultural innovation. Faint reminders of the short-lived cultural renaissance tumble

---

* Coauthored with Tatiana Mikhailova.

raspily through *Geograf*, but only a scant few: namely, the slogan "Happiness isn't behind the mountains" (an art object by Boris Matrosov), the job affiliation of one of the characters, and the album of contemporary art in Perm' that the hero receives as a birthday gift. The scarcity of these echoes is not overly confounding—first, because the novel was written prior to these events, though the screenwriters decided to situate the story in present-day Perm' rather than the 1990s. Second, and more significantly, despite the designation of protagonist Viktor Sluzhkin (Khabenskii), a former biologist and current teacher of geography in an ordinary high school, as a modern *intelligent*, his actual interests are limited to alcohol, friends, and, of course, tourism—more specifically, rafting the perilous rivers of the Urals. Cultural novelties and politics are altogether nonexistent for him. At the same time, his constant drinking and meager salary (in the beginning of the film, he pretends to be deaf in order not to pay the train fare) do not impede his status as a man-star, attractive to many women, excepting his wife Nadia (Elena Liadova), who feels disheartened by the poverties of their life.

Sluzhkin's profile quickly reminded critics of such films from the late-Soviet era as Roman Balaian's *Polety vo sne i naiavu* (*Flights in Dreams and Reality*, 1982) and Vitalii Mel'nikov's *Otpusk v sentiabre* (*Vacation in September*, 1979, released in 1987; based on Aleksandr Vampilov's *Utinaia okhota* [*The Duck Hunt*]). Veledinsky directly alludes to Balaian's film through paraphrases of its memorable scenes: Sluzhkin's teetering on a children's swing and his "disappearance" from the balcony in the finale recall Makarov (Oleg Iankovskii) swinging on the *tarzanka* (a primitive bungee-jumping rope), ending in his faked death and disappearance. Another important point of reference for *Geograf* is *American Beauty*: a recurring photograph of a sinking love letter distinctly reminds of the flying plastic bag in Sam Mendes's film. This reference is especially meaningful since Sluzhkin's story is also one of love toward a teenage girl. The arc of his romance ends in similar waters as Lester Burnham's in *Beauty*: Sluzhkin does not seize the chance to have sex with his beautiful student Masha Bol'shakova (Anfisa Chernykh), though he plainly is in love with her, and though the girl eagerly offers herself to him. These references cement the context in which the authors situate their film.

However, in a seeming contradiction to this system of coordinates, Aleksei Ivanov has insisted on a parallel between Sluzhkin and Dostoevsky's Prince Myshkin. As the novelist said in an interview,

> He [Sluzhkin] is ideal, but not in the sense of "the best" or "flawless." He lives according to an ideal. Sluzhkin as a culturological type—this is a type of the harmonious man, which harks back not to "superficial men" of Russian literature (Zilov from *Utinaia okhota*, Makarov from *Polety vo sne i naiavu*), but to Prince Myshkin. As a teacher, he is a complete failure. But he is a true human being, he teaches not through pedagogical techniques, but through his own existence in given circumstances. He is confused neither in his relationships with women, nor in life in general. He clearly knows what is good and what is bad. He won't be reaching his goal by walking on human heads, he won't betray, and won't be arrogant about his morals, because pride is a mortal sin. He is not an alcoholic, he drinks when he has to do something improper, perform a small everyday betrayal that would improve his life. When drinking, he replaces this meanness by misbehavior, without reproaching others by his righteousness. (Kul'chitskii 2013)

Frankly, this interpretation produces more questions than answers. First of all, what is that ideal according to which Sluzhkin lives? In one of the film's scenes, he explicitly describes his position as that of a secular saint who wants to depend on no one and wants no one to depend on him, while preserving love for everyone. However, in the film (as well as in the novel) this profession is ironically corroborated by an immediately ensuing cheerful tryst with his former classmate Vetka (Anna Ukolova), who remains pleased by Sluzhkin's sexual virility but more so amazed by his rejection of personal pleasure. More seriously, his moral bearing can be seen in his nonobjection to his wife's affair with his best friend Budkin (Aleksandr Robak); yet as another character suggests, this might be also read as Sluzhkin's strutting of his "moral superiority" over both adulterers—coupled, we might add, with his reluctance to provide for the family. From a practical standpoint, Sluzhkin's principle means that he feels liberated from any responsibilities to his wife and daughter and would readily leave Nadia to her own devices if her needs brought too much pressure on his freedom. If he is a saint, then he has managed to elevate cynicism to the state of sainthood; this, to be sure, is a seminal achievement.

As to alcohol, Ivanov's description is best illustrated by a scene in which Sluzhkin drinks himself into oblivion and passes out in a bathtub when he could be sleeping with his beautiful colleague Kira (Evgeniia Brik), seductively and cynically offering herself to him. A pattern seems to emerge: Sluzhkin also opts for liquor over Vetka's invitation to spend the night at her place after his birthday party, although this sacrifice is somewhat devalued by their later sex in the scene described above.

Diverging from Ivanov, the film director suggests a different pedigree for Sluzhkin:

> We thought a lot about classical characters closest to our Sluzhkin. We recalled Oblomov, Prince Myshkin—"the idiot." Shukshin's "oddballs," Vampilov's characters, Balaian's film. [. . .] We decided that he has to be a jester [*shut gorokhovyi*], the holy fool who through his misbehavior exposes to us our sins. He is like a mirror reflecting our society—this is probably why those who watched the movie liked him so much. (Kichin 2013)

This appraisal (also supported by Dmitry Bykov) invites the concept of the trickster, which appears even more relevant for today's cultural climate (as discussed earlier in the case of Pussy Riot).

However, the practical application of this approach to Sluzhkin is disappointing at best. Admittedly, just about everyone around him acts as a seasoned cynic: even tender Sashen'ka (Evgeniia Kregzhde), a kindergarten instructor who spends all her time at the gym, instantly metamorphoses from nymph into merciless boss in conversation with her subordinate, exhibiting a cynical multiplicity of personae. Even an unnamed schoolgirl articulates her first impression of the new geographer with a simple "I'd blow him." Sluzhkin blends effortlessly into this milieu with his constant drinking, card playing with students, and instructorship in a subject about which he knows nothing—"teaching" by dictations from a textbook. However, his eccentricities are so mild and unmemorable that they can hardly qualify as those of a trickster: his supposed holy foolishness is indistinguishable from the other characters' cynicism.

Imbibing with his unruly student Gradusov (Andrei Prytkov) and afterward improvising rap bars instead of guiding the class during the first leg of their field trip on the river, is probably the sole episode that might merit the trickster seal. This scene (minus the rapping) also appears in the novel but carries there a tactical meaning that is lost in the film. Ivanov's Sluzhkin develops a particular pedagogical program manifested most clearly during the river excursion: he eschews his own authority as teacher and intentionally unseats himself from the position of power—what better method of self-sabotage is there than getting sloshed at the start of their journey, compelling his students to usurp him? He wants to teach his pupils to act as free, and therefore self-sufficient, persons, and while placing utter responsibility for the expedition and their survival onto them, he tactfully aids his kids when a lack of knowledge or practical skills arises. This strategy proves to be soaringly effective, up to and through the novel's climax, when the students, without Sluzhkin, manage to traverse a dangerous batch of rapids. Dmitry Bykov accurately described Sluzhkin's method: "This is a cruel but effective technique—just to place them [the students] into a situation when they will have to decide. When they have one choice only: either to cross the rapid, or to stay in the woods and die. He does not have to be a lonely hero anymore—now his students have to make a heroic effort" (Bykov 2013).

However, Bykov unwittingly mixes up the novelistic and filmic representations of the drunkard-geographer. His words match Ivanov's rendition of Sluzhkin, who primes the students' success by his honest, though not didactic, communication with "fathers" (as he calls his students) throughout the entire narrative. This is not true of Veledinsky's Sluzhkin, whose pedagogical program remains completely imperceptible in the movie. Everything that transpires between Sluzhkin and his pupils in the film happens by accident, and his communication with them is reduced to muted lectures and angry, yet banal, philippics. Even the students' final triumph is prepared by a *lecture* (also muted) about this particular rapid and the ways to cross it. In other words, the cinematic Sluzhkin, unlike his literary counterpart, remains within a conventional teacher-student paradigm; the driving theme of the novel is obfuscated in adaptation, lost in transmediation.

Tellingly, while endorsing the analysis of Sluzhkin as a secular saint, Ivanov did not participate in sculpting the script, which was coauthored by Veledinsky, Rauf Kubaev, and Valery Todorovsky (also one of the film's producers). Probably, the writer reinterpreted his own novel (after all, it was written about twenty years ago), but having reread the book recently, we cannot help noticing some other significant differences between characterizations of the protagonist on the screen versus on the page.

The novel endows Sluzhkin with far greater complexity than Veledinsky's film does. On the one hand, it does not hide his irresponsible infantilism. He drinks with his favorite students, and while being drunk, he breaks his leg sliding down a snow hill. His pedagogical repertoire includes *repeat* beatings of the most obnoxious students—in the film we see only Sluzhkin's very moderate (and justified!) physical reprimand of the unruly student Gradusov. His flirtation with Masha is not limited to a tender yet restrained embrace as in the movie but also involves sticking his hands under her jeans, groping, and so on. Furthermore, his risky behavior during the river trip results in a number of life-threatening situations that befall his wards, including confrontations with inebriated locals.

On the other hand, the harbors of Sluzhkin's sensitivity and artistry are deeply plumbed in the novel. Unlike his Khabenskii-helmed on-screen embodiment, in Ivanov's vision he sparkles with quotations from his and others' poetry, and his speech is oversaturated with diverse cultural and historical references, while in the film he recites ad nauseam one and the same stanza from Pushkin's *Skazka o mertvoi tsarevne* (*Tale of a Dead Princess*), which supposedly expresses his free spirit but in fact belongs to the toddlers' reading list. The novel has him truly enraptured with the Urals' history and nature (much as Ivanov himself is), while the movie's Sluzhkin stands by impassively as Masha responds to his lecture about the Kama docks: "This is not interesting to you either . . ." Across the pages of the novel, he vividly transfigures the whitewater field trip into his pupils' immersion in the deep currents of history, retracing with them a journey from the forgotten ancient life of native tribes to the Gulag; the frames of the film preserve only his banalities and a crude joke about mammoths' petrified shit.

This complexity could have justified the representation of Sluzhkin as a "superfluous man" who is too bright to fit into a new repressive social condition, beneficial for more primitive souls like Budkin, who plainly introduces himself as "Corruptioner." The movie, in contrast, mercilessly flattens the central character, retaining from the "superfluous man" dossier only references to Balaian and Mendes. What's more, these references apparently operate in Veledinsky's film as decorative replacements for the protagonist's missing "depth." In Inna Denisova's words,

> The principal difference between the character played by Khabenskii and Ivanov's hero (as well as Iankovskii's Makarov) is that the latter travels along a certain [intellectual] path. Ivanov describes his character's internal journey in the second part of the book, when the teacher with the students takes a river trip. During this trip, Sluzhkin performs immense internal work, making his way from the lack of love to true love. [. . .] But the [filmic] protagonist amazes not only by the fact that he doesn't evolve but also by the fact that the idea of the character's internal development didn't cross the minds of either the director or the scriptwriters. (Denisova, Koretskii, and Ruzaev 2013)

Following suit with the hero's flattening, other characters in the film are also sheared of any strand of complexity. This is especially evident in the representation of Sluzhkin's wife, Nadia. The novel depicts her as a woman fatigued not only by a life of limited means and a deficiency of perspective but also by Sluzhkin's ceaseless drinking, womanizing, and general infantilism. Elena Liadova reduces this character to an irate bitch, a nag who iniquitously berates her husband for not having the money to buy a car and penalizes him by withholding sex and cheating with his best friend. Such a portrayal of Nadia obviously paints Sluzhkin as the victim and grants him a mother lode of viewers' empathy. (Notably,

Ivanov's novel presents all its female characters besides Nadia as one-dimensional stereotypes: nymph, vixen, calculating user, etc.; in this respect, the film duly follows the original.) Similarly, if in the novel each student in Sluzhkin's crew has a unique face and persona, the film allocates some individuality only to Masha and Gradusov, the rapping urinator. The purpose of this simplification is the same as with Nadia: contrasted with an indistinguishable mass of coarse teenagers Sluzhkin can pose as Hamlet.

Naturally, the question arises, why is this film, with its relentless pancaking of characters, so successful among critics and educated viewers? Or, to put it another way, why is *Geograf*'s representation of the contemporary *intelligent* so comforting to the contemporary Russian audience? Anzhelika Artiukh, in her review article "Losers and Patriots," identifies in Veledinsky's film a bitter verdict laid on the entire present generation of Russian intelligentsia—the one to which Sluzhkin, Khabenskii, Veledinsky, and Ivanov, born in the 1960s, brought up and educated in the late-Soviet days, and reaching the stride of their mature years in the post-Soviet age, together belong: "Veledinsky's artistic and personal honesty lies in the following: through the protagonist of his 'school movie' he demonstratively explicates that his generation cannot teach anybody anything. [. . .] The post-Soviet period with its shift from the cult of education to the cult of money signified an absolute failure of the Enlightenment project, for which intelligentsia was responsible in Soviet society. The descendants of intelligentsia either have degraded to Sluzhkins or become petty bourgeois completely forgetful about their social origins" (Artiukh 2013). Inna Denisova is more specific: she detects in Sluzhkin the reflection of a particular stratum of intelligentsia—namely, the scientific-technological intelligentsia, who encompassed avid readers of the Strugatsky brothers and ardent fans of the modern bards; thus *Geograf* appears as a recent installment in the ITR culture, which was discussed above:

> Much like many film viewers, I first read Ivanov's book, from which becomes perfectly clear what milieu has formed the protagonist. He is a former scientist, who is left unemployed, because in the 1990s research institutions have closed. And he

gives up. He loses identification in the time of social troubles and cataclysms. In other words, we are observing his tragedy. In the movie, the action takes place in our days, which produces a disorienting effect—it appears that the protagonist gives up for no reason, because he is an egotist, eternal child, antihero, who does not give a damn about anybody. What is this film about then? (Denisova 2013)

Echoing Denisova, we wish to stress once again that all these imperative social contexts—the broad intelligentsia's and its scientific representatives' crises—are omitted from Veledinsky's *Geograf globus propil*. We believe, however, that their invisible presence in the audience's perception serves as the chief predicate for the film's *positive* effect. By cutting off all direct lines to these contexts from the cinematic representation (the sole remaining trace being the movie's title), its creators tried to achieve a very clear aim: to refigure the defeat of Sluzhkin, of the entire stratum of intelligentsia symbolically tethered to him, as the *victory*; hence, his name—Viktor. This is why Sluzhkin is ultimately beatified as the one who does not betray himself, being a "true human being" (in Ivanov's words), indeed a new Prince Myshkin and a holy fool, although, as mentioned above, it remains ultimately unclear what values and, most importantly, what deeds his "victory" does entail.

In this light, the discrepancy between the novel and the film is quite telling. The novel, written in the 1990s, remained hopeful; in a nutshell, its message was yes, we, the intelligentsia, are economically and socially marginalized—but we manifest freedom and can teach the next generation to be free. The film, portraying today's Sluzhkin, is thoroughly hopeless, despite its seemingly upbeat atmosphere and despite its creators' intentions. The picture is hopeless because Sluzhkin's freedom cannot be distinguished from his peers' cynicism, because instead of analyzing the intelligentsia's failed post-Soviet mission, it recommends that we accept and admire the protagonist for what he is. In lieu of questioning, it substitutes a nonentity for an idealist.

Khabenskii in his performance as Sluzhkin essentially faces one key challenge: to make this static nobody lovable. The actor, unfortunately, succeeds, and his Sluzhkin oozes charm. No wonder so many viewers have excitedly claimed to recognize themselves in Sluzhkin: this hero's delightful vagueness and shapelessness expressly invite us to project our own insecurities onto him. Undoubtedly, such representation is flattering to intelligentsia viewers; it offers a soothing indulgence for being what they are, not apologizing, not problematizing their social and cultural functions. This flattery also befuddles the flatness of the cinematic representation of the intelligentsia. In this respect, *Geograf* is a truly historical film: it has tangibly and vividly captured the gloomiest symptom of the post-Soviet intelligentsia's defeat—the state of denial.

Lost in Translation:
Short Stories by Mikhail Segal

After the events of March 2014, many things appear not exactly as before. Mikhail Segal's (b. 1974) renowned film *Rasskazy* (*Short Stories*, 2012) is no exception. When the picture was released, it was prevailingly received as a witty, well-crafted absurdist comedy. Now, a change in political context has imbued this charming comic flick with new meaning and refigured it to reveal something deeper—probably despite its author's intentions.

Rasskazy brought Mikhail Segal, already known for his understated war drama *Franz + Polina* (2006, based on Boris Vakhtin's famous novella *Odna absoliutno schastlivaia derevnia* [*One Absolutely Happy Village*]), the reputation of a dazzling creator of "(sm)art mainstream" (Abdullaeva 2012), one of those rare talents whose work is equally captivating to an undergraduate audience as to a sophisticated viewer equipped to detect its carnivalesque motifs and Foucauldian epistemology (Nemchenko 2013). *Rasskazy*'s accretion of prizes and awards looks mammoth but consists mainly of critics' commendations and a Grand Prix from only a second- (if not third-) rate festival. This is of course with the exception of Kinotavr, which discovered Segal by virtue of his short *Mir krepezha* (*The World of Fixtures*, 2011; Grand Prix for Best Short), later resubmitted as the first segment of *Rasskazy*, where it helped to secure the 2012 Kinotavr Prize for Best Screenplay and the diploma of the Guild of Film Critics and Film Scholars.

Many critics linked the *al'manakh* structure of *Rasskazy*, consisting of four "novellas," to the director's previous experience in music-video production, alleging that the film inherits the notorious "clip-based consciousness." Zara Abdullaeva has expressed this thought in the most nuanced manner: "This card-film is composed of fragments and splinters (of a mirror). The fragment is a respectable genre of Romanticism, but not the only correct way (as is often believed) to reflect on stereotypes or just visualize the superficiality of the contemporary 'clip-like' or 'mosaic' consciousness. Segal tells of these stereotypes, of this consciousness and even of the 'collective unconscious' lucidly, bitingly, and from a distance" (2012).

Instead of chiding *Rasskazy* for its "clip-based consciousness," I would like to argue that Segal masterfully emulates the fragmentary structure as one of the key justifications for his artistic logic, while at the same time furtively unraveling his vision in a single coherent thread, from the movie's first episode to its last. Segal presents his fragmented composition as a replacement to a "big and totalizing form," about which, in the frame narrative of the movie, the publishing house's editor in chief dreams aloud while rejecting the young author's book of titular short stories.

In an interview that accompanied the screening of *Rasskazy* at Kinotavr in 2012, Segal said that the entire film had already been shot in his head when he was making *Mir krepezha*. (This explains how he managed to spin a fifteen-minute short into a feature-length picture within two summer months.) The director emphasized that he did not envision *Rasskazy* as an *al'manakh* but as a "whole" work. Yet Segal also argues that each installment toys with its own film genre—comedy, satire, thriller, and melodrama. The dissimilarity of the novellas in style and in genre serves the same purpose: to effect the condition of multiple overlapping and coexisting dimensions as the setting for the filmic narrative.

The first ("seed") novella, "The World of Fixtures," intoned with a deadpan black humor, plays with the "European/Russian" dichotomy and is set to a brilliant performance of "Fly Me to the Moon" by Polina Kasianova with a *baian* accompaniment. This opposition has a tangential relationship to the next segment, the satirical parabola "Circular Movement" ("Krugovoe dvizhenie"), which illustrates the motion of bribes in Russian society and bears no relation whatsoever to the mock-mystical thriller "Energy Crisis" ("Energeticheskii krizis"), about a clairvoyant from a provincial library who conveys her revelations through verses stylized along the lines of Pushkin's poetry. Then one can sense the opposition resurfacing in the final novella, "Inflamed" ("Vozgoritsia plamia"), among the most elegant of the four installments in terms of its plot: here, the love affair of two new "Russian Europeans" displays a deep generational conflict that eventually leads to *Rasskazy*'s most frequently quoted line, "What do we have to fuck about?!" (*O chem s toboi trakhat'sia?!*).

The dim interior of the café that becomes the stage for plotting out one's entire life in the first novella contrasts with the next segment's motley transformations of the backdrop, from a dirty labyrinth of garages to the shining decorum of the president's vast estate. The mystical provincial coloring of the third novella is likewise irreconcilable with the Moscow milieu favored by the "creative class" in the fourth. These are not just different stories; these are also disparate Russias, which exist without noticing each other, in parallel, yet inevitably overlapping. Thus, the formal structure of *Rasskazy* manifests the film's thematic crux: multiple realities, or more precisely, multiple post-Soviet realms, each with its own language (or lack thereof) or, at least, its own semiotics.

In Lilya Nemchenko's words, "All the characters of *Rasskazy* are formally united through the location, and conceptually through the absence of a common language, not on the level of semantics and syntax, but on the level of contextual memory. No fixtures will help here: 'The link of time is out of joint'" (2013). I'd rather engage a more optimistic characterization: *Rasskazy* is, altogether, a film about attempted translations and transactions between these manifold realms and dissimilar semiotics.

In "The World of Fixtures," an unflappably professional organizer of family events (Andrei Merzlikin), hired to plan the wedding and the entire subsequent life of a young couple, appears as a superb translator who connects the present with the future and weds an imaginary "European" style and recognizably "Russian" traditions of wild celebration. In "Circular Movement," a stack of bills serves as the universal translator, crossing hands toward ever-higher planes of authority until a modest editor who pays a bribe for his car to pass technical inspection is linked to the surreal president (brilliantly played by Igor' Ugol'nikov). The president doubles the operation of universal conversion: first, he elegantly "translates" cynical political manipulations into lofty quotations from Lev Tolstoy, Vasily Kliuchevsky, or Nikolai Karamzin, and vice versa. Second, he translates Russian "cultural tradition" into a malleable virtual reality: during his conversation with the governor who has delivered a bribe for his "reelection," the president angelically strolls against the background of a shining green landscape, most reminiscent of Microsoft Windows' preprogrammed desktop wallpaper, and at the end of his heartfelt monologue transmutates into a TV broadcast. In the third novella, "Energy Crisis," the film's unifying principle is presented in its most obvious form: here, the police major Oleg Ivanovich (Viktor Molchan) "translates" Anna Petrovna's (Tamara Mironova) stylized, versified visions into a "normal human language"—that is, a stream of obscenities.

Indeed, the procedures of translation between "European" and "Russian," between present, past, and future, constitute the essence of the post-Soviet epoch. Yet in *Rasskazy* the only successful translation appears to be the one associated with money: this is the sole universal language that functions effectively. However, the destructive effect of this successful communication leaves no doubts. All other attempts, based on the languages of rationality, culture, or historical memory, either hopelessly fail or will inevitably fail (as in "The World of Fixtures").

This becomes painfully obvious in the fourth novella, "Inflamed," where an inspired love affair between the middle-aged editor Max (Konstantin Iushkevich) and the stunning young beauty, tellingly deprived of a name (Liubov' Novikova), ends with the man's disappointment in his female lover: it turns out that the girl has never heard of the Cheka, thinks that Dzerzhinsky was a writer, believes that Lenin lived until 1940, and minimizes the number of victims during Soviet history. Striking scenes of intimacy (probably among the best in contemporary Russian cinema) testify that the heroes are perfectly compatible sexually, but they fail to find a mutually understandable language of communication.

Max's representation is a trap set by the filmmaker for the viewer. (Segal's aptitude for such traps revealing the viewers' misjudgment is even more obvious in his next feature, *A Film about Alekseev* [*Fil'm pro Alekseeva*, 2014].) The majority of critics and viewers enthusiastically took Max's side, detecting in this character their own frustrations with the post-Soviet generation, governed by consumerist rather than cultural or historical signifiers. For some reason, however, many of Max's fans failed to notice that his wisdom is an agglomeration of the intelligentsia's clichés (including criminal songs, as sardonically noted by Abdullaeva [2012]) and that his girlfriend sincerely wants to learn from him, which he finds rather irritating. "We should talk more!" (*Nam nuzhno bol'she razgovarivat'*), she repeats as a mantra after each séance of their sensational sex.

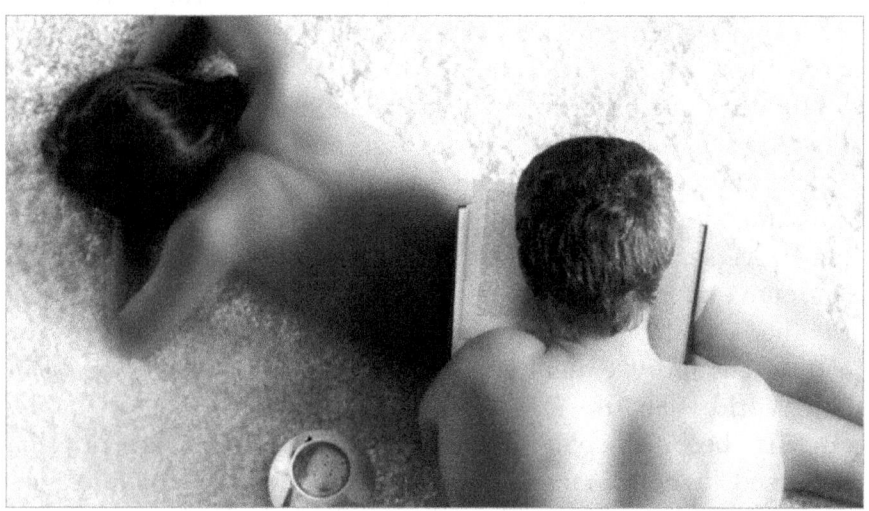

Fig. 3. Max and his nameless young lover

The culminating scene in the car and afterward, when Max conflates sexual pleasure with an increasingly cruel examination of his lover's knowledge of Soviet history, is almost painful to watch. In fact, he amplifies his sexual domination by the assumed position of a strict and unforgiving teacher, when—with obvious pleasure—he first humiliates and then dumps his lover on the grounds of her intellectual inferiority. Max's arrogance in these scenes borders on sadism, which admittedly only increases his pleasure.

Max is a member of the "creative class," an editor and, possibly, a writer, who obviously sees himself as the heir to the Russian intelligentsia. He only prefers to forget that the Russian intelligentsia held itself responsible for translations between social languages and for (pardon my pathos) the enlightenment of those who need to be enlightened. So it is also Max's fault that his girlfriend does not understand his values. He could have taught her: she was eager to learn. He forgets about these banalities not by accident: it's just much more pleasant to feel angry and disappointed. His noble anger effectively proves—and even more effectively embodies—his cultural and social superiority over post-Soviet consumerist *"bydlo"* (trash). And this is the key to his character: wearing the clout of the Russian intelligentsia, he has exchanged obligations associated with this affiliation for the position of symbolic power nicely fused with hedonism.

In "Energy Crisis," the librarian Anna Petrovna perishes in flames together with a book, which a girl lost in the woods has burned in the hope of keeping warm. This is also a signification of the intelligentsia's failure—in this case stemming from the cult of classical tradition, the identification with "sacred" literature. But at least Anna Petrovna tried to provide a translation, through her comically and lofty pseudo-Pushkinian revelations. On the contrary, Max's refusal to be patient, his anger at the girl who does not know the basics of the intelligentsia's lexicon but looks into his eyes with trust and admiration, in the view of recent Russian history reads as an unforgiving explanation of the yawning gap between the liberal intelligentsia and the notorious 86 percent of Russian citizens who applaud the annexation of Crimea, the war against Ukraine, rabid anti-Americanism, nationalist hysteria, and other niceties of the current political situation.

The abandonment of attempts to translate and adapt the intelligentsia's language and values to the worldview of the rest of the population has left a vacuum that has promptly been filled by "fixtures" in the form of quotations from Russian classics adapted to immediate political needs and, especially, by the nationalist rhetoric about "CrimeaIsOurs," the aggressive United States, and the decaying "Gayrope."

With its title and its framework setting in a publishing house specializing in fiction, *Rasskazy* places *literature* at the center of *cinema*. Oddly enough, nobody seemed to notice this splendid paradox. All of the film's parts are about the power of literature—or at least they include such a motif. The main character in "The World of Fixtures" presents a perfect writer for contemporary Russia, albeit of a new kind: one who has already absorbed the symbolist-futurist-Socialist Realist Pelevin-vs.-Baudrillard lessons of live creation, life construction, and hyperreality of simulacra. Indeed, he masterfully imagines the future in minute detail, extracting the psychological profile of a client and instantly casting actors for roles in the future play of life. Correspondingly, the president in "Circular Movement" epitomizes a perfect reader and cocreator, who with virtuoso artistry utilizes decontextualized fragments of the sacred classics to justify a cynical regime of universal corruption. Anna Petrovna and Max appear as the professional priests of the cult of literature: a librarian and an editor. However, they present contrasting scenarios: the former implements her dedication in an archaic way more fitting to the nineteenth than the twenty-first century, while the latter abandons his intelligentsia duty for the sake of hedonism. Although both fail, they do not fail to enjoy the position of symbolic power and superiority over their "folk."

How did we rejoice in the end of Russian logocentrism and literature-centrism in the 1990s, how many tears were shed about it in the 2000s (some, especially advanced Western analysts, seem to be catching up with this trend only now—see Brooks 2015). Yet all in vain. *Rasskazy* clearly demonstrates that the Russia of the 2010s remains a literature-centric country. Literature-centrism certainly has its obvious cultural benefits (one may call them culture-specific), along with less palpable political disadvantages. Segal's film is about the latter.

Rasskazy proves that literature-centrism, as a version of much-maligned logocentrism in its post-Soviet incarnation, has become more savvy and more ubiquitous, albeit less obvious than before. Yet like any form of logocentrism, it feeds the illusion of the intelligentsia's innate superiority and lends itself to corrupt power as a respectable outfit (remember "writers" dancing around their desks at the opening ceremony of the Sochi Olympics?). In other words, it secures positions of authoritarianism, political or symbolic, which in today's world does not help cultural communication, but interrupts it; does not translate but preserves the untranslatability of authoritative languages as the foundation of power. This is why the "Internationale" reworked into rap in the finale of *Rasskazy* is not such a silly idea as at first it might seem. After all, Segal has made a truly anti-authoritarian film that not only foreshadows failures of the liberal intelligentsia but also suggests the direction of a further quest that might revoke the triumph of logocentric authoritarianism.

Works Cited

Abdullaeva, Zara. 2011. *Postdok: Igrovoe/neigrovoe.* Moscow: NLO.
― ― ―. 2012. "Oskolki. 'Rasskazy.' Rezhisser Mikhail Segal." *Iskusstvo kino* 8. http://kinoart.ru/archive/2012/08/oskolki-rasskazy-rezhisser-mikhail-segal.
Adorno, Theodor W. 2005. "The Meaning of Working through the Past." In *Critical Models: Interventions and Catchwords*, translated by Henry W. Pickford, 89–103. New York: Columbia University Press. https://signale.cornell.edu/text/meaning-working-through-past.
Adorno, Theodor W., with Max Horkheimer. 2002. *Dialectic of Enlightenment.* Translated by Edmund Jephcott. Stanford, CA: Stanford University Press.
Agamben, Giorgio. 1995. *Homo Sacer: Sovereign Power and Bare Life.* Translated by Daniel Heller-Roazen. Stanford, CA: Stanford University Press.
Akulova, Vera. 2013. "Pussy Riot: Gender and Class." In *Post-Post-Soviet? Art, Politics & Society in Russia at the Turn of the Decade*, edited by Marta Dziewanska, Ekaterina Degot, and Ilya Budraitskis, 279–87. Warsaw: Museum of Modern Art in Warsaw.
Akunin, Boris. 2014. *Ognennyi perst (sbornik).* Moscow: AST.
Alexandrov, Vladimir E. 1991. *Nabokov's Otherworld.* Princeton, NJ: Princeton University Press.
― ― ―, ed. 1995. *The Garland Companion to Vladimir Nabokov.* New York: Garland.
Appel, Alfred, Jr. 1974. *Nabokov's Dark Cinema.* New York: Oxford University Press.
― ― ―. 1991. *The Annotated "Lolita": Revised and Updated.* New York: Vintage.
Arendt, Hannah. 1970. *On Violence.* Orlando, FL: Harcourt.
Artiukh, Anzhelika. 2013. "Luzery i patrioty (esse o sovremennom rossiiskom kino)." http://www.arterritory.com/ru/stilj/kino/3069-luzeri_i_patrioti/.
Babcock-Abrahams, Barbara. 1975. "'A Tolerated Margin of Mess': The Trickster and His Tales Reconsidered." *Journal of the Folklore Institute* 11 (3): 161–65.

Bakhtin, Mikhail. 1981. *The Dialogic Imagination: Four Essays.* Edited by Michael Holquist. Translated by Caryl Emerson and Michael Holquist. Austin: University of Texas Press.
———. 1983. *Problems of Dostoevsky's Poetics.* Edited and translated by Caryl Emerson. Minneapolis: University of Minnesota Press.
———. 1996. *Speech Genres and Other Late Essays.* Edited by Caryl Emerson and Michael Holquist. Austin: University of Texas Press.
Balabanova, Irina. 2001. *Govorit Dmitrii Aleksandrovich Prigov.* Moscow: OGI.
Basinskii, Pavel. 2000. "'Kak serdtsu vyskazat' sebia?" *Novyi mir* 4. http://magazines.russ.ru/novyi_mi/2000/4/basin.html.
Baudrillard, Jean. 1994. *Simulacra and Simulation.* Translated by Sheila Faria Glazer. Ann Arbor: University of Michigan Press.
Bauman, Zygmund. 2001. *The Bauman Reader.* Edited by Peter Beilharz. Oxford: Blackwell.
Beissinger, Mark R. 1995. "The Persisting Ambiguity of Empire." *Post-Soviet Affairs* 11 (2): 149–84.
Beliakov, Sergei. 2009. "Istoki i smysl 'novogo realizma.'" *Rossiiskii pisatel'.* http://rospisatel.ru/konferenzija/beljakov.htm.
Belkovskii, Stanislav. 2012a. "Perestroika 2: Mezhdu krovavoi gebnei i liberalami." OpenSpace. http://www.openspace.ru/society/projects/31848/.
———. 2012b. "Putin, perestroika i smert'." OpenSpace. http://www.openspace.ru/society/projects/31848/details/33763/.
Benjamin, Walter. 1978. *Reflections: Essays, Aphorisms, Autobiographical Writings.* Translated by Edmund Jephcott. New York: Harcourt.
———. 1985. *The Origin of German Tragic Drama.* Translated by John Osborne. London: Verso.
Bessarab, Maia. 2003. *Tak govoril Landau.* Moscow: Fizmatlit. http://www.ega-math.narod.ru/Landau/Dau2003.htm#ch01.
Beumers, Birgit, and Mark Lipovetsky. 2009. *Performing Violence: Literary and Theatrical Experiments of New Russian Drama.* Bristol: Intellect.
Bhabha, Homi K. 1994. *The Location of Culture.* London: Routledge.
Bogdanov, Konstantin. 2011. "Fiziki vs. liriki: K istorii odnoi 'pridurkovatoi' diskussii." *Novoe literaturnoe obozrenie* 111. http://nlobooks.ru/rus/magazines/nlo/196/2556/2561/.
Bol'shakova, Alla. 2009. "Sovremennyi literaturnyi protsess: Tendentsii i perspektivy." *Rossiiskii pisatel'.* http://www.rospisatel.ru/konferenzija/bolshakova-doklad.htm.
Bonnell, Victoria. 1999. *Iconography of Power: Soviet Political Posters under Lenin and Stalin.* Berkeley: University of California Press.
"Borat: Selves and Others." 2008. *Slavic Review* 67 (1): 1–87.

Borenstein, Eliot. 2000. *Men without Women: Masculinity and Revolution in Russian Fiction, 1917–1929*. Durham: Duke University Press.

———. 2012. "Kseniia Sobchak, Puzzled by Sexism." NYU Jordan Center, October 24. http://jordanrussiacenter.org/news/ksenia-sobchak-puzzled-by-sexism/#.UPoXmhy5JX8.

Boym, Svetlana. 2001. *The Future of Nostalgia*. New York: Basic Books.

Brand, Dana. 1987. "The Interaction of Aestheticism and American Consumer Culture in Nabokov's *Lolita*." *Modern Language Studies* 17 (2): 14–21.

Brinkema, Eugenie. 2014. *The Forms of the Affect*. Durham: Duke University Press.

Brooks, David. 2015. "The Russia I Miss." *New York Times*, September 11. http://www.nytimes.com/2015/09/11/opinion/david-brooks-the-russia-i-miss.html?_r=2.

Brubaker, Rogers. 1998. "Myths and Misconceptions in the Study of Nationalism." In *The State of the Nation: Ernest Gellner and the Theory of Nationalism*, edited by John A. Hall, 272–305. Cambridge: Cambridge University Press.

Buck-Morss, Susan. 2000. *Dreamworld and Catastrophe: The Passing of Mass Utopia in East and West*. Cambridge, MA: MIT Press.

Burbank, Jane, Mark von Hagen, and Anatolii Remnev, eds. 2007. *Russian Empire: Space, People, Power, 1700–1930*. Bloomington: Indiana University Press.

Bykov, Dmitry. 2002. "Ivanovo otrochestvo, ili Rebiata s nashego dvora." Bykov-quickly: Vzgliad –32, *Russkii zhurnal*, March 15. http://www.russ.ru/ist_sovr/2002315_b.html.

———. 2003a. "Filosoficheskie pis'ma." In *Khroniki blizhaishei voiny*. http://old.russ.ru/columns/bikov/20031216_b.html.

———. 2003b. "Lokhotron, ili Vodka iz gorlyshka." *Iskusstvo kino* 1:27–33.

———. 2005. *Evakuator*. Moscow: Vagrius.

———. 2013. "Proiti porog." *Moskovskie novosti*, November 1. http://www.mn.ru/oped/20131101/361232510.html.

Chizhevsky, Dmitry. 1952. *Outline of Comparative Slavic Literatures*. Survey of Slavic Civilization, vol. 1. Boston: American Academy.

Clark, Katerina. 2000. *The Soviet Novel: History as Ritual*. 3rd ed. Bloomington: Indiana University Press.

Dargis, Manohla. 2011. "A Tale of Russia Haunted by Ghosts and the Living Dead." *New York Times*, September 29. http://movies.nytimes.com/2011/09/30/movies/my-joy-directed-by-sergei-loznitsa-review.html?_r=0.

Deleuze, Gilles, and Félix Guattari. 1986. *Kafka: Toward a Minor Literature*. Translated by Dana Polan. Minneapolis: University of Minnesota Press.

Denisova, Inna. 2013. "Konstantin Khabenskii: 'Roman—muzhskoi? Ponimaete?'" *Colta*, November 7. http://www.colta.ru/articles/cinema/1060.
Denisova, Inna, Vasilii Koretskii, and Denis Ruzaev. 2013. "Pochemu ia ne Sluzhkin." *Colta*, November 8. http://www.colta.ru/articles/cinema/1073.
Derrida, Jacques. 1990. *Mémoires d'aveugle: L'autoportrait et autres ruines*. Paris: Ministère de la culture, de la communication, des grands travaux, et du bicentenaire: Réunion des musées nationaux.
Dobrenko, Evgenii. 1993. Metafora vlasti: Literatura stalinskoi epokhi v istoricheskom osveshchenii. Munich: Verlag Otto Sagner.
Dolin, Anton. 2010. "Drugie russkie." *Gazeta.ru*, May 19. http://www.gazeta.ru/culture/2010/05/19/a_3370110.shtml.
Doty, William G., and William J. Hynes. "Historical Overview of Theoretical Issues: The Problem of the Trickster." In *Mythical Trickster Figures: Contours, Contexts, and Criticisms*, edited by William J. Hynes, 13–32. Tuscaloosa: University of Alabama Press, 1993.
Dubin, Boris. 2001. *Slovo-pis'mo-literatura: Ocherki po sotsiologii sovremennoi kul'tury*. Moscow: NLO.
———. 2010. *Klassika, posle i riadom: Sotsiologicheskie ocherki o literature i kul'ture*. Moscow: NLO.
———. 2011. *Rossiia nulevykh: Politicheskaia kul'tura, istoricheskaia pamiat', povsednevnaia zhizn'*. Moscow: Rossiiskaia politicheskaia entsiklopediia (ROSSPEN).
Dugum, Daniil. 2012. "Prekrasnyi, to est' vtorostepennyi pol." *Colta*, March 29. http://os.colta.ru/art/events/details/35486/.
Epshtein, Alek. 2012. *Iskusstvo na barrikadakh: Pussy Riot, "Avtobusnaia ostanovka" i protestnyi aktivizm*. Moscow: Kolonna.
Ermolin, Evgenii. 2006. "Sluchai novogo realizma." *Kontinent* 128. http://magazines.russ.ru/continent/2006/128/ee27.html.
Etkind, Alexander. 2002. "Bremia britogo cheloveka, ili Vnutrenniaia kolonizatsiia Rossii." *Ab Imperio* 1:265–98.
———. 2003. "Russkaia literatura, XIX vek: Roman vnutrennei kolonizatsii." *Novoe literaturnoe obozrenie* 59:103–24.
———. 2011. *Internal Colonization: Russia's Imperial Experience*. Cambridge: Polity.
———. 2013. *Warped Mourning: Stories of the Undead in the Land of the Unburied*. Stanford, CA: Stanford University Press.
Etkind, Alexander, and Mark Lipovetsky. 2008. "The Return of a Triton: The Soviet Catastrophe and the Post-Soviet Novel." *Novoe literaturnoe obozrenie* 94: 174–206. Published in English (2010) in *Russian Studies in Literature* 6 (4): 6–48.

Etkind, Alexander, Dirk Uffelmann, and Ilya Kukulin, eds. 2012. *Tam, vnutri: Praktiki vnutrennei kolonizatsii v kul'turnoi istorii Rossii.* Moscow: NLO.
Fanailova, Elena. 2009. *The Russian Version.* Translated by Genya Turovskaya and Stephanie Sandler. New York: Ugly Duckling Presse.
Fiedler, Leslie. 1972. *Cross the Border—Close the Gap.* New York: Stein and Day.
Fitzpatrick, Sheila. 2005. *Tear Off the Masks! Identity and Imposture in Twentieth-Century Russia.* Princeton, NJ: Princeton University Press.
Florida, Richard. 2000. *The Rise of the Creative Class: And How It's Transforming Work, Leisure, Community and Everyday Life.* New York: Basic Books.
Foucault, Michel. 1970. *The Order of Things: An Archeology of the Human Knowledge.* New York: Pantheon Books.
Freud, Sigmund. 1955. *The Standard Edition, vol. 17 (1917–1919): An Infantile Neurosis and Other Works.* Translated and edited by James Stracheu with Anna Freud. London: Hogarth Press and the Institute of Psycho-Analysis.
Gapova, Elena. 2012. "Delo 'Pussy Riot': Feministskii protest v kontekste klassovoi bor'by," *Neprikosnovennyi zapas* 85 (5). http://www.nlobooks.ru/node/2794.
Gasparov, Boris. 2003. "Istoriia bez teleologii (Zametki o Pushkine i ego epokhe)." *Novoe literaturnoe obozrenie* 59. http://magazines.russ.ru/nlo/2003/59/gas3.html.
Geertz, Clifford. 1973. *The Interpretation of Cultures.* New York: Harper and Collins.
Genis, Aleksandr. 2002. *Rassledovaniia: Dva!* Moscow: Eksmo.
———. 2004. "Skazka dlia gnostikov: V. Sorokin *Put' Bro.*" *Radio Svoboda*, September 18.
Gerasimov, Ilya, Sergei Glebov, Jan Kusber, Marina Mogilner, and Alexander Semyonov, eds. 2009. "New Imperial History and the Challenges of Empire." In *Empire Speaks Out: Languages of Rationalization and Self-Description in the Russian Empire*, 3–32. Leiden: Brill.
Gerasimov, Ilya, Sergei Glebov, and Marina Mogilner. 2013. "The Postimperial Meets the Postcolonial: Russian Historical Experience and the Postcolonial Moment." *Ab Imperio* 2:97–135.
Gessen, Masha. 2014. *Words Will Break Cement: The Passion of Pussy Riot.* New York: Riverhead Books.
Gladil'shchikov, Iurii. 2002a. "Novyi, russkii." *Izvestiia*, September 18. http://www.izvestia.ru/culture/article24061.
———. 2002b. "Putevodnaia *Zvezda*: Novyi fil'm dolzhen vyrazit' natsional'nuiu ideiu." *Izvestiia*, April 9. http://izvestia.ru/news/260595.

Goscilo, Helena. 1996. *Dehexing Sex: Russian Womanhood during and after Glasnost*. Ann Arbor: University of Michigan Press.
Gudkov, Lev. 2004. *Negativnaia identichnost': Stat'i 1997–2002*. Moscow: NLO, 2004.
———. 2005. "The Fetters of Victory: How the War Provides Russia with Its Identity." Translated by Misha Gabowitch. *Eurozine*, March 5. http://www.eurozine.com/articles/2005-05-03-gudkov-en.html.
Gudkov, Lev, and Boris Dubin. 2009. *Intelligentsiia: Zametki o literaturno-politicheskikh illiuziiakh*. St. Petersburg: Izd. Ivana Limbakha.
Gulin, Igor'. 2011. "'Schast'e moe' Sergeia Loznitsy." *Kommersant-Weekly*, April 22. http://www.kommersant.ru/doc/1621572.
Gumbrecht, Hans-Ulrich. 2004. *Production of Presence: What Meaning Cannot Convey*. Stanford, CA: Stanford University Press.
Gusev, Aleksei. 2011. "Bezymiannaia t'ma." *Seans*, March 31. http://seance.ru/blog/my-joy/.
Hanisch, Carol. 1969. "The Personal Is Political." http://www.carolhanisch.org/CHwritings/PIP.html.
Hyde, Lewis. 1998. *Trickster Makes This World: Mischief, Myth, and Art*. New York: North Point Press.
Iampol'skaia, Elena. 2011. "Chuzhoe schast'e." *Izvestiia*, March 30. http://izvestia.ru/news/373039.
Iampol'skii, Mikhail. 2012. "Tri sloia teksta na odnu izvilinu vlasti." *Novoe vremia*, August 13. http://www.newtimes.ru/artilces/print/55977/.
Ivanov, Sergei. 2005. *Blazhennye pokhaby: Kul'turnaia istoriia iurodstva*. Moscow: Iazyki slavianskoi kul'tury. In English: Ivanov, Sergey A. 2006. *Holy Fools in Byzantium and Beyond*. Translated by Simon Frank. Oxford: Oxford University Press.
Jameson, Fredric. 2016. "Revisiting Postmodernism." Interview by Nico Baumach, Damon R. Young, and Genevieve Yue. *Social Text 127* 34 (2): 143–60.
Jung, C. G. 1972. "On the Psychology of the Trickster Figure." In *The Trickster: A Study in American Indian Mythology*, by Paul Radin with commentaries by Karl Kerényi and C. G. Jung, 195–211. New York: Schocken Books.
Jurich, Marilyn. 1998. *Scheherazade's Sisters: Trickster Heroines and Their Stories in World Literature*. Westport, CT: Greenwood.
Kerényi, Karl. 1972. "The Trickster in Relation to Greek Mythology." In *The Trickster: A Study in American Indian Mythology*, by Paul Radin with commentaries by Karl Kerényi and C. G. Jung, 173–91. New York: Schocken Books.
Khapaeva, Dina. 2007. *Goticheskoe obshchestvo: Morfologiia koshmara*. Moscow: NLO.

Khoroshilova, Tatiana. 2004. "Frankenshtein — nash syn i brat." *Rossiiskaia gazeta*, June 25. http://www.rg.ru/2004/06/25/frankenstein.html.
Kichin, Valerii. 2013. "Aleksandr Veledinskii: Bez liubvi pravda — lozh'." *Rossiiskaia gazeta*, November 5. http://www.rg.ru/2013/11/04/veledinskiy-site.html.
Knabe, Georgii S. 1993. *Materialy k lektsiiam po obshchei istorii kul'tury i kul'ture antichnogo Rima*. Moscow: RGGU.
"Kniga kak sobytie." 2015. *Novoe literaturnoe obozrenie* 136 (6). http://www.nlobooks.ru/node/6781.
Kochetkova, Natalia. 2004. "Ia literaturnyi narkoman, kak i vy, no ia eshche umeiu izgotovliat' eti narkotiki." *Izvestiia* 170, pp. 11–12.
Kononenko, Natalie, and Svitlana Kukharenko. 2008. "Borat the Trickster: Folklore and the Media, Folklore in the Media." *Slavic Review* 67 (1): 8–18.
Kormer, Vladimir. 1970. "Dvoinoe soznanie intelligentsii i psevdokul'tura." http://www.litmir.net/br/?b=113014.
Koval'skaia, Elena. 2015. "Eduard Boiakov: 'Poezdki na Afon i v Pskovsko-Pecherskii monastyr', dumaesh', bessledno prokhodiat?'" *Colta*, October 7. http://www.colta.ru/articles/theatre/8787.
Kristeva, Julia. 1982. *Powers of Horror: An Essay on Abjection*. Translated by Leon S. Roudiez. New York: Columbia University Press.
———. 1991. *Strangers to Ourselves*. Translated by Leon S. Roudiez. New York: Columbia University Press.
Kukulin, Ilya. 2007. "Alternativnoe sotsial'noe proektirovanie v sovetskom obshchestve 1960–1970-kh godov, ili Pochemu v sovremennoi Rossii ne prizhilis; levye politicheskie praktiki." *Novoe literaturnoe obozrenie* 88:169–201.
———. 2010a. "'Kakoi schet?' kak glavnyi vopros russkoi literatury." *Znamia* 4. http://magazines.russ.ru/znamia/2010/4/ku19.html.
———. 2010b. "Sozdat' cheloveka, poka ty ne chelovek. . ." *Novyi mir* 1. http://magazines.russ.ru/novyi_mi/2010/1/ku11.html.
———. 2012. "'Vnutrenniaia postkolonizatsiia': Formirovanie postkolonial'nogo soznaniia v russkoi literature 1970–2000-kh godov." In *Tam, vnutri: Praktiki vnutrennei kolonizatsii v kul'turnoi istorii Rossii*, edited by Alexander Etkind, Dirk Uffelman, and Ilya Kukulin, 846–909. Moscow: NLO.
Kul'chitskii, Bogdan. 2013. "Aleksei Ivanov: 'Ekaterinburg—paradoksal'nyi splav idealizma i ambitsii.'" *66.ru*, November 24. http://66.ru/news/society/146875/.
Kuz'min, Dmitrii. 2001. "Postkontseptualizm: Kak by nabroski k monografii." Novaia Literaturnaia Karta Rossii. http://www.litkarta.ru/dossier/kuzmin-postkonts/.

Kuznetsov, Sergei. 2016. "My ochen' khoteli byt' nad skhvatkoi." *Otkrytyi Universitet*. https://openuni.io/course/1/lesson/2/.
LaCapra, Dominick. 1998. "An Interview with Professor LaCapra by Amos Goldberg." Shoah Research Center, June 9. http://www1.yadvashem.org/odot_pdf/Microsoft%20Word%20-%203648.pdf.
Larsen, Susan. 2003. "National Identity, Cultural Authority, and the Post-Soviet Blockbusters; Nikita Mikhalkov and Aleksei Balabanov." *Slavic Review* 62 (3): 490–511.
Ledeneva, Alena V. 1998. *Russia's Economy of Favours: Blat, Networking and Informal Exchange*. Cambridge: Cambridge University Press.
— — —. 2002. *How Russia Really Works: The Informal Practices That Shaped Post-Soviet Politics and Business*. Ithaca, NY: Cornell University Press.
Lehmann, Hans-Thies. 2006. *Postdramatic Theatre*. Translated by Karen Jürs-Munby. London: Routledge.
Leiderman, Daniil. 2008. "Vkhodit Trikster." *Neprikosnovennyi zapas* 62 (6): 139–48.
Leiderman, Naum. 2010. *Teoriia zhanra: Issledovaniia i razbory*. Ekaterinburg: Ural'skii gos. pedagog. universitet.
Liashchenko, Vladimir. 2011. "Schast'e moe, ia tvoi khaos." *Gazeta.ru*, March 23. http://www.gazeta.ru/culture/2011/03/29/a_3568857.shtml.
Likhachev, Dmitrii. 1973. *Razvitie russkoi literatury XI–XII vekov: Epokhi i stili*. Leningrad: Nauka.
Lipovetsky, Mark. 2002a. "Explosive Compromises of Russian Postmodernism." In *Postmodernism and Postcolonialism*, edited by Sylvia Albertazzi and Donatella Possamai, 57–74. Bologna: Il Poligrapho.
— — —. 2002b. "PMS: Postmodernizm segodnia." *Znamia* 5:200–211.
— — —. 2008. *Paralogii: Transformatsii (post)modernistskogo diskursa v russkoi kul'ture 1920–2000-kh godov*. Moscow: NLO.
— — —. 2010. "'Metel'' v retrobudushchem: Sorokin o modernizatsii." *OpenSpace*, September 13. http://www.openspace.ru/literature/projects/13073/details/17810/.
— — —. 2011. *Charms of the Cynical Reason: The Trickster's Transformations in Soviet and Post-Soviet Culture*. Boston: Academic Studies Press.
— — —. 2012. "Sovetskie i postsovetskie transformatsii siuzheta vnutrennei kolonizatsii." In *Tam, vnutri: Praktiki vnutrennei kolonizatsii v kul'turnoi istorii Rossii*, edited by Alexander Etkind, Dirk Uffelmann, and Ilya Kukulin, 809–45. Moscow: NLO.
— — —. 2016. "A Culture of Zero Gravity." *Boundary 2* (forthcoming).
Luk'ianenko, Sergei. (1997) 2004. *Zvezdy—kholodnye igrushki*. Moscow: AST.
— — —. 2006. *Dozor*. Moscow: AST.

L'vovskii, Stanislav. 2012. *Vse nenadolgo*. Moscow: NLO.
Makarius, Laura. 1993. "The Myth of Trickster: The Necessary Breaker of Taboos." In *Mythical Trickster: Figures, Contours, Contexts, and Criticism*, edited by William J. Hynes, 66–86. Tuscaloosa: University of Alabama Press.
Martin, Terry. 2001. *The Affirmative Action Empire: Nations and Nationalism in the Soviet Union, 1923–1939*. Ithaca, NY: Cornell University Press.
Marusenkov, Maxim. 2012. *Absurdopediia russkoi zhizni Vladimira Sorokina: Zaum', grotesk i absurd*. St. Petersburg: Aleteia.
Medvedev, Kirill. 2012. *It's No Good*. Translated by Keith Gessen. New York: N+1 / Ugly Duckling Presse.
Meletinskii, E. M. 1975. *Poetika mifa*. Moscow: Nauka.
"[Mikhail] Leont'ev: Nikto ne izvlechet urokov iz dela Pussy Riot." 2012. *Aktual'nye kommentarii*, August 17. http://actualcomment.ru/news/47010/.
Mogilner, Marina, and Alexander Etkind. 2011. "Razgovor o neklassicheskom kolonializme I: Interv'iu s Aleksandrom Etkindom." *Ab Imperio* 1:117–30.
Moskvina, Tat'iana. 2002. "Pro Ivana i Dzhona." *Iskusstvo kino* 7:21–25.
Mulder, Anne-Claire. 2006. *Divine Flesh, Embodied Word: Incarnation as a Hermeneutical Key to a Feminist Theologian's Reading of Luce Irigaray's Work*. Amsterdam: Universiteit Van Amsterdam.
Murav'ev, Aleksei. 2012. "'Tri shchelchka popu,' ili Novoe iurodstvo kak refleks." *Polit.ru*, April 23. http://www.polit.ru/article/2012/04/23/Riot_three_kicks/.
Nabokov, Vladimir. 1977. *Lolita*. New York: Vintage.
― ― ― . 2001. *Lolita*. St. Petersburg: Symposium.
Nancy, Jean-Luc. 2008. *Corpus*. Translated by Richard A. Rand. New York: Fordham University Press.
"Naval'nyi vstupilsia za Pussy Riot, khotia i priznal ikh aktsiiu idiotskoi." 2012. *RBK*, October 7. http://www.rbcdaily.ru/politics/562949983174898.
Nemchenko, Lilya. 2013. "Mikhail Segal: *Short Stories* (*Rasskazy*, 2012)." *KinoKultura* 39. http://www.kinokultura.com/2013/39r-rasskazy.shtml.
Neuberger, Joan. 2003. *Ivan the Terrible*. London: I. B. Tauris.
Novikova, Liza. 2008. "Vladimir Sorokin: V Mavzolee dolzhen lezhat' Ivan Groznyi." *Kommersant*, August 22.
Novodvorskaia, Valeriia. 2012. "Tranzit na Arkanar." *Medved'*, November 21. http://www.medvedmagazine.ru/articles/Valeria_Novodvorskaya_o_bratiah_Strugatskih.1831.html.
Nuriev, Vitalii. 2011. "Vladimir Sorokin: Podmorozhennaia Rossiia." *Nezavisimaia gazeta*, July 5. http://www.srkn.ru/interview/podmorozhennaya-rossiya.html.

Osminkin, Roman. 2016. *Not a Word about Politics! / Ni slova o politke!* New York: Cicada Press.
Oushakine, Serguei. 2001. "The Terrifying Mimicry of Samizdat." *Public Culture* 13 (2): 191–214.
———. 2010a. *The Patriotism of Despair: Nation, War, and Loss in Russia.* Ithaca, NY: Cornell University Press.
———. 2010b. "Totality Decomposed: Objectalizing Late Socialism in Post-Soviet Biochronicles." In "Documentary Trends in Contemporary Russian Culture," edited by Birgit Beumers and Mark Lipovetsky. Special issue, *Russian Review* 69 (4): 638–69.
———, ed. 2013a. "Ob"ekty affekta: K materiologii emotsii." *Novoe literaturnoe obozrenie* 120:29–93, and 121:10–45.
———. 2013b. "Remembering in Public: On the Affective Management of History." *Ab Imperio* 1:269–302.
Parry, Albert. 1966. *The New Class Divided: Science and Technology versus Communism.* New York: Macmillan.
Pelevin, Viktor. 2012. *S.N.U.F.F.* Moscow: Eksmo.
Pifer, Ellen. 1995. "*Lolita.*" In *The Garland Companion to Nabokov,* edited by Vladimir E. Alexandrov, 305–20. New York: Garland.
Platt, Kevin M. F. 2012. "Examining International Media Coverage and Responses to Pussy Riot." Center for Global Communication Studies blog, September 6. http://cgcsblog.asc.upenn.edu/2012/09/06/examining-international-media-coverage-and-responses-to-pussy-riot-by-kevin-m-f-platt/.
Pomerantsev, Vladimir. 1953. "Ob iskrennosti v literature." *Novyi mir* 12. English translation (abridged) at http://www.thedrawers.net/pomerantsev.htm.
Ponomariov, Alexander. 2013. "The Pussy Riot Case in Russia: Orthodox Canon Law and the Sentence of the Secular Court." *Ab Imperio* 1:187–216.
Prigov, Dmitrii. 2015. *Moskva.* Edited by Georg Witte and Brigitte Obermayr. Moscow: NLO.
Proffer, Carl. 1968. *Keys to "Lolita."* Bloomington: Indiana University Press.
Prokhorov, Aleksandr. 2007. *Unasledovannye diskursy: Stalinistskie tropy v kul'ture ottepeli.* St. Petersburg: Akademicheskii proekt.
"Pussy Riot i iurodstvo." 2012. Sakharov Center, June 16. http://www.sakharov-center.ru/discussions/?id=1663.
"Pussy Riot's Closing Statements." 2012. *n+1,* August 13. http://nplusonemag.com/pussy-riot-closing-statements.
Rancière, Jacques. 2001. "Ten Theses on Politics." http://www.after1968.org/app/webroot/uploads/RanciereTHESESONPOLITICS.pdf.
Rasskazova, T. 1992. "Vladimir Sorokin: 'Tekst kak narkotik.'" In *Sbornik rasskazov* by Vladimir Sorokin, 119–126. Moscow: Russlit.

Roll, Serafima. 1996. *Postmodernisty o postkul'ture*. Moscow: NLO.
Rossa, Boryana. 2012. "Pussy Riot kak vozhdelenie." PosleZavtra, November 8. http://poslezavtra.be/optics/2012/11/08/pussy-riot-kak-vozhdelenie-pochemu-ya-podderzhivayu-pussy-riot-no-ne-razdelyayu-argumentov-v-ih-zaschitu.html.
Rubinshtein, Lev. 2001. *Here I Am: Performance Poems*. Translated by Joanne Turnbull. Glas: New Russian Writing, vol. 27. Moscow: Glas.
Rudik, I. 2008. "Vladimir Sorokin: 'Ia pochuvstvoval, chto seichas poidu i prosto-naprosto ub'iu ego.'" *Konkurent*, April 2. http://www.konkurent-krsk.ru/index.php?id=1259.
Rutten, Ellen. 2012. "Impotent-intelligent: Seksualizatsiia vnutrennei kolonizatsii." In *Tam, vnutri: Praktiki vnutrennei kolonizatsii v kul'turnoi istorii Rossii*, edited by Alexander Etkind, Dirk Uffelmann, and Ilya Kukulin, 789–808. Moscow: NLO.
———. 2017. *Sincerity after Communism: A Cultural History*. New Haven, CT: Yale University Press.
Rymbu, Galina. 2014a. *Peredvizhnoe prostranstvo perevorota*. Moscow: Argo-Risk.
———. 2014b. "Sobytie-sobranie: K poetike Fainy Grimberg." In *Faina Grimberg: Stat'i i materialy*, 3–8. Moscow: Argo-Risk, Knizhnoe obozrenie.
Said, Edward W. 1979. *Orientalism*. New York: Vintage Books.
Sakharov, Andrei. 1968. "Progress, Coexistence and Intellectual Freedom." Sakharov Center. http://www.sakharov-center.ru/asfconf2011/english/articleseng/1.
Saprykin, Iurii. 2012. "'Dumaete, zapadnaia publika liubit sovremennoe iskusstvo? Ni figa podobnogo?' Boris Grois o Pussy Riot, fundamentalistakh i pobede video." *Afisha*, June 1. http://www.afisha.ru/article/boris-grojs-o-pussy-riot-fundamentalistah-i-zasile-videorolikov/.
Satarov, Georgii. 2012. "Koshchunstvo vmesto iurodstva." *Ezhednevnyi zhurnal*, August 27. http://www.ej.ru/?a=note&id=12178.
"*Seansu* otvechaiut. . . *Moi svodnyi brat Frankenshtein*." 2005. *Seans* 21/22. http://seance.ru/category/n/21-22/films2004/frankenshtein/mnenia.
Semenova, Oksana. 2002. "Vladimir Sorokin: 'Uboinoe salo': 'Ia khotel napolnit' russkuiu literaturu govnom.'" *MK-Voskresen'e*, July 21–27.
Senderovich, Savely, and Elena Shvarts. 1999. "*Lolita*: Po tu storonu pornografii i moralizma." *Literaturnoe obozrenie* 2:63–72.
Shakina, Ol'ga. 2010. "Sergei Loznitsa: 'Ni cherta ne srastetsia.'" OpenSpace, August 25. http://os.colta.ru/cinema/events/details/17550/?attempt=1.
Shalamov, Varlam. 1998. *Sobranie sochinenii*. 4 vols. Moscow: Khudozhestvennaia literatura.

Shapoval, Sergei. 1998. "Vladimir Sorokin: 'V kul'ture dlia menia net tabu...'" In *Sobranie sochinenii* by Vladimir Sorokin, vol. 1, 8–20. Moscow: Ad Marginem.
Sharogradskii, Andrei. 2012. "Obozrevatel' RS Kirill Kobrin o smesi Govorukhina s Mikhalkovym." *Radio Svoboda*, July 31. http://www.svoboda.org/content/article/24662246.html.
Shute, Jenefer. 1995. "Nabokov and Freud." In *The Garland Companion to Nabokov*, edited by Vladimir E. Alexandrov, 412–19. New York: Garland.
Sidorov, Dmitri. 2000. "National Monumentalization and the Politics of Scale: The Resurrections of the Cathedral of Christ the Savior in Moscow." *Annals of the Association of American Geographers* 90 (3): 549–72.
Sirivlia, Natal'ia. 2002a. "Igra v mashinki." *Iskusstvo kino* 2:47–48.
———. 2002b. "Voina bez mira." *Novyi mir* 7:209–13.
Sitkovskii, Gleb. 2002. "Kirdyk po-russki." *Iskusstvo kino* 7:30–32.
Skakov, Nariman. 2016. "Typographomania: On Prigov's Typewritten Experiments." *Russian Review* 75 (2): 241–61.
Slatina, Elena. 2002. "Idet 'Voina' narodnaia." *Ekspert*, March 18, 72–74.
Sloterdijk, Peter. 1987. *Critique of Cynical Reason*. Translated by Michael Eldred. Minneapolis: University of Minnesota Press.
Smirnov, Igor'. 2000. *Megaistoriia: K istoricheskoi tipologii kul'tury*. Moscow: Agraf.
Snow, Charles Percy. (1956) 1998. *The Two Cultures.* Cambridge: Cambridge University Press. Citations refer to the 1998 edition.
Sobchak, Kseniia. 2012. "Valeriia Novodvorskaia o politicheskom performance: Ia ne Pussy—ia tikhii, prilichnyi chelovek." *TV Rain*, December 12. http://tvrain.ru/articles/valerija_novodvorskaja_o_politicheskom_performanse_ja_ne_pussy_ja_tihij_prilichnyj_chelovek-334155/.
Sobchak, Kseniia, and Elena Sokolova. 2012. "Ekaterina Samutsevich. Neraschekhlennaia." *Snob*, October 19. http://www.snob.ru/selected/entry/53946.
Sokolovskaia, Ianina. 2002. "Liubka Shevtsova i Marilyn Monroe: Kommunisticheskii roman 'Molodaia gvardiia' stanet komiksom." *Izvestiia*, July 12, 1, 10.
Solzhenitsyn, Aleksandr. 1973. "Raskaianie i samoogranichenie kak kategorii natsional'noi zhizni." http://www.vehi.net/samizdat/izpodglyb/05.html.
Sorokin, Vladimir. 1998. *Sobranie sochinenii*. 2 vols. Moscow: Ad Marginem.
———. 2006. *Den' oprichnika*. Moscow: Zakharov.
———. 2011. *Day of the Oprichnik*. New York: Farrar, Straus and Giroux.

———. 2014. "Russia Is Slipping Back into an Authoritarian Empire." *Der Spiegel* interview with Vladimir Sorokin. In *Late and Post-Soviet Literature: A Reader*, edited by Mark Lipovetsky and Lisa Ryoko Wakamiya, 279–80. Boston: Academic Studies Press.

Staten, Henry. 1993. "How the Spirit (Almost) Became Flesh: Gospel of John." *Representations* 41:34–57.

Stishova, Elena. 2004. "Semeinaia khronika vremen neob"iavlennoi voiny." *Iskusstvo kino* 7. http://kinoart.ru/archive/2004/07/n7-article5.

Strel'tsov, Mikhail. 2012. "Vse ne prosto Rait." *Kontr@banda*, September 3. http://kbanda.ru/index.php/culture-miscellaneous-2/obshchestvo/261-obshchestvo/2770-vsjo-ne-prosto-rajt-razmyshleniya-v-otpuske.html.

Strugatsky, Arkady, and Boris Strugatsky. 1980. *Beetle in the Anthill*. Translated by Antonina W. Bouis. New York: Macmillan.

———. 2000–2003. *Sobranie sochinenii*. 11 vols. Donetsk: Stalker; St. Petersburg: "Terra Fantastica" izd. doma "Corvus."

———. 2014. *Hard to Be a God*. Translated by Olena Bormashenko. Chicago: Chicago Review Press.

Suny, Ronald. 2001. "Imperiia kak ona est': Imperskaia Rossiia, 'natsional'noe' samosoznanie i teorii imperii." *Ab Imperio* 1–2: 10–72.

Suslova, Evgeniia. 2013. "Praktika sub"ektivatsii." *Novoe literaturnoe obozrenie* 124. http://magazines.russ.ru/nlo/2013/124/18s.html.

Tolstaya, Tatiana. 2002. *Izium*. Moscow: Podkova.

Tuula, Maksim. 2011. "Skazka so strashnym kontsom: Interv'iu s Sergeem Loznitsei." *Booknik*, April 12. http://booknik.ru/context/all/skazka-so-strashnym-kontsom/.

Tynianov, Iurii. 1977. *Poetika. Istoriia literatury. Kino*. Edited by E. Toddes, A. Chudakov, and M. Chudakova. Moscow: Nauka.

Uffelmann, Dirk. 2006. "*Led tronulsia*: The Overlapping Periods in Vladimir Sorokin's Work from the Materialization of Metaphors to Fantastic Substantialism." In *Landslide of the Norm: Language Culture in Post-Soviet Russia*, edited by Ingunn Lunde and Tine Roesen, 100–125. Slavica Bergensia 6. Bergen: University of Bergen.

———. 2012. "Podvodnye kamni vnutrennei (de)kolonizatsii Rossii." In *Tam, vnutri: Praktiki vnutrennei kolonizatsii v kul'turnoi istorii Rossii*, edited by Alexander Etkind, Dirk Uffelmann, and Ilya Kukulin, 53–104. Moscow: NLO.

Vail', Petr, and Aleksandr Genis. 2003. *60-e: Mir sovetskogo cheloveka*. In Vail' and Genis, *Sobranie sochinenii*, vol. 1, 507–948. Ekaterinburg: U-Faktoriia.

Verigina, Marina. 2012. "O roli sado-mazo v dele Pussy Riot." Forum.msk.ru, August 7. http://forum-msk.org/material/society/9550027.html.

Vishnevetsky, Ignatiy. 2015. "*Hard to Be a God* Will Take You to a World of Shit." *A.V. Club*, January 29. http://www.avclub.com/review/hard-be-god-will-take-you-world-shit-214434.
Volkova, Elena. 2016. "Khristianskaia apologiia Pussy Riot." Academia.edu. https://www.academia.edu/_Pussy_Riot.
Voznesenskii, Aleksandr. 2006. "Vladimir Sorokin: 'Zakony russkoi metafiziki.'" Srkn.ru, October 26. http://www.srkn.ru/interview/voznesenski.shtml.
Willems, Joachim. 2013. *Pussy Riots Punk-Gebet: Religion, Recht und Politik in Russland*. Berlin: Berlin University Press.
Wölfflin, Heinrich. 1996. *Renaissance and Baroque*. Ithaca, NY: Cornell University Press.
Worland, Rick. 2007. *The Horror Film: An Introduction*. London: Blackwell.
Yakhina, Guzel'. 2015. *Zuleikha otkryvaet glaza*. Moscow: AST.
Yurchak, Alexei. 2006. *Everything Was Forever, until It Was No More: The Last Soviet Generation*. Princeton, NJ: Princeton University Press.
Žižek, Slavoj. 1989. *The Sublime Object of Ideology*. London: Verso.
———. 2001. *Did Somebody Say Totalitarianism? Five Interventions in the (Mis)Use of a Notion*. London: Verso.
Zubok, Vladislav. 2009. *Zhivago's Children: The Last Russian Intelligentsia*. Cambridge, MA: Belknap Press of Harvard University Press.

INDEX

Ab Imperio, 56
Abdullaeva, Zara, 240-241, 244
Adorno, Theodor W., 27, 44
Agamben, Giorgio, 44, 128
Aigi, Aleksei, 199n2
Aitmatov, Chingiz, 152
Akhmatova, Anna, 91
   Requiem, 91
Aksenov, Vasilii, 40
   Colleagues (Kollegi), 40
   Our Golden Iron (Zolotaia nasha Zhelezka), 40
Akulova, Vera, 139n6
Akunin, Boris, 57
   Fiery Finger (Ognennyi perst), 76
   History of the Russian State, The (Istoriia rossiiskogo gosudarstva), 76
   A Part of Europe, (Chast' Evropy), 77
   A Part of Asia, (Chast' Azii), 77
Al'brekht, Vladimir, 36
Alekhina, Mariia, 135
Alekseeva, Liudmila, 36
Alov, Aleksandr, 195
Altaev, O. see Kormer
Al'tshuler, Boris, 36
Amenábar, Alejandro, 162
Andersen, Hans Christian, 114
Anufriev, Sergei, 173
Appel, Alfred, 14n1, 19, 25
Arendt, Hanna, 54, 68
Artaud, Antonin, 110

Artiukh, Anzhelika, 237
Arzhak, Nikolai, 38n4
Authoritarainism (authoritarian), 124, 138, 142, 144, 247
Babel, Isaak, 131, 176n4
Baitov, Nikolai, 103
Bakhtin, Mikhail, 13, 110, 145, 222-223
Bakuradze, Bakur, 96n3
Balabanov, Aleksei, 90, 172, 177-179, 182-183, 187, 189-192, 200, 204-205
   Brother (Brat), 190, 204-205
   Brother 2 (Brat 2), 90, 172-173, 190, 2-4
   War (Voina), 172, 177-180, 183-194, 200
Balabanova, Irina, 104
Balaian, Roman, 231, 233, 236
Baron Cohen, Sasha, 144n13
Barskova, Polina, 105-106, 154, 160, 167
   Directory of Leningrad Front Poets, 1941–45 (Spravochnik leningradskikh poetov-frontovikov, 1941-45), 160
   Living Pictures (Zhivye kartiny), 167
Bashkirtseva, Mariia, 158
Basinskii, Pavel, 88, 151
Batkin, Leonid, 43
Baudelaire, Charles, 14
Baudrillard, Jean, 20, 246
Bauman, Zygmund, 174-175, 183n5

Beissinger, Mark R., 56
Bekmambetov, Timur, 45, 80
Beliakov, Sergei, 88
Belkovskii, Stanislav, 34
Benjamin, Walter, 30-31, 97, 119
Berezovsky, Boris, 132, 141
Beria, Lavrentii 63, 72
Bessarab, Maia, 37, 39n5, 47n8
Beumers, Birgit, 9-10, 94, 157n6, 221
Bezrodnyi, Mikhail, 152
Bhabha, Homi, 55-57
Bikini Kill, 139
Bildungsroman, 222
Blok, Aleksandr, 14
Blue Noses Group, 132
Bodrov Jr., Sergei, 183, 204
Bogart, Humphrey, 31
Bogdanov, Konstantin, 38
Boiakov, Eduard, 157
Bolotnaia Square, 159
Bol'shakova, Alla, 88
Bondarchuk, Fedor, 200
Bondarchuk, Sergei, 195, 211
Bonnell, Victoria, 89
Borat, see Baron Cohen, Sasha
Borenstein, Eliot, 9, 144n11-12, 176-177n4
Bosch, Hieronymus, 64, 124
Boym, Svetlana, 181-182
Brand, Dana, 24
Brik, Evgeniia, 233
Brinkema, Eugenie, 164
Brodsky, Joseph, 90
Bromfield, Andrew, 82
Brooks, David, 246
Brooks, Mel, 208
Brubaker, Rogers, 56
Bruskin, Grisha, 152
Buchenwald, 74
Buck-Morss, Susan, 183
Buddhism, 147
Bukovskii, Vladimir, 36

Bulgakov, Mikhail, 131
Burbank, Jane, 56
Bykov, Dmitry, 45, 48, 57, 75, 79-80, 90, 97-98, 100, 144, 155, 186, 189-190, 192n7, 233-234
  Evacuator, The (Evakuator), 79
  Living Souls (ZhD), 45, 90, 97-98
Bykov, Vasil', 225
Catullus, 14
Chadov, Aleksei, 183
Chebotarev, Vladimir, 196n1
Chechen War, 176, 178, 198, 200, 205, 213
Chechnya, 184, 190, 198, 213, 216
Cheka, 45, 120, 243
Chekhov, Anton, 113-114, 158
Chernikova, Larisa, 171
Chernykh, Anfisa, 231
Chernykh, Valentin, 199
Chizhevsky, Dmitry, 88
Chkheidze, Rezo, 195
Chukovskii, Kornei, 152
Christ (Christian), 125-126, 136, 139, 188, 226
Cimino, Michael, 202
Civil War (Russian), 45, 93-94, 151, 170
Clark, Katerina, 188, 206
Comedy Club, 43
Crimea (annexation), 52, 56, 81, 82n24, 102, 145, 155-156, 245-246
Dante Alighieri, 14
Dapkunaite, Ingeborga, 184
Dargis, Manohla, 221
Deleuze, Gilles, 149
Delone, Vadim, 36
Democratic Union Party, 78
Denisova, Inna, 236-238
Derevianko, Pavel, 179
Derrida, Jacques, 30, 44, 193
Dietrich, Marlene, 19, 25, 31
Diogenes, 125

Disney, 19, 25, 169
Disneyland, 20, 25
Dobrenko, Evgeny, 180
Dolin, Anton, 219
Dostoevsky, Fyodor, 14, 17, 110, 114, 232
Dovlatov, Sergei, 91, 146, 152
Dubin, Boris, 34, 43, 72, 137, 148-149, 217
Dugum, Daniil, 140
Dzerzhinsky, Feliks, 120n14, 243
Efremov, Mikhail, 155
Ehrenburg, Ilya, 38n3, 131
Eikhenbaum, Boris, 145
Eisenstein, Sergei, 89
Elizarov, Mikhail, 97-100
Eltang, Lena, 106
Emelin, Vsevolod, 43
Epshtein, Alek, 130n2
Ermolin, Evgenii, 88
Erofeev, Venedikt, 131
Esenin-Vol'pin, Aleksandr, 36
E.T.I., 132
Etkind, Alexander, 53-55, 60, 63-64, 68, 97-98, 101-103, 225
Eucharist, 115, 121, 126
Evtushenko, Evgenii, 40, 43, 91
Facebook, 80n23, 152-154, 164
Fadeev, Aleksandr, 169-170
Family (life, values), 18, 36, 95-96, 105, 177n4, 184, 190, 196-218, 232
Fanailova, Elena, 105, 154, 160-162, 164
Fedorchenko, Aleksei, 96n3
Feminism, 52, 70, 82, 127, 138-139, 148, 174
Fiedler, Leslie, 90
Fitzpatrick, Sheila, 34
Flaubert, Gustav, 14, 16
Florida, Richard, 34, 51-52
Formalism (formalist), 145, 147, 152

Foucault, Michel, 44, 153
Franklin, Benjamin, 146
Freud, Sigmund, 94, 201-202
Freudianism, 18, 23, 97, 102
FSB (Federal Security Service), 101, 184, 186
Gai Germanika, Valeriia, 96n3
Gaidai, Leonid, 40, 43
  Operation "Y", 40
  Ivan Vasilievich: Back to the Future (Ivan Vasil'evich meniaet professiiu), 40
  Kidnapping, Caucasian Style (Kavkazskaia plennitsa), 40
Gaidar, Arkadii, 170-171
Galanter, Eugene, 60
Galich, Alexander, 35
Gapova, Elena, 139n6
Garmash, Sergei, 178, 203
Gasparov, Boris, 87
Gasparov, Mikhail, 152
Gazarov, Sergei, 214
Gazmanov, Oleg, 139
Geertz, Clifford, 59-60
Genis, Aleksandr, 36, 39, 47, 112, 116, 118
Gerasimov, Ilya, 10, 54, 56, 58
Gerasimov, Sergei, 169
German, Aleksei, 64, 75-72, 92,
Germany (Germans), 146, 174, 198, 219-220, 224, 226-227
Gerstenhaber, M., 60
Gessen, Masha, 130n1
Ginzburg, Lidiia, 106, 152, 158
Girard, René, 191
Gladil'shchikov, Iurii, 182, 205
Glebov, Sergei, 54
Gol'dshtein, Aleksandr, 92n2, 103, 106
Golovin, Vladimir, 220
Goralik, Linor, 154, 167
Goscilo, Helena, 9-10, 70
Gospel, see John's Gospel

Govorukhin, Stanislav, 40, 43,139, 178-179, 182, 189
   Vertical, The, 40, 43
   Voroshilovskii strelok, 178-180, 189
Granin, Daniil, 40
Great Patriotic War, see World War II
Great Terror, 54, 225
Grebenshchikov, Boris, 139
Greene, Graham, 25
Gremina, Elena, 154, 160
   Hour and Eighteen (Chas vosemnadtsat'), 160
   September.doc, 154
Grimberg, Faina, 161, 164
Grishkovets, Evgenii, 43, 90, 155-157
   +1, 157
   Dreadnoughts, 157
   House, The, 157
   How I Ate a Dog, 157
   Planet, The, 157
Grois, Boris, 136, 148
Grossman, Vasily, 91
Guattari, Félix, 149
Gudkov, Lev, 34, 43, 137, 197-198, 202, 213
Gudlin, Vladimir, 199n2
Guerrilla Girls, 139
Gulag, 55, 62-63, 102, 119, 152, 171, 136
Gulin, Igor', 219
Gumbrecht, Hans-Ulrich, 164
Gusev, Aleksei, 219
Gverdtsiteli, Tamara, 139
Halva, Helen, 9-10, 151, 156n5, 163n10, 166n12
Hanisch, Carol, 148
Hashamova, Yana, 9, 11
Hemingway, Ernest, 43
Hiroshima, 47
Hitler, Adolf, 116, 198
Hollander, John, 18

Hollywood, 19-23, 83, 170n1, 177
Holocaust, 103, 197
Horkheimer, Max, 27, 44
Iakovleva, Elena, 204
Iampol'skaia, Elena, 219-220, 227
Iampolskii, Mikhail, 134-135
Iankovskii, Oleg, 179, 231, 236
Iarmol'nik, Leonid, 199n2, 200
Ideology (ideological), 20, 35-45, 49, 54, 56, 59-60, 82, 85, 90-91, 101-104, 108, 112-113, 119-121, 126-127, 134, 138, 142, 145-146, 155, 158-162, 177n4, 181, 188-192, 196, 200, 205, 224, 227-228
Intelligentsia, 8-9, 33-52, 59-60, 63, 70-71, 75, 79-80, 85, 126, 137, 139, 142, 153, 171, 187, 200-202, 207, 209-211, 216-217, 230, 237-239, 244-247
Intertext, 14, 16, 114
Irigaray, Luce, 127
ITR, 33-35, 37, 38n3, 40-52, 59 237
I.Grekova, 39
Il'f, Ilya, 131
Il'ianen, Aleksandr, 153, 167
Il'ina, Marianna, 207
Imperialist (imperialism), 9, 52, 55-58, 70, 81, 85, 103, 155, 191, 200, 213
Internet, 34, 52, 80, 92, 146, 149-150, 153-155
Iskander, Fazil', 55, 131
Isolationism, 9, 52
Iushkevich, Konstantin, 243
Ivanov, Aleksei, 230, 232-238,
Ivanov, Sergei, 134-135
Ivashchenko, Aleksei, 172
Izvestiia, 169-171
Jakobson, Roman, 145
Jameson, Fredric, 8
Jencks, Charles, 170
John's Gospel, 125-127

Joyce, James, 14
Jung, C. G., 26
Jurich, Marilyn, 132, 141, 143
Kanevskaya, Marina, 32n8
Kantor, Maksim, 98
Kapitsa, Petr, 36
Karloff, Boris, 200, 204, 207
Kasianova, Polina, 241
Kelly, Ian, 184
KGB, 37
Khabenskii, Konstantin, 230
Khapaeva, Dina, 47
Kharitonov, Evgenii, 152
Khemlin, Margarita, 107
   Investigator, The, (Doznavatel'), 107
   Klotsvog, 107
   Last One, The (Krainii), 107
Khersonskii, Boris, 105
Khlebnikov, Boris, 96n3, 211n6
   Free Floating (Svobodnoe plavanie), 96n3
   Help Gone Mad (Sumasshedshaia pomoshch'), 96n3
   Koktebel', 211n6
Khoroshilova, Tatiana, 200
Khrzhanovsky, Andrei, 90
Kichin, Valerii, 233
Kidman, Nicole, 161n8
Kirill, Patriarkh, 139
Kirillov, Viktor, 169
Knabe, Georgii, 88
Kobrin, Kirill, 141
Kobzon, Iosif, 139
Kochetkova, Natalia, 123
Kokh, Alfred, 139
Komsomol'skaya Pravda, 38n3
Kononenko, Natalie, 144n13
Kononov, Nikolai, 103, 106
Koretskii, Vasilii, 236
Kormer, Vladimir, 36, 46-48, 51
Kopylov, Gertsen, 39
Kotcheff, Ted, 202
Kott, Aleksandr, 172, 179, 181-182
Kovalev, Sergei, 36
Kovalov, Oleg, 203n4
Koval'skaia, Elena, 157
Kregzhde, Evgeniia, 233
Kristeva, Julia, 127, 202, 210, 218
Krupin, Vladimir, 139
Krusanov, Pavel, 172-3
KSP (*klub samodeiatel'noi pesni*, amateur song club), 35, 42, 46
Kubaev, Rauf, 235
Kukharenko, Svitlana, 144n13
Kukulin, Ilya, 50, 55, 62-63, 105
Kul'chitskii, Bogdan, 232
Kulidzhanov, Lev, 195
Kulik, Oleg, 132
Kul'tura, 219
Kurdizis, E., 184
Kuvaev, Oleg, 132
Kuz'min, Dmitrii, 104
Kuzmin, Mikhail, 152
Kuznetsov, Sergei, 146
KVN (a televised competition of wits), 35, 43, 46
LaCapra, Dominick, 94-96
Landau, Lev, 37, 47n8
Laodicean synod, 136
Larsen, Susan, 190
Lawrence, T. E., 65
Lebedev, Nikolai, 172, 178-180, 182, 200
Ledeneva, Alena V., 131-132
Lee, Rowland V., 208
Lehmann, Hans-Thies, 160, 164
Leiderman, Daniil, 9, 144n13
Leiderman, Naum, 88
Lemon, Alaina, 59n1
Lenin, Vladimir, 112, 145, 243
Leningrad blockade, 105-106
Leningrad Polytechnic, 40
Leont'ev, Mikhail, 139, 142-143
Lermontov, Mikhail, 16, 163, 163n10

Levada, Iurii, 44
Levinson, Alexei, 34
Levkin, Andrei, 92n2, 103
  Golem, Russian Version (Golem, russkaia versiia), 92n2
  Marple, 92n2
  Mozgva, 92n2
Liadova, Elena, 231, 236
Liashchenko, Vladimir, 219
Liberal (liberalism), 9, 34-35, 37, 40-43, 46, 48, 51, 57-60, 78, 80, 82, 85, 86, 90, 98, 103, 112, 128, 137-142, 144n11, 146, 150-151, 155, 157, 169, 193, 196, 200, 207, 216-217, 245-247
Likhachev, Dmitrii, 88
Limonov, Eduard, 158
Lipkin, Semen, 55
LiveJournal, 152-153
Lotman, Yurii, 40, 145
Loznitsa, Sergei, 96, 219-229
  My Joy (Schast'e moe), 96, 219-229
  In the Fog (V tumane), 225
Luk'ianenko, Sergei, 43, 45, 57, 75, 80-85, 139
  Day Watch (Dnevnoi dozor), 80
  Night Watch (Nochnoi dozor), 80
  Stars Are Cold Toys (Zvezdy – kholodnye igrushki), 80, 82, 85
  Twilight Watch (Sumerechnyi dozor), 80
  World of Watches (Vselennaia "Dozorov"), 45
Lungin, Pavel, 172, 182
  Oligarch, The (Oligarkh), 172
Lutsik, Petr, 173
  Outskirts (Okraina), 173
L'vovskii, Stanislav, 105, 154, 160, 164-166
  Rendered by Alien Words (Chuzhimi slovami), 160

Soviet Drinking Songs (Sovetskie zastol'nye pesni), 105, 160
Lyotard, Jean-François, 44
Maeterlinck, Maurice, 19, 26
Magical Historicism, 97-103, 225
Magnitsky, Sergei, 159
Magun, Artemii, 59n1
Maidan, 102
Makanin, Vladimir, 39
Makarius, Laura 133
Makarevich, Andrei, 139
Makarov, Vladimir, 9, 33n1
Malevich, Kazimir, 135
Mamardashvili, Merab, 44
Mamyshev-Monro, Vladislav, 132
Mandelstam, Osip, 33, 113
Masing-Delic, Irene, 9-10, 151, 156n5, 163n10, 166n12
Martin, Terry 54
Marychev, Viacheslav, 132
Marusenkov, Maxim 116n10
Matizen, Viktor, 206
Matrosov, Boris, 231
Mavrodi, Sergei, 132
Medvedev, Dmitry, 141
Medvedev, Kirill, 154, 159
Medvedev, Zhores, 36
Meletinskii, E. M., 176
Mel'nikov, Vitalii, 231
Mendes, Sam, 231, 236
Mérimée, Prosper, 14, 16, 31
Merzlikin, Andrei, 242
Meskhiev, Dmitrii, 199n3
Mikhailova, Tat'iana, 11, 230
Mikhal'chuk, Sergei, 199n2
Mikhalkov, Nikita, 90, 139, 172
Miller, Henry, 117
Minaev, Sergei, 43
Mironova, Tamara, 243
Mizgirev, Aleksei, 96n3
Modernism (modernist), 13-15, 17, 27-28, 41, 88-93, 97, 105, 158
Mogilner, Marina, 10, 54-55

Molchan, Viktor, 243
Morozov, Pavlik, 206
Moscow State University, 39
Moskvina, Tat'iana, 190
Mulder, Anne-Claire, 127
Muratova, Kira, 92
Murav'ev, Aleksei 134n3
Mutu, Oleg, 219
Myth of the Great Family, 190, 196, 206
NKVD, 74, 99, 151
Nabokov, Vladimir, 13-32, 93
   Despair 13
   Eye, The 13
   Gift, The 15
   Invitation to a Beheading, 15
   King, Queen, Knave, 15
   Lolita 13-32
   Luzhin Defence, The 15
   Speak, Memory, 15n4
Nancy, Jean-Luc, 44, 126
Narinskaya, Anna, 151
Nasha Russia, 43
Nathans, Benjamin, 59n1
Nationalism (nationalist), 9, 33, 41, 44, 52, 57, 80-81, 83, 90, 98, 116, 152, 155, 189-190, 197, 199n3, 200, 204, 245-246
NATO, 156
Naumov, Vladimir, 195
Naval'nyi, Aleksei, 139-140
Nazi (camp, state) 62, 73-74, 101, 106, 119, 174, 227
Nazism, 103, 198
Nekrasov, Vsevolod, 104
Nemchenko, Lilya, 240, 242
Nemets, Viktor, 220
Nemtsov, Boris, 139, 141
Neuberger, Joan, 89
New Drama, 89, 94-96, 154-155, 157, 167, 221, 223, 229
New Realism (realists), 97-98, 107, 158
New Russians, 179, 187-189
New York Times, 219, 221

Novikova, Liubov', 243
Novikova, Liza, 122
Novodvorskaia, Valeriia, 53, 78,
Novoe Literaturnoe Obozrenie, NLO, (New Literary Review), 149, 153
Nuriev, Vitalii, 124
Obama, Barak, 156
Okhlobystin, Ivan, 141
Okudzhava, Bulat, 91
Old Songs about the Main Things (Starye pesni o glavnom), 94, 171-173
Olesha, Iurii, 66, 131, 176n4
Orientalism, 70-71, 79, 151
"Orthodox Russia, My History, 20th Century: From the Great Shocks to the Great Viktory," 157
Orwell, George, 180
Osminkin, Roman, 154, 160-161
Ostrovskii, Gennadii, 200
Oushakine, Serguei, 94, 146n1, 165
Ovid, 14
Parry, Albert, 35
Pasternak, Boris, 38n4, 91
Paul I, 146
Pavlenskii, Petr, 167
Pavlovskii, Gleb, 50
Pelevin, Viktor, 48-51, 57, 75, 80, 82-85, 90, 97, 100, 102, 132-133, 146-147, 173, 246
   Buddha's Little Finger (Chapaev i Pustota), 49
   Empire V (Ampir V), 101
   Generation "P", 49, 90, 101
   Omon Ra, 50, 100
   Operation "Burning Bush", 101
   Sacred Book of the Werewolf (Sviashchennaia kniga oborotnia), 100-101, 132-133
   Seer, The (Smotritel'), 146-147
   S.N.U.F.F., 82-83, 85, 101

Peppershtein, Pavel, 173
Perestroika, 9, 34, 92-93, 95, 112, 145, 155
Performativity (performative), 63, 154-155, 159, 164-167, 216
Petrov, Evgenii, 131
Pervomaiskii, Leonid, 196n1
Picasso, Pablo, 146
Pifer, Ellen, 28
Plakhov, Andrei, 205
Platonov, Andrei, 93, 176, 196n1, 222
  Foundation Pit, The (Kotlovan), 93, 222
  "Future October, The," 176
  Happy Moscow (Schastlivaia Moskva), 93
  "Return, The"("Vozvrashchenie"), 196n1
Platt, Jon, 161n7
Platt, Kevin, 134
Pliaskin, Leonid, 170n1
Poe, Edgar Allan, 14-17, 31
  "Annabel Lee", 14, 20, 22, 27
Poland, 198
Poletaev, Igor' Andreevich, 38n3
Pomerantsev, Vladimir, 91
Ponomariov, Alexander, 130n1
Popogrebskii, Aleksei, 96, 211n6
  How I Ended This Summer (Kak ia provel etim letom), 96
  Koktebel', 211n6
Popular culture (mass, pop-culture), 8, 14, 18-28, 30, 44, 89, 92, 94, 132, 170-173, 177
Postconceptualism, 104
Postmodernism (postmodernist), 27, 32, 41, 52, 82, 88-92, 97, 103-104, 132, 147-148, 152, 155, 158-159, 171-176, 182, 188, 193
Post-Soc, 148, 169-194

Post-Soviet, 8, 10, 34, 41, 44, 47-48, 54-62, 74-75, 80, 82, 85, 87-90, 92, 94, 97- 103, 108, 121, 124-125, 130-133, 137, 147-149, 152n4, 155, 172-174, 177, 186-187, 193, 197-201, 204, 206, 209-213, 217-221, 224-225, 229, 237-239, 242-246
Pravda, 117
Presniakov brothers, 95
  Playing the Victim (Izobrazhaia zhertvu), 95
Prigov, Dmity, 103-105, 115, 129, 132-133, 154-155, 173
Prilepin, Zakhar, 43, 155, 158
Proffer, Carl, 14n1
Progressor, 49, 53-86
Prokhanov, Aleksandr, 98, 139, 193
Prokhorov, Aleksandr, 196
Proskurina, Svetlana, 96n
Protest, 9, 51-52, 79, 108, 130, 133-134, 138, 140-141, 145-146, 223
Prytkov, Andrei, 234
Puchkov, Dmitrii (Goblin), 139
Pugacheva, Alla, 179
Pushkin, Aleksandr, 87, 113, 152, 235, 242, 245
Pussy Riot, 52, 130-144, 148, 159-160, 167, 233
Putin, Vladimir, 9, 78-79, 130, 136-137, 140, 142-145, 148, 158, 194, 197
Rakhmanova, Irina, 180
Rancière, Jacques, 166
Rasputin, Valentin, 139
Rasskazova, T., 109
Remnev, Anatolii, 56
Riazanov, El'dar, 139
Rimbaud, Arthur, 14
Riot Grrrl, 139
Robak, Aleksandr, 232
Rodionov, Andrei, 154, 160, 164

Rogozhkin, Aleksandr, 178
Roll, Serafima, 111
Romanticism, 14-17, 41, 241
Romm, Mikhail, 40, 43, 46
Rossa, Boryana, 142n9
Rostov University, Department of Physics and Mathematics, 41
Rozanov, Vasilii, 152, 158,
Rubinshtein, Lev, 104, 115, 152, 171-172
Rudik, I., 123
Russian Orthodox Church, 130, 136-138
Rutten, Ellen, 66, 155
Ruzaev, Denis, 236
Rybakova, Maria, 106
Rymbu, Galina, 154, 162-164
Said, Edward W., 60n5, 65, 70-71
Sakharov, Andrei, 36-37, 41-42, 44
Samutsevich, Ekaterina, 136, 139n6, 140-141
Sandler, Stephanie, 161n8
Saprykin, Iurii, 136
Satarov, Georgii, 134n3
Sebald, W. G., 106
Segal, Mikhail, 11, 240-247
   Film about Alekseev, A (Film pro Alekseeva), 244
   Franz+Polina, 240
   Short stories (Rasskazy), 11, 240-247
   World of Fixtures, The (Mir krepezha), 240-241
Semenova, Oksana, 109-110
Senchin, Roman, 158
Senderovich, Savely, 14n2
Serebrennikov, Kirill, 95
   Playing the Victim (Izobrazhaia zhertvu) (film), 95-96
Serov, Valentin, 152
Shakespeare, William, 14, 22, 114
Shakina, Ol'ga, 220, 223, 228

Shalamov, Varlam, 106
Shalimov, Artem, 204
Sharov, Vladimir, 101-103
Shapoval, Sergey, 109, 118
Shargunov, Sergei, 158
Sharogradskii, Andrei 142
Shelley, Mary, 202, 217
Shchedrovitskii, Georgii, 50
Shepit'ko, Larisa, 196n1
Shishkin, Mikhail, 92, 103, 105
   Letter-Book (Pis'movnik), 92, 105
   Maidenhair (Venerin volos), 92n2, 105
   Taking of Izmail (Vziatie Izmaila), 92n2, 105
Shklovsky, Viktor, 145, 149, 158
Sholokhov, Mikhail, 210
Shute, Jenefer, 23n5
Shvarts, Elena, 14n2
Sidorov, Aleksei, 230
Sidorov, Dmitrii, 137
Sigarev, Vasilii, 96n3
Silver Age (of Russian modernism), 91-93, 101, 106
Siniavsky, Andrei, 152
Sirivlia, Natal'ia, 180-181, 186, 188, 190
Sitkovskii, Gleb, 189n6
Skakov, Nariman, 113, 155
Slatina, Elena, 186, 192n7
Slavnikova, Olga, 97-98, 100
   2017, 98
   Immortal, The (Bessmertnyi), 97
   Light-Headed (Legkaia Golova), 97
Sloterdijk, Peter, 50-51, 125, 127, 131
Smirnov, Igor', 88
Snow, Charles P., 39
Sobchak, Kseniia, 53n2, 78, 139n6, 140, 144n11
Sochi Olympics, 247
Socialist Realism, 38, 89, 91, 94, 113-114, 117, 151, 158, 169-194, 200, 246

Sokolova, Elena, 139n6, 140, 144n11
Sokolovskaia, Ianina, 170-171,
Sokurov, Aleksandr, 92
Solov'ev, Dmitrii, 178
Solov'ev, Sergei, 178
Solov'ev, Vladimir, 139
Solzhenitsyn, Aleksandr, 38n4, 39n6, 41-42, 44n7, 55, 91, 117, 158
   Cancer Ward, The (Rakovyi korpus), 91
   First Circle, The (V kruge pervom), 91
   Gulag Archipelago, 158
   One Day in Life of Ivan Denisovich, 38n4
Sorokin, Vladimir, 8, 90, 101-103, 109-129, 131, 146, 155, 172-173, 193
   4, 124
   Anniversary (Iubilei), 114
   Blizzard (Metel'), 101, 113, 120, 123-124
   Blue Fat (Goluboe salo), 90, 114, 116, 119, 122-124, 128
   Cabbage Soup, (Shchi), 119, 122
   Confidence (Doverie), 116
   Day of the Oprichnik (Den' oprichnika), 101, 113, 116-117, 120, 122-123, 128
   Deti Rozentalia, 124
   Drift (Zanos), 116
   Dostoevsky-Trip, 114, 123
   Dumplings (Pel'meni), 121
   Feast, The (Pir), 122
   First Saturday Workday, The (Pervyi subbotnik), 112, 114-115
   Hearts of Four, The (Serdtsa chetyrekh), 112, 116, 123, 128
   Ice Trilogy (Led; Put' Bro; 23,000), 90, 172
   Kopeck (Kopeika), 114
   Marina's Thirtieth Love (Tridtsataia liubov' Mariny), 117, 119
   Monoclone (Monoklon), 101, 120
   Month in Dachau, A (Mesiats v Dakhau), 121
   Moscow, 112
   Norm, The (Norma), 111, 121
   Queue, The (Ochered'), 128
   Russian Grandmother (Russkaia babushka), 115
   Roman, 114, 116, 121, 128
   "San'kina Liubov'", 112
   Sugar Kremlin (Sakharnyi Kreml'), 101, 116, 120, 123
   Target (Mishen'), 114, 116, 123-124
Spivakovskii, Daniil, 200-201, 207
Stalin, Iosif, 35, 99, 116, 122-123, 195
Stalinism, 34, 48, 93-94, 97, 99, 103, 122, 148, 171-172, 196-197, 201, 206
State Institute of Cinematography (VGIK), 40
Staten, Henry, 126-127
Stepanova, Mariia, 105, 154, 160, 164
   Four Operas (Chetyre opery), 160
   "Prose of Ivan Sidorov, The" (*Proza Ivana Sidorova*), 105
Stishova, Elena, 211
Strel'tsov, Mikhail, 134n3
Strugatsky, Arkady, 40, 53, 57, 59
Strugatsky, Boris, 40, 53, 57,
Strugatsky brothers, 40, 43, 45-46, 48, 50, 58-86, 237,
   Anxiety (Bespokoistvo), 65n10
   Beetle in the Anthill (Zhuk v muraveinike), 58, 61, 67, 71
   Dead Alpinist Hotel, The (Otel' "U pogibshego al'pinista"), 58, 61

Distant Rainbow, The (Dalekaia raduga), 61
Doomed City, The (Grad obrechennyi), 72
Escape Attempt (Popytka k begstvu), 58, 62-63
Hard to be a God (Trudno byt' bogom), 58, 61, 63-64, 66-67, 72, 72
Inhabited Island (Obitaemyi ostrov), 58, 61, 63, 67, 72-73
Kid from Hell, The (Paren' iz preispodnei), 58, 61
Monday Begins on Saturday (Ponedel'nik nachinaetsia v subbotu), 46, 58, 71
Overburdened with Evil, (Otiagoshchennye zlom), 72
Poor Angry People (Bednye zlye liudi), 58
Predatory Things of the Century (Khishchnye veshchi veka), 58
Roadside Picnic (Piknik na obochine), 58, 61, 63
Second Invasion of Martians, The (Vtoroe nashestvie marsian), 58
Snail on the Slope (Ulitka na sklone), 45, 58, 65, 68-69, 71
Space Mowgli, The (Malysh), 58, 61
Time Wanderers, The (Volny gasiat veter), 58, 61, 72
Ugly Swans, The (Gadkie lebedi), 58, 61
White Bishop, The (Belyi ferz'), 73
Sukharev, Dmitrii, 39
Suny, Ronald, 56
Suslova, Evgeniia, 166
Tamas, Pal, 59n1
Tarkovsky, Andrei, 92, 211n6
Telegin, Semen, see Kopylov, Gertsen

Temple, Shirley, 25
Terekhov, Aleksandr, 97-100, 102
Ter-Oganian, Avdei, 135
Terts, Abram, 38n4
Thaw, 35, 38-39, 48, 59, 86, 92-93, 149, 195-196
Todorovsky, Valery, 178, 199-218, 235
  Lover, The (Liubovnik), 178
  My Stepbrother Frankenstein (Moi svodnyi brat Frankenshtein), 199-218
Tolokonnikova, Nadezhda, 133-136, 141, 148
Tolstaya, Tatiana, 102, 175n2, 203n4
Tolstoy, Aleksei, 131
Tolstoy, Lev, 113-114, 188, 243
  Anna Karenina, 114
Totalitarianism (totalitarian), 14, 58, 60-61, 63, 93, 101, 116, 119, 122, 128, 172-174, 177, 180, 183, 189, 192-196
Traditionalist (neotraditionalist), 43, 116-117, 120-121, 138, 142, 188, 193
Transcendentalism (transcendental), 8, 13-32, 50, 95, 100, 115-116, 119, 123-124, 126, 128, 204, 212
Trauma (historical), 63, 93-108, 174, 197, 202-203, 207, 209, 211n6, 213, 216, 218, 220, 224-226
Trifonov, Iurii, 92, 201
Trickstar, 132, 135, 136, 140-141, 143-144
Trickster, 82, 130-136, 143-144, 233-234
Tsekalo, Aleksandr, 172
Tullan synod, 136
Turchin, Valentin, 36
Turnbull, Joanne, 171
Tuula, Maksim, 227
Tvardovskii, Aleksandr, 131

Tynianov, Iurii, 145, 149-150, 152, 167
Turovskaya, Genya, 161n8
Uffelmann, Dirk, 10, 55, 60, 63, 111, 113, 120n13,
Ugarov, Mikhail, 154
Ukolova, Anna, 232
Ukraine, 52, 56, 81-82, 103, 156, 219-220, 245
Ul'ianov, Mikhail, 179
Ulitin, Pavel, 152
Ulitskaya, Liudmila, 97, 100, 150, 152
Ursuliak, Sergei, 94
USSR, 37, 54-55, 58, 94, 100, 112, 197-198
Vaenga, Elena, 139
Vail', Petr, 36, 38, 47
Vampilov, Aleksandr, 231, 233
Vasil'ev, Georgii, 172
Vasil'eva, Zinaida, 59n1
Vattimo, Giorgio, 43
Veledinsky, Aleksandr, 230-239
   Brigade (Brigada), 230
   Geographer Drank His Glove Away (Geograf globus propil), 230-239
   Russian, The (Russkoe), 230
   Alive (Zhivoi), 230
Veller, Mikhail, 43
Venttsel, Elena, see I. Grekova
Verigina, Marina 142n9
Verzilov, Petr, 141
Violence, 16, 44, 54, 63, 66-67, 72, 95-96, 100, 107, 110, 114-121, 138, 164, 172, 184, 187, 191-201, 209, 213-217, 221-229
Vishnevetsky, Ignatiy, 64
Vishnevetsky, Igor', 106
Voina (performance group), 132
Volkova, Elena, 134n3
Volodin, Aleksandr, 91
Von Hagen, Mark, 56

Votrin, Valerii, 107
Voznesenskii, Aleksandr, 114
Voznesenskii, Andrei, 40, 43, 91
VTsIOM (the All-Russia Center for the Study of Public Opinion), 141, 197
Vyrypaev, Ivan, 96n3
   Oxygen (Kislorod), 96n3
   Euphoria (Eiforiia), 96n3
Vysotskii, Vladimir, 35
Waldstein, Maxim, 59n3
Whale, James, 200, 204n5, 208
Willems, Joachim, 130n1
Wölfflin, Heinrich, 88
Worland, Rick, 204n5
World War II, 44, 170, 176, 178, 188, 195, 197-199, 211, 213, 215, 218, 220-221, 223, 225-226
Yakhina, Guzel', 150-152
Yakubovsky, Dmitry, 132
Yurchak, Alexei, 152
Zav'ialov, Sergei, 106
Zhirinovsky, Vladimir, 132
Zholkovsky, Aleksandr, 152
Ziuganov, Gennady, 141
Žižek, Slavoj, 158
Zubok, Vladislav, 35, 35n2, 36-39, 59n1

www.ingramcontent.com/pod-product-compliance
Lightning Source LLC
Chambersburg PA
CBHW051112230426
43667CB00014B/2550